The Future
of New Religious Movements

The Future
of New Religious Movements

EDITED BY

David G. Bromley

AND

Phillip E. Hammond

·MERCER·

ISBN 0-86554-237-6

The paper used in this publication meets
the minimum requirements of American National Standard
for Information Sciences—Permanence of Paper
for Printed Library Materials, ANSI Z39.48-1984.

∞™

Library of Congress Cataloging-in-Publication Data
The future of new religious movements.

Based on papers presented at a three-day conference held in
Oct. 1983 in Berkeley, California, and sponsored by the New
Ecumenical Research Association.
    Includes bibliographies.
    1. Cults—History—20th century—Congresses.
2. Sects—History—20th century—Congresses.   I. Bromley,
David G.   II. Hammond, Phillip E.   III. New Ecumenical Re-
search Association (Unification Theological Seminary)
BP603.F88 1987   291.9'09'048   86-33239
ISBN 0-86554-237-6 (alk. paper)
ISBN 0-86554-238-4 (pbk.)

· CONTENTS ·

A Recent History of the Future Of New Religious Movements

David G. Bromley
Phillip E. Hammond

In October 1983 a three-day conference on the future of new religious movements was held in Berkeley, California. The articles comprising this book were prepared by scholars invited to participate in that conference because they are involved in the study of new religious movements. Our objective was to gain a historical and comparative perspective on the problems and prospects facing these new movements. This introduction is devoted to discussing the way in which the conference influenced the organization and content of this volume.

THE CONFERENCE

Conference Planning

The conference began as a result of casual discussions between the editors since both of us have closely followed contemporary forms of religious expression. Like other scholars who have been studying new religious movements over the past decade, we had been informally discussing issues such as how this latest cohort of new religious movements compares with its historical counterparts, what the implications are of various organizational developments occurring within specific groups, and, in general, what the future holds for these groups. Although there has been widespread informal discussion of such matters among interested scholars and a substantial body of search has been amassed, little formal attention has been paid to assessing the future of new religious groups. In our initial conversations we discussed how general social science knowledge about social movements could inform our understanding of these contemporary new religious groups, on the one hand, and how accumulating knowledge about new religious groups could inform social science knowledge, on the other hand. We became convinced that there was a real potential for making progress on both of these fronts and that a number of other scholars shared with us an interest in doing so.

Our initial plan divided the conference into three major segments: the first to deal with factors associated with the success or failure of earlier new religions, which might establish a comparative base for the analysis of contemporary groups; the second to analyze factors associated with the success or failure of contemporary groups; the third to integrate ideas emerging from the first two segments and thus discuss alternative scenarios for the future of contemporary new religious movements. In commissioning papers for the conference we decided not to stipulate definitions of ''success'' and ''failure'' so that this question could be a matter for discussion at the conference and so that scholars would be free to approach the conference theme from different perspectives. We also extended to authors the option of concentrating either on a single factor that they viewed as having been critical in the development of new religious groups in general or on a set of factors that, taken together, had significantly influenced the course of a single group.

We decided to limit to three the number of groups to be the focus of paper presentations in the second segment of the conference so that the discussions would not become fragmented. The Church of Scientology, the Holy Spirit Association for the Unification of World Christianity (Unification Church), and the International Society for Krishna Consciousness (Hare Krishna) were selected because all three have been at the center of the ''cult controversy'' (and hence the objects of considerable research) and, at the same time, they present a real diversity of ideology, cultural traditions, goals, and organizational structure.

As our planning proceeded, it occurred to us that it would add an interesting dimension to the conference to invite spokespersons from each of these groups to participate as discussants. The voluminous body of social science research on new religious groups compiled over the last decade constitutes the assessments of outsiders. Having representatives from the groups present to respond to social scientists' projections and express their own reactions to having been the objects of intensive social science investigation for more than a decade offered a unique opportunity for feedback and interchange. Two papers by representatives of new religious groups are included in the book to incorporate that perspective.

Sponsorship of the Conference

The conference was sponsored by the New Ecumenical Research Association (New ERA), which is formally affiliated with the Unification Theological Seminary in Barrytown, New York. Since sponsorship of conferences for scholars by organizations affiliated with the Unification Church has been relatively controversial in the intellectual community, we felt it was particularly important to describe the relationship between the conference participants and its sponsor. New ERA sponsors a variety of conference series, one of which is "special theme conferences." Several of these, like this one, have addressed issues primarily of interest to social scientists. Previous social science-oriented conferences have resulted in books such as Bryan Wilson (ed.), *The Social Impact of New Religious Movements,* and Joseph Fichter (ed.), *Alternatives to Mainline American Churches.*

There are several features of New ERA conferences that have made them attractive to scholars such as ourselves. The availability of funding is, of course, an important factor. Although funding creates the potential for these events, scholars choose to participate for other reasons. The conferences allow small groups to meet for several days of uninterrupted formal and informal discussion on a topic of common interest. Such opportunities are now relatively uncommon in academe. Simply because of the extended time available and the mutuality of interests, there is a greater opportunity for exchange of ideas than at annual conferences sponsored by professional associations. In view of the overwhelming amount of research on new religious groups and the rapid change in the groups themselves, the opportunity for exchange of new ideas and information is particularly valuable.

We followed the usual procedure of submitting a conference proposal to the governing board of New ERA. The proposal contained a presentation of the conference goals and organization and was approved on that basis. The selection of topics to be discussed, the individuals to be invited, the publication arrangements for papers presented, and the content and discussion of individual sessions were entirely under the control of the editors. New ERA did stipulate the *number* of participants and the *luxury* of the hotel accommodations for budgetary reasons, but otherwise we, as conveners and editors, enjoyed complete freedom.

A few scholars, when offered invitations to the conference, demurred because of its sponsorship. For the most part, however, those invited expressed enthusiasm about the conference theme because of its salience to their own work. Naturally, some scholars are perceived by new religious groups to be less "fair and balanced" in their work than others, but no objections came on this score from the conference sponsors, and it is important to note that no bargaining on the list of invited participants occurred. Indeed, the final list included more than one scholar regarded by one or another of the groups to be less than sympathetic.

The Conference

Several developments during the conference gave rise to our emerging conception of how a book should be fashioned out of the conference papers. First, discussion on the initial day of the conference made it apparent that no consensus would be reached on definitions of success and failure. There were some participants who argued that nothing short of full denominationalization of a new religious movement constituted success, that there were but a handful of such successes at best, and that therefore our discussions were in fact largely discussions of relative failure. Others argued for specific quantifiable indices of success and failure such as longevity and membership size. Still others argued for typing groups and for composite definitions that would include less easily measured qualities such as the development of a viable, meaningful life-style for members.

However, this discussion revealed that, although participants were operating on the basis of rather different definitions of "success" and "failure," substantial agreement existed on the kinds of developmental problems confronting new religious groups. Since Rodney Stark and Bryan Wilson had independently developed the most general models identifying major social factors influencing the course of new religious movements, presentation and discussion of subsequent papers made frequent references to them. A common perspective was thus developing, and we decided to elicit the insights that were emerging. Specifically we proposed, and the authors agreed, that most would revise their papers in light of the Stark and Wilson models. Stark and Wilson agreed to revise their papers to incorporate additional insights gleaned from the conference discussions. A second development during the conference also influenced this volume. Discussants had been enlisted for the traditional role of critiquing papers. However, in several cases, discussants, including representatives of the new religious groups, pursued independent lines of thought that we requested be developed into papers to be included in the book. Some of these papers even analyzed religious groups other than the three originally selected; so the book contains a more diverse comparative base than we had originally envisioned. In all instances, however, the basic themes and arguments of these papers were integral to the conference discussion.

Finally, throughout the conference it became apparent that individual scholars were reluctant to make concrete, specific predictions—even about groups they knew quite well. Time and again they cited the complex combination of factors that would influence the future life of these groups, but then indicated their inability to know all those factors in advance. While there was some speculation about the future in the course of our discussions, *most of the scholars concentrated on identifying critical developmental problems rather than predicting outcomes.* In order to address the issue of the future more directly, therefore, we commissioned three papers to be prepared after the conference. While they were to incorporate the conference papers and discussions, they were also to address specifically the matter of the new religions' futures.

ORGANIZATION OF THE VOLUME

The three papers comprising the first section of this book provide a historical, comparative context for the study of contemporary new religious groups. Melton's paper is included in this section since he focuses on the general issue of the role of culture in spawning successive waves of new religious movements. It is clear from his analysis that we should expect new religious groups to appear again in the future, and this conclusion only serves to underline the importance of the models developed in the other two papers. Stark and Wilson present more general models that enumerate characteristics of both new religions and the kinds of sociocultural environments that facilitate or inhibit their development. Both address the issue of success and failure. Stark sets an exceedingly rigorous standard for success, "the degree to which a religious movement is able to dominate one or more societies," which by definition most groups could not achieve. However, this strategy allows him to delineate sharply those qualities characterizing the ultimate survivors. Wilson approaches the issue of success and failure from a more contemplative perspective, observing the numerous pitfalls awaiting efforts to attach those labels to specific groups.

Stark's focus on success and Wilson's on failure appear to lead them in somewhat different directions. Most new religious groups fail by even the most basic criterion—surviving for more than a brief period—so the fact that relatively few groups do survive thus constitutes impressive evidence that most soon encounter one or more organizational problems they are unable to resolve. In analyzing failure, therefore, Wilson is dealing with a large sample and emphasizes the myriad organizational incongruences and environmental challenges that can derail new religious movements. In analyzing success, by contrast, Stark distills the essence of the ultimately "dominant" survivors rather than depicting the process by which dominance was achieved. In a very real sense, however, the analyses are reciprocal: Wilson's analysis suggests there are many ways to fail, Stark's that there are few ways to succeed.

There are some other differences in emphasis that flow out of the authors' respective concerns with success and failure. Wilson, for example, stresses external and Stark internal factors. Since hostility and repression have been most pronounced early in the life histories of social movements, failed groups do not exist long enough to have to face internal problems. Similarly, Wilson is more concerned and Stark less with ideology, again perhaps because ideology tends to be a greater determinant of individual and organizational behavior in the early stages of new religions' development. However, the degree of complementarity between the two models is much more striking than the differences.

Stark's analysis of success stresses the advantage for new groups in preserving some cultural continuity; Wilson describes the enormous hostility and resistance new religious groups almost inevitably encounter during the formative years. Stark speaks of the importance of engendering high levels of commitment among members; Wilson observes that some of the most common relational forms new religious groups have used to link individual and group (for example, communal, therapeutic) have proven inherently unstable in the long run. Stark asserts the importance of a normal demographic profile; Wilson notes the limited constituency to which most new religious groups initially appeal. In these and other elements of both models, there is a real congruence of analysis. This congruence is important for it suggests that irrespective of how success and failure are defined and of where boundaries are drawn, new religious movements must solve a limited, identifiable set of organizational, developmental and relational problems. Stark and Wilson have made significant strides toward specifying these, albeit by peering through opposite ends of the telescope.

Part Two of the volume contains seven papers, each of which analyzes one or more structural elements of a new religious movement. These papers reflect authors' assessments of major sources of strength or weakness for each movement and how these will bear upon their futures. Most of the papers deal with Hare Krishna, the Unification Church, and Scientology, but other groups such as the Children of God and Nichiren Shoshu are discussed as well. While the Stark and Wilson essays have provided a common framework for addressing the problems and prospects confronting new religious movements, within this framework authors have handled the various elements in the models in very different ways. Some authors have singled out one element while others have considered several simultaneously. For example, in her analysis Barker delineates a whole series of problems that she sees looming in the future of the Unification Church. Rochford, by contrast, focuses primarily on the techniques of accommodation Hare Krishna has employed to lower a very high level of tension with the surrounding society. Most of the authors broaden and add to the models in various ways. Bainbridge takes on Stark's notion of cultural continuity and argues that although Scientology manifests little religious continuity with the Judeo-Christian tradition, it does have strong ties to the popular science fiction subculture and harmony with contemporary scientific cosmology. Lofland undertakes an innovative analysis of the relative "richness" or "poverty" of movement cultures and relates this to Unificationism's success and failure. The authors also differ in their assessments of what the future holds in store for various groups. Shinn foresees the potential of a more stable and noncontroversial future for Hare Krishna since the problem of succession apparently has been resolved, especially if fundraising and recruitment practices are modified. Wallis, by contrast, expects Scientology to lose its capacity to resonate with the larger culture and expects it thus to languish despite enormous economic resources. This dialogue and debate should not be allowed to obscure the underlying consensus that (1) although the problems of specific groups may vary, the set of problems new religions will encounter is highly predictable and (2) the prospects for the current cohort of new religious movements do not appear any brighter than for those of the past.

The third section of the book contains three essays examining the implications of social science research on new religious groups. Two are written by representatives of the Unification Church and Hare Krishna, two persons who have personally lived through some of the problems raised by papers in the preceding sections. They candidly examine their feelings about being the objects of scholarly scrutiny and offer their own assessments of the major issues confronting their movements. They also make clear that movement leaders recognize and seek to address many of the organizational problems social scientists have identified. While representatives of the new religions have either the hope or the expectation of resolving these problems, social scientists obviously are much less sanguine about their prospects. The third paper is authored by three social scientists who thus consider some of the problems and responsibilities that inhere in the process of conducting research in this area.

The volume concludes with four essays that look to the future. What will happen to the anticult movement, currently rather strong? What if any lasting impact will today's new religious movements have on the shape of tomorrow's social order? And what does all this analysis tell us about these new religious movements at the beginning of the next century and beyond?

• PART I •
GAINING PERSPECTIVE

· CHAPTER TWO ·

How New Religions Succeed:
A Theoretical Model*

Rodney Stark

A<small>lmost</small> every day, somewhere in the world a new religion appears. Nevertheless, it is very difficult to study how such movements succeed, for the fact is that virtually all new faiths rapidly fail. Moreover, nearly all of the others can be rated as successes only in comparison with the absolute failures, for they too seldom become more than footnotes in the history of religions. We must keep these harsh realities in mind when we examine new religious movements. For when we seek the common characteristics of these movements, we often are distilling the characteristics of failure. That is, among the things a selection of new religious movements has in common are the features that prevent them from succeeding. To know why and how religious movements succeed, it is necessary to isolate features that distinguish the rare successes from the multitudes of failures.

Unfortunately, it is hard to make such comparisons because nearly all the cases of success are obscured by the fog of unrecorded history. It has been fourteen centuries since Mohammed rode out of the desert to found the last new religion to achieve major success. The other world religions are even older and their formative days even more poorly recorded. (Of course, I am excluding sects since they are only new organizations, not new religions).

For this reason, in recent work I have suggested that the Mormons are a priceless gift to sociologists of religion. Even very pessimistic projections suggest they will become a major world faith over the next century, having anywhere from 60 to 265 million members worldwide by 2080 (Stark, 1984). Thus the Mormons permit sociologists to witness a movement rise from ob-

*I am indebted to Larry W. Hurtado for saving me from several serious errors about the history of the Pauline Church. I also must thank my old friend Jeff Hadden for pointing out the need for explicit treatment of socialization in the model.

scurity to success for even their earliest days are exquisitely documented.

I have utilized the Mormons to seek insights about why and how religious movements succeed or fail. This led me to a provisional theoretical model. To test and refine the model I next applied it to a host of contemporary new religious movements, finding that they typically violate what I theorize to be the conditions for success. Here Christian Science proved of great significance since this movement began with very rapid and substantial growth, and then crumbled (Stark, forthcoming). Most recently I have been doing what I can with available historical materials on Pauline Christianity and on Islam during the life of Mohammed.

In what follows, primary emphasis will be given to presenting and explaining my theoretical model of religious success, illustrating each element by drawing on my work on the Mormons, Christian Science, the Pauline church, and Islam. While the model has not been tested rigorously, it is a theory, not simply a description, and it was fully stated before being applied to most of the available cases.

However, before examining the model, we need to say a few words about the definition of success. While it seems obvious that a religious movement succeeds only insofar as it attracts and holds a significant following, some who have commented on drafts of this essay have asked to be comforted by the sound of splitting hairs. It has been suggested that we attend to the goals of individual movements, for some of them may have aimed only to attract a few members and to remain in obscurity and therefore must be rated a success in terms of *their own* goals. Frankly, I suspect that few movements ever begin with such modest aims; they adopt them only after they have lost hope of doing better (Stark and Roberts, 1982). In any event, social science is not constrained to accept outside judgments of the definitions it employs; and clearly there is sociological merit in distinguishing between religious movements that matter, that gain a wide following and influence the course of history, from those that do not.

I define success as a continuous variable based on the *degree to which a religious movement is able to dominate one or more societies*. Such domination could be the result of conversion of the masses, of elites, or both. By dominate, I mean to influence behavior, culture, and public policy in a society. Elsewhere I have argued that no single religion ever truly monopolizes faith in any society, that even in the most repressive situation heresies arise and persist (Stark and Bainbridge, 1985). Hence, I expect the topmost end of the dominance continuum to be only hypothetical. Nonetheless, this definition of success seems adequate for the task at hand: to test propositions about what factors lead to success or failure.

A MODEL OF SUCCESS

New religious movements are likely to succeed to the extent that they:

1. Retain *cultural continuity* with the conventional faiths of the societies in which they appear or originate.
2. Maintain a *medium* level of *tension* with their surrounding environment; are deviant, but not too deviant.
3. Achieve *effective mobilization:* strong governance and a high level of individual commitment.
4. Can attract and maintain a *normal age and sex* structure.
5. Occur within a *favorable ecology,* which exists when:
   a. the religious economy is *relatively unregulated;*
   b. conventional faiths are *weakened* by secularization or social disruption;
   c. it is possible to achieve at least *local success* within a *generation.*
6. Maintain *dense* internal network relations without becoming isolated.
7. Resist *secularization.*
8. Adequately *socialize* the young so as to:
   a. limit pressures towards secularization;
   b. limit defection.

These conditions should be regarded as continuous variables, not as dichotomies. In general I predict that the more fully a movement fulfills each of these conditions, the greater its success. Moreover, I suggest that failure minimally to fulfill any single condition will doom a movement. Keeping these claims in mind, let us now pursue each condition in detail.

CULTURAL CONTINUITY

Mormon missionaries do not ask Christians to discard their religious heritage and adopt a new one. Rather, they ask Christians to add to their religious culture—not to discard the Old and New Testaments, but to add a third testament. Mormonism does not present itself as an alternative to Christianity, but as its fulfillment. Joseph Smith did not disavow the prevailing religious culture but claimed to bear more recent tidings from the conventional source, tidings for a *latter* day.

Two thousand years ago the "latter-day saints" were the Christians. Christians did not ask Jews to discard their traditional scriptures, but to add to them. Perhaps even more important is the extent to which the Pauline church was culturally continuous with classical paganism. For the past century Christian historians have recognized that the face Christianity presented to the pagan world was relatively familiar (Harnack, 1908; Nock, 1933; Smith, 1980; Kee, 1983; Wilken, 1984). To the traditional messianic elements of Judaism, the emerging church in the West added the familiar "Son of God" tradition of paganism—the impregnation of a mortal female by a god. Granted that, as Brown (1977) has argued so forcefully, many of the early church fathers drew a sharp distinction between these pagan traditions (and the lusty nature they imputed to the gods) and the virginal conception of Jesus. But the essential point here is not what the church fathers believed, but what appeared *to pagans* as familiar cultural material. In similar fashion, the story of the Magi in Matthew's account of the birth of Jesus may not have been intended to sustain the familiar pagan notions of astrological signs and portents of divinity, but this is how the passage would have struck pagans (and how, since early childhood, it has always struck me). Whatever the theological reasons that the church fathers gave for abandoning the Jewish sabbath for a celebration of the "Lord's Day" on Sunday, the fact remains that this put them "in step" with the pagan observance of Sunday, while the Jews of the diaspora remained "out of step." In time Christianity made many other adjustments to pagan culture, including setting the date of Christmas to overlay the winter solstice—the primary pagan holiday.

We also must recognize how the Pauline decision to accept gentiles directly into Christianity without their also becoming Jews increased the continuities between Christianity and the pagan world at the level of everyday cultural patterns—that is, it was enough that they accept a new religion; they did not also have to adopt a new ethnicity.

In similar fashion, Islam presented itself as the final unfolding of a prophetic tradition embracing both Old and New Testaments, thus maintaining continuity with Judeo-Christian culture (indeed, Mohammed expected acceptance from neighboring Christian and Jewish communities). Parrinder (1983) reports the existence of a number of Jewish and Christian settlements in Arabia in Mohammed's time, and a substantial amount of contact between Arabs, Christians and Jews because of trade. "Knowledge of these two religions was important," according to Parrinder (1983:465), "for it prepared those who came in contact with them to receive the closely related teachings of Mohammed, and thus ultimately contributed to the actual rise and development of Islam."

Of course, Mohammed's own Arab people were pagans. Yet, Islam achieved an extraordinary degree of continuity with this religious culture too. Thus, while the Arabs worshiped many gods, their pantheon included a superior deity called Allah (albeit his functions were obscure). Therefore, in asserting the existence of one, all-powerful god called Allah, Mohammed was not introducing an unknown deity. Moreover, the annual pilgrimage to Mecca to perform rites during a holy month had been a prominent part of Arab religion since long before Mohammed's time. Hence, here too Mohammed built upon the familiar. Finally, Mohammed maintained that he was a Hanif. Although little is known about this group, we do know they were Arabs and that they claimed spiritual descent from Abraham. Clearly, they enjoyed special spiritual standing among Arabs, and it is likely that they were some kind of reformist ascetic order perhaps akin to the Essenes. In claiming that the new revelations he preached were a continuation of Hanifi teachings, Mohammed again laid claim to and utilized familiar culture.

Confucius went so far as to deny that there was anything new in his teachings, but that he had merely "transmitted what was taught me without making up anything of my own," (*Analects, 7.*1). He based this claim on his use of the archives of the Chou kings as relics of a golden age, but, of course, he did create an ethical and moral system from these materials.

Let me make it clear that I do not imply that any of these founders of great religions engaged in conscious "product-engineering" in order to have the greatest market appeal. I mean only to note that founders whose revelations are rooted in familiar cultural material are the ones likely to succeed.

In contrast, many new religious movements are wholly discontinuous with the conventional religious culture. Many reflect an alien culture—Hindu and Buddhist groups in the West, for example. Indeed, some claim cultural continuity with aliens of the extraterrestrial variety. Such movements suffer from asking converts to reject their whole religious heritage and thus risk being defined as too deviant. In this regard, it must be noted that Mormon foreign missions have had their greatest success among Christians and in those parts of Asia where Christianity has had the greatest impact. Moreover, the Mormons are doing best in those parts of Asia that are the most industrialized and therefore *westernized,* thus enabling citizens to adopt only a new religion, not a new ethnicity too. (A young American official in the Unification church once told me that before she became a Moonie, she had spent some time with Hare Krishnas but had rejected their efforts to convert her because "I couldn't see myself trying to act like an Indian.")

It also seems significant that imported faiths appear to do best if and when they are taken over by locals and modified to include familiar cultural elements. Thus, the spread of Christianity to western and northern Europe was associated with rapid expansion of the list of Saints as local pagan deities were incorporated. So too has the rapid and extraordinary spread of Christianity in sub-Saharan Africa been accomplished by a proliferation of syncretic sects (Barrett, 1968; 1982).

Is it impossible for a new religion to make its way if it lacks continuity with conventional religious culture? I am inclined to say yes, at least until a religion has succeeded in at least one society. Even then, religious movements will spread more readily to the extent that they build upon the familiar.

MEDIUM TENSION

I have mentioned that faiths with a wholly alien doctrine may be regarded as too deviant. By this I mean to suggest that religious movements can be in so high a state of tension with their environment that conversion is all but impossible. Against the potential rewards of converting, people must weigh the costs of membership. When society is sufficiently hostile towards a group, these costs can be very high indeed. Granted, that under some conditions the attractions of membership can offset even the risk of martyrdom, as happened in the day of the Pauline church. Still, repression and stigmatization are not assets for a movement.

However, the movement must maintain a substantial sense of difference and considerable tension with the environment if it is to prosper. Without significant differences from the conventional faith(s) a movement lacks a basis for successful conversion. Thus, it must maintain a delicate balance between conformity and deviance. This balance is likely to be constantly shifting and will be influenced greatly by the extent to which the religious economy is regulated.

EFFECTIVE MOBILIZATION

While it is convenient to speak of organizations doing this or that, we must always keep in mind that, in fact, organizations never do anything. Only people ever act. And individual actions can be interpreted as those of an organization only to the extent that they are coordinated and controlled. Put another way, organizations come into existence and gain the capacity to function only to the extent that individual humans are mobilized to act on behalf of the collective interests expressed in the organization and their activity is given coherence by leaders.

Ineffective mobilization is chronic among new religious movements. Melinda Wagner's (1983) description of the Spiritual Frontiers Fellowship as a virtual non-organization, almost devoid of the capacity for coordinated action, could be applied to many new religious movements. Indeed, Elaine Pagels (1979) attributes a similar inability to mobilize to the Christian Gnostic movements. Moreover, while religious movements having a guru authority system can generate intense levels of individual member commitment, they are very fragile organizations for lack of effective governance. As Larry Shinn (1984) has so elegantly demonstrated for the Hare Krishnas, guru authority systems are inimical to effective organization and are subject to constant fission and schism, since members are committed to a particular guru, not to a larger organization.

It was perhaps the greatest achievement of the early Christian church that it forged so effective and lasting a system of governance (Pagels, 1979; Meeks, 1983). Granted, there always were problems in maintaining central authority over all congregations and areas. But from the start, the local congregation seems to have been a strong organization, not some loose affinity group of adepts or fellow "seekers" (Holmberg, 1978). Thus it was possible for the Christian movement to pursue long-range goals by consistent and rational means, to endure in the face of persecution and social disorganization, to negotiate for privileges and political alliances, and, quite simply to outlast the competition.

Elsewhere I stress the extraordinary mobilization of Mormons, combining both a very strong system of central authority and very high levels of rank-

and-file participation in governance. Their efforts to produce and maintain a universal male priesthood having real pastoral duties and authority succeed to a remarkable degree. For example, the Mormons are able to put as many full-time missionaries in the field as can the combined Christian denominations of North America. This is possible only because so large a proportion of young Mormons volunteer for an eighteen-month missionary tour and pay all of their own expenses.

Some contemporary new religious movements also generate high levels of mobilization. Many of them differ from the Mormons, however, because they achieve and sustain their mobilization by removing converts from the normal secular world. This procedure results in isolation and in reliance on collective economic activities (which may deflect from religious goals); often such a high level of mobilization inhibits fertility and family life. In contrast, even Mormon bishops and stake presidents are unpaid volunteers who continue to earn a living in secular society.

Converts to the Pauline church did not follow the admonitions of Jesus to drop out and follow him as full-time devotees. They remained in the world, thus giving the growing Christian movement influence in secular affairs. Let us acknowledge that such influence was not trivial since, contrary to popular wisdom and Marxist doctrine (Kautsky, 1953), Christian converts probably were not primarily from the lower strata of society. Study of local leaders mentioned in the Pauline letters or other early documents shows that they had considerable social standing (Meeks, 1983). Moreover, all available studies of converts to contemporary new religious movements show them to be very overselected from privileged backgrounds (Stark and Bainbridge, 1985). The average Moonie, for example, is not some unemployable high school dropout but is instead unusually well educated and able (Barker, 1981). When such people are withdrawn from secular life, much is lost to the movement that recruited them.

The interplay of doctrine and organization also seems to deserve closer attention than contemporary sociologists have paid it. While most writing on religion suffers from dealing with nothing other than accounts of theology and rite, I confess that my work has suffered from paying too little attention to the *content* of doctrine. I am indebted to Elaine Pagels (1979) for her persuasive demonstration that the content of doctrine can facilitate or impede organizational structure. The failure of the Gnostics surely was inherent in their elitist and personalistic doctrines of secret knowledge to be sought through private, individual enlightenment. Loose networks of individual adepts could not withstand the mobilized might of the Pauline church. Indeed, Paul's major success was not to have founded so many congregations, but to have successfully imposed his model of effective organization upon them—that was the rock on which the church was built.

A NORMAL AGE AND SEX STRUCTURE

Religious movements that appeal only to a limited segment of a population are thereby prevented from becoming a dominant faith. The negative impact of limited appeal is especially potent when it results in a population composition incapable of sustaining its ranks. Such groups forever stand in risk of rapidly disappearing. In contrast, a religious movement can sustain substantial growth through fertility alone, given an appropriate age and sex composition.

An appropriate contrast here is between the Shakers and the Mennonites. The Shakers prohibited sex and had no member fertility. When the flow of new converts began to decline, the organization also began rapidly to shrink. In fact, however, the Shakers probably would have declined rather rapidly for want of fertility even had they permitted sex because, from the beginning, they disproportionately attracted female members (Bainbridge, 1982). In contrast, it has been a century or two since the Mennonites attracted converts, and each generation produces a substantial number of defectors. Yet, each year the Mennonites are more numerous due to their normal demographic composition and their high level of fertility.

The great majority of new religious movements resembles the Shakers more than the Mennonites. Census data from the 1920s, for example, show that members of new religious movements in the United States were disproportionately female and older (Stark, Bainbridge and Kent, 1981). Indeed, this demographic pattern holds the key to the rapid failure of Christian Science. In the first generation, Christian Science achieved a truly remarkable rate of growth—much more rapid even than that of the Mormons. However, the massive overrecruitment of older females who either did not have children or whose children were already grown before their mothers' conversion resulted eventually in an extraordinary mortality deficit as first-generation members began to die without leaving offspring within the faith. From then on, substantial rates of conversion failed to produce growth because they were offset by mortality.

A major asset of Mormonism is its ability to appeal to young people of both sexes. The 1920s data showed the age and sex composition of the Mormons was virtually identical with that of the general population, and Mormons have long had higher than average fertility. Thus the Mormon movement would grow even without a flow of converts, although, given its very successful missionary efforts, it grows rapidly. Similarly, fragments of historical evidence suggest that Pauline Christianity primarily recruited family units and thus began with the demographic capacity to sustain itself (Meeks, 1983).

A FAVORABLE ECOLOGY

It is vital to recognize that the fate of new religious movements depends greatly on features of the environment within which they appear. Here three environmental features seem important. First is the degree to which the religious economy is *regulated*. Second is the *condition of the conventional* faith or faiths against which the new movement must compete. Third is the size and structure of the environment as these place practical limits on first generation *perceptions of success*.

When a single religious organization has been granted monopoly rights in a religious economy, backed by the coercive power of the state, it will be more difficult for new faiths to flourish. It will not be impossible, however, and in fact even under the most repressive conditions numerous blackmarket faiths will exist. Still, other things being equal, it will be much easier to build a new faith where such activity is legal, and even easier when all religions have equal standing vis-à-vis the state and the legal system. The special favors granted the established state churches in Europe seem to impede the successful rise of sects as well as of new faiths. In the United States, in contrast, the most obscure religious group has precisely the same legal privileges, such as tax exemptions, as do the most powerful bodies. Interestingly enough, American tax laws induce new religious movements to become formally organized at a very early date and thus may make them visible sooner than is true of similar groups in Europe. As a result, the primary regulators of our religious economy are state and federal tax collectors. This situation is reflected in the fact that founders and leaders of new religious movements appear to be the single highest risk group in terms of prosecution for tax violations. Unwittingly perhaps, the IRS serves as a functional equivalent of the Holy Inquisition in the officially unregulated religious economy of the United States.

However, even in the least regulated religious economies, new religious movements will *not* succeed so long as conventional religious organizations are *effectively serving* market demand. As with any market, firms already established enjoy many advantages over newcomers. Therefore, to succeed, new religions must appear in the right place at the right time—where and when the older firms have become ineffectual. Major religious organizations, and even the traditions they represent, can crumble for several reasons. An obvious one is secularization, which can empty them of the potency that produced their original success. Second, sudden social disruptions can overwhelm the capacity of the older faiths to serve market needs.

In a number of recent essays, Bainbridge and I have argued that secularization is a universal feature of religious economies (Stark and Bainbridge, 1985). Secularization *reflects at the societal level the process by which sects are tamed and transformed into churches*. That is, at least since the work of Niebuhr (1929), sociologists have accepted that if sect movements flourish they thereby undermine their ability to maintain relatively high tension with their environment and thus lose the power to provide potent otherworldly religion. If this conclusion applies at the level of specific organizations, it must follow that at any given moment the more significant higher-tension organizations are moving in the direction of lower tension and that long-established organizations will be in quite low tension, which is simply to say, societies always display the process of secularization. They do not ever become truly secularized, however. That is, religion does not ever finally wither away. Instead, secularization produces its own countervailing trends elsewhere in a religious economy. The most common of these is sect formation. As a given organization becomes too worldly to fulfill market requirements, schisms occur and higher-tension movements appear—sects. Once in a while, too many episodes of transformation of sects into churches (secularization) undermine the whole religious tradition of a given society, and at those moments new religions have the opportunity to take over the market.

Of course, it is not only secularization that can produce market opportunities for new faiths. This also can occur when severe social disruptions shatter confidence in prevailing faiths. Indeed, Anthony F. C. Wallace (1957) has argued forcefully that new religions succeed only during times of grave crisis and social disorganization.

Social crises make conventional religions vulnerable in two ways. First of all, a crisis such as a plague, natural disaster, or conquest by an enemy can place *demands* upon a conventional religion that it *appears unable to meet*. For example, when the American Indians found their traditional religions unable to provide them with the means to resist European encroachments, they evolved new religions and discarded the old (Mooney, 1896). Bryan Wilson has surveyed many similar episodes from around the world (1975).

Social turmoil can weaken conventional faiths in another important but less dramatic way: it can *disrupt the social ties* by which most people are bound to social institutions, including religion. Thus, in the aftermath of a plague that has randomly destroyed half the population, the survivors will not only wonder why the gods failed them, the depletion of their networks will cause many of them to become loose social atoms unrestrained from radical realignments.

However, conventional institutions can be eroded by much less dramatic sources of social disorganization. No plague has turned the West Coast of the United States into a place lacking solid networks—communities of strangers and newcomers. A high level of geographic mobility, however, prevents substantial social integration in the Far West and accounts for the very high rates of involvement in new religions. It is interesting to recall that the Mormons also arose in an area disorganized by rapid mobility. Mormonism began among displaced New Englanders in the process of drifting West (Hansen, 1981). Indeed, Mormons built their first great centers in Ohio, Missouri, and Illinois where they drew upon the flow of westward migration.

I think it especially important that, insofar as the historical record can be read, Pauline Christianity also exploited weak social integration caused by geographic mobility. That is, Christianity built its vital base in the Greek cities of the eastern provinces of the Roman Empire. Many of these cities had only just been founded or refounded—sometimes as retirement compensation for veterans of the legions. As new cities, they were made up of strangers, many of whom were being exposed for the first time to city life and to the unusually disorganized cosmopolitanism created by the sudden mixing of diverse cultures (Rostovetzeff, 1957; Bowersock, 1965; Levick, 1967; Meeks, 1983). Thus, in addition to the crises that beset the empire, especially after the first century, chronic social disruption and disorganization provided a sufficient opening for new religious movements.

We come now to the crisis of confidence that awaits most new religious movements as members of the founding generation reach the end of their lives. I think the record of new faiths suggests that unless the movement achieves a persuasive appearance of major success within the first generation, the founders will lose hope and turn the movement inward—adopt a new rhetoric that de-emphasizes growth and conversion.

When movements arise in small societies, it is within their capacity to become the dominant religion within a few years. This is especially true if a new religious movement can appeal to a small ruling elite. However, when movements aimed at the general public arise within large societies, the same absolute number of converts that would spell success in a small society is an insignificant fragment of the larger population. When we analyze growth rates in terms of reasonable arithmetic assumptions about the social surface of the group—its contacts and connections with outsiders—even with very high rates of conversion it takes a generation to assemble even 20,000 followers (Stark and Roberts, 1982). In societies of several million or more, that is not an influential number (unless, of course, the 20,000 are concentrated among the upper nobility or other ruling elite).

In my judgment this dismal arithmetic of first generation growth crushes the confidence out of most new movements. But not always. Why not? In the case of the Mormons, the answer seems clear. They headed to the empty West and founded their own society and religious economy, thus turning a modest absolute number of followers into a dominant majority. That is, the Mormons in effect created a homeland where they have since experienced life as members of a dominant religion. Secure in their triumph in one society, the Mormons have gone out to add to their kingdom.

To keep their confidence, new religious movements need such an early victory. Within the lifetime of the first generation, they need to perceive serious success. While the record is, of course, extremely fragmentary, it appears that the Pauline church became a major body in some of the eastern cities of the empire within the lifetime of Paul and the Apostles. It may indeed have been the dominant faith in some of these cities (keep in mind that these were very small cities, often having only several thousand residents). Given the local outlook that prevailed at that time, local successes probably were sufficient to inspire faith that Christianity was the wave of the future. Moreover, these local successes gave the church the power to withstand persecution— mass crucifixions in Rome could be borne by a movement well entrenched in the provinces.

In the case of Islam, major success came swiftly. Arabia was inhabited by a number of independent tribes. Thus, Mohammed was able to convert a "society" simply by converting one of these tribes, which required him to make but a rather small number of converts. Indeed, since upon the conversion of the head of a large extended family or clan all members converted too, success hinged on even fewer actual converts. Having gained ascendency in one tribe, Mohammed then recruited the rest of the Arabs as whole tribes converted on the basis of treaties or conquest. In this way the Prophet amassed great secular power within his lifetime and was able to merge religious and political authority.

NETWORK TIES

In order to have effective mobilization, any religious movement needs to have a dense network of internal attachments among its followers. Such attachments tie individuals to the group. They also can serve as a major source of rewards by which commitment is maintained—affection and self-esteem are among the most vital exchange commodities within social movements. To the extent that movements are made up of a collection of casual acquaintances, they will lack energy, commitment, and salience as the current condition of the liberal Christian denominations demonstrates (Stark and Glock, 1968). Indeed, this is a common failure of new religious movements. Bryan Wilson (1961) noted the remarkable absence of social relations among Christian Scientists, and Melinda Wagner (1983) observed the same condition in the Spiritual Frontiers Fellowship.

Weak networks seem to be the primary impediment facing Scientology at present, limiting the ability of the group to mobilize effectively and, more important, to prevent massive movement from active to inactive membership. The basic unit of Scientology is the dyad: the auditor and the person undergoing therapy. The movement has failed to discover organizational means to create bonds among those undergoing auditing; hence whenever members suspend their therapy sessions (which most must do periodically because of the great expense involved), the risk they will drop out altogether is high—there is nothing to tie them to the group. Several Scientology officials have told me that at any given moment only about 10 to 15 percent of those who have been active in the movement remain active. Efforts to make Scientology considerably more "churchlike" with a much richer group life may mend this weakness.

But, if many religious movements suffer from weak social relations among members, many others suffer from internal networks that are too all-embracing and impede the ability of members to form or to maintain attachments with outsiders. In the absence of such attachments, a movement will be unable to make converts, for it is through attachments that people are recruited to movements. In full recognition of this problem, Mormon publications admonish members against "exclusiveness" and urge them to seek non-Mormon friendships. In similar fashion, in the early 1960s Miss Kim recognized that her young converts to the Unification Church were beginning to spend too much time with one another, and thus the outer social surface of the group was diminished. Therefore she dispersed the group into cells of two or three members in an effort to help them obtain new external attachments.

As with tension, here too a delicate balance must be maintained between internal and external attachments. Successful movements consist of dense but *open* social networks.

SECULARIZATION

To succeed, a new religious movement must not make its peace with this world too rapidly or too fully. A faith too accommodated to worldliness lacks the power for continued conversion. Elsewhere I argue that Christian Science was short-lived partly because it so rapidly watered down central doctrines in an effort to gain respectability. Indeed, in her last years Mrs. Eddy herself took the lead in secularizing her movement.

If I am correct about the nature of religious economies, only rarely could there exist a shortage of secularized religious bodies. Hence, to become like them offers no market edge—indeed, since secularization is how religious organizations die, this is not an enviable condition. During their rise, successful religious movements do not abandon their original cultural content.

Here again the Mormons fill the bill. While they have made several adjustments in doctrine in order to prevent their level of tension from becoming harmfully high—abandoning polygamy being a prime example—they have not softened the radical doctrines that are the heart of their faith. While seminarians at famous Protestant schools no longer assert the existence of a personal God, Mormons remain confident that eventually each of them will become God of a universe. Compared with mere salvation, that is an extraordinary expectation for the afterlife.

A major reason why the Mormons seem uninclined to back away from their traditional theology can be found in simple arithmetic of growth. Even with a fairly low rate of growth (even one well below that maintained by the Mormons in fact), the majority of members of a movement will *always be first-generation converts*. Thus while the stereotypical Mormon is someone born in Utah or Idaho of Mormon ancestors, in reality the average Mormon converted in his or her late teens or early twenties.

There is considerable truth in the old saying that a convert is holier than the Pope. People who adopt a new faith are not eager to have changes made in its central doctrines. Thus, so long as a religious movement maintains a significant rate of growth, it will remain a movement primarily made up of converts. In this way it is strengthened against the forces leading to secularization.

ADEQUATE SOCIALIZATION

Finally, provision must be made for effective socialization of those born into the faith. Lacking this, a movement will develop powerful internal pressures toward secularization. Elsewhere I have analyzed the many ways in which generations born into, rather than converted to, a religious movement often will prefer to reduce the level of tension between it and the social environment (Stark and Bainbridge, 1985). Here I merely note that this tendency can be minimized by socialization, especially as it implants a sense of superiority over those outside the movement.

It also is obvious that without effective socialization a movement will suffer damaging rates of defection as its youngest members grow up and leave the faith. Clearly, no movement has learned how to prevent all such defections, especially if we recognize that much defection does not involve official withdrawal but is the silent defection of inactivity and skepticism (Mauss, 1969; Brinkerhoff and Burke, 1980; Albrecht and Bahr, 1983). Movements differ greatly in their ability to hold the young. For example, while the Shakers had no children born into the faith, they pursued a policy of adoption for many years. At eighteen the adoptive children were given the choice of staying or leaving: nearly all of them left (Bainbridge, 1982; forthcoming). The Amish, on the other hand, seem to have but modest defection rates. How do groups hold their younger members, especially during periods when the group still is regarded as deviant?

I suggest that successful movements find important things for young people to do on behalf of their faith, that early on they provide ways by which youth can exhibit and build commitment. Here the Mormon practice of basing its primary missionary effort on teenage volunteers stands out. Not only does this custom make it possible for the church to put more than 30,000 missionaries in the field each year; it has extraordinary impact on the commitment of the best and brightest of its young people in each generation. Nothing will so build one's faith as going out and spending eighteen months bringing that faith to others (cf. Festinger, Riecken, and Schachter, 1956). Consider too the moral obligations engendered by converting others—to defect is to betray their trust. Moreover, close contact with new converts exposes young Mormons to the appeal of unsecularized forms of the faith at just the time when young people in many other faiths begin to question and modify their initial religious socialization.

How early Christians socialized their young and kept them committed is unknown. What we do know is that the church has never deferred full membership until adulthood but has confirmed people at the start of their teens and has sought to involve them in religious roles at a young age.

CONCLUSION

This essay presents the skeleton of my theory of religious innovation, of how new religions succeed. I have given a few empirical examples of each of the propositions. But it will take a detailed analysis of many cases to see the adequacy or the shortcomings of the model. I suspect that such research will confirm that these propositions represent *necessary* conditions for success: that any movement failing to fulfill one or more of these conditions will not succeed. But I also suspect that this set may not yet state the *sufficient* conditions for success. That is, the model may well need expansion. Taking the model as it stands, I think it needs more development in several places.

First of all, much more needs to be known about socialization and its connections with effective mobilization. I think it evident that not only must a religious movement be able to demand sacrifices from its members, but that these demands are, in turn, crucial to building and maintaining commitment, especially as a part of socialization. Indeed, it appears to me that people rate the value of religion not only on the basis of what it gives them, but on how much it costs them—that people place little value on religion that is cheap and prefer religions that are relatively costly. But costly in what ways? In general, I think people prefer costs of time and money as opposed to costs in terms of stigma. But this is a topic needing a great deal of investigation.

I almost hesitate to admit it, but I think the model needs greater development in terms of ideological or theological elements. I have suggested that cultural continuity matters and that theology can also impede or facilitate organization. But we probably need to confront the possibility that some theologies are inherently more plausible; some are more easily and effectively communicated; some are more able to satisfy deeply felt needs of large numbers of people; indeed, some probably are inherently more interesting, even exciting, than others.

I have touched on some of these matters in my recent work on secularization. I have suggested that when religions surrender a vivid, close-at-hand conception of the supernatural they can no longer satisfy basic needs for which religions exist. But this is an immense subject; and, despite the vast libraries generated by scholars of religion—especially comparative religions—it has hardly been touched. One reason is that many dangers lurk for scholars who presume to rate the comparative plausibility, clarity, or inherent interest of religious doctrines. Nonetheless, these are jobs that need to be done.

Moreover, we must pose some of these questions, not simply at the individual level, but at the level of societies as whole systems. Let me close with two examples with which I may, eventually, concern myself.

It has often been suggested that Christian doctrines *per se* served the needs of various groups of individuals within the Roman world, although there has been heated disagreement whether these groups were on the bottom of society or in the middle or higher. But I think it might be possible to develop the thesis that Christian doctrine solved major, widespread, intellectual and cultural problems of the empire—problems that affected *all* groups.

Rome produced a substantial political and economic unity within its boundaries. By doing so, however, it caused cultural disunity. Roman expansion produced cultural chaos, a helter-skelter bringing together of local cultures to which Rome reacted by eclecticism, which simply sustained the problem. Until the rise of Christianity, there was no successful attempt to formulate a universal culture. Was there need of one? I suggest that the capacity of Christianity to serve as a potent and expanding cultural core, even after the political and economic unity of the empire had collapsed, reveals its contribution to the relevant social systems.

In similar fashion I would be prepared to develop the thesis that, contrary to fashionable intellectual dogma, the Enlightenment and the rise of science and technology in the West were not accomplished *despite* Christianity, but were *inherent* in the cultural legacies of the Pauline church. What strikes me as distinctive about Christianity, especially medieval Christianity, is its commitment to reason, to the rules of logic (in clear continuity from Greek rhetoric). The great intellectual figures in church history, from Paul to Pascal, were men of the word, not men of the mystery; men of logic, not men of the ineffable and unexpressible. And, whatever specific conflicts occurred between people such as Galileo and church officials, it was the tradition of deductive logic and the rule of reason, sustained by the church and by Christian culture in general, that produced modern science.

These last remarks would seem to take us far afield from what makes religious movements succeed. But perhaps not. Perhaps the most important *cultural continuity* of Christianity (and therefore of those that would follow it) was with the *rational intellectual* tradition of the Greeks and Romans; the terminal weakness of paganism lay in the vulnerability of its elaborate magic and mysteries to this same rationalism. What that suggests is that paganism suffered from the flowering of classical science and philosophy (deVries, 1967) in much the same way that traditional Christianity has been eroded by the rise of modern science. And that would confirm once again that there is no new thing under the sun. In the past, in the present, and so in the future, secularization will prompt revivals and the rise of new religions.

REFERENCES

Albrecht, Stan L., and Howard M. Bahr
    1983   "Patterns of Religious Disaffiliation," *Journal for the Scientific Study of Religion* 22:366-79.
Bainbridge, William Sims
    1982   "Shaker Demographics 1900-1940," *Journal for the Scientific Study of Religion* 21:352-65.
    Forthcoming   "The Decline of the Shakers."
Barker, Eileen
    1981   "Who'd Be a Moonie?" In Bryan Wilson, ed., *The Social Impact of New Religious Movements*. New York: Rose of Sharon Press.
Barrett, David B.
    1968   *Schism and Renewal in Africa*. New York: Oxford.
    1982   *World Christian Encylopedia*. New York: Oxford.
Boorstin, Daniel J.
    1983   *The Discoverers*. New York: Random House.
Bowersock, Glen W.
    1965   *Augustus and the Greek World*. 2 vols. Oxford: Clarendon.
Brinkerhoff, Merlin B., and K. L. Burke
    1980   "Disaffiliation," *Sociological Analysis* 41:41-54.
Brown, R. E.
    1977   *Birth of the Messiah*. Garden City NY: Doubleday.
de Vries, Jan
    1967   *Perspectives on the History of Religions*. Berkeley: University of California Press.
Festinger, Leon, Henry W. Reicken, and Stanley Schachter
    1956   *When Prophesy Fails: A Social and Psychological Study of A Modern Group That Predicted the Destruction of the World*. New York: Harper.
Hansen, Klaus J.
    1981   *Mormonism and the American Experience*. Chicago: University of Chicago Press.
Harnack, Adolf von
    1908   *The Mission and Expansion of Christianity in the First Three Centuries*, 1962 reprint, New York: Harper and Row.

Holmberg, Bengt
     1978   *Paul and Power.* Philadelphia: Fortress.

Kautsky, Karl
     1953   *Foundations of Christianity.* New York: Russell and Russell.

Kee, Howard Clark
     1983   *Miracle in the Early Christian World.* New Haven: Yale University Press.

Levick, Barbara M.
     1967   *Roman Colonies in Southern Asia Minor.* Oxford: Clarendon Press.

Mauss, Armand L.
     1969   ''Dimensions of Religious Defection,'' *Review of Religious Research*
             10:128-35.

Meeks, Wayne A.
     1983   *The First Urban Christians.* New Haven: Yale University Press.

Mooney, James
     1896   *The Ghost Dance Religion and the Sioux Outbreak of 1890.* Washington:
             U.S. Government Printing Office.

Niebuhr, H. Richard
     1924   *The Social Sources of Denominationalism.* New York: Henry Holt.

Nock, A. D.
     1933   *Conversion: The Old and the New in Religion from Alexander the Great
             to Augustine of Hippo.* Oxford: Oxford University Press.

Pagels, Elaine
     1979   *The Gnostic Gospels.* New York: Random House.

Parrinder, Geoffrey
     1983   *World Religions.* New York: Facts on File Publications.

Rostovtzeff, Mihail
     1957   *The Social and Economic History of the Roman Empire,* 2 vols. 2nd ed.
             revised by P. M. Fraser. Oxford: Clarendon Press.

Shinn, Larry D.
     1984   ''Conflicting Networks: Guru and Friend in ISKCON,'' *Religious
             Movements: Genesis, Exodus, and Numbers,* edited by Rodney Stark.
             New York: Rose of Sharon Press.

Smith, Morton
     1980   ''Pauline Worship as Seen by Pagans,'' *Harvard Theological Review*
             73:241-49.

Stark, Rodney
     1984   ''The Rise of a New World Faith,'' *Review of Religious Research* 26.
     Forthcoming   ''The Rise and Fall of Christian Science.''

Stark, Rodney and William Sims Bainbridge
     1984   *The Future of Religion: Secularization, Revival, and Cult Formation.*
             Berkeley: University of California Press.

Stark, Rodney, W. S. Bainbridge, and Lori Kent
  1981   "Cult Membership in the Roaring Twenties," *Sociological Analysis*
          42:137-62.
Stark, Rodney and Charles Y. Glock
  1968   *American Piety*. Berkeley: University of California Press.
Stark, Rodney and Lynne Roberts
  1982   "The Arithmetic of Social Movements," *Sociological Analysis* 43:53-
          68.
Wagner, Melinda Bollar
  1983   "Spiritual Frontiers Fellowship." In *Alternatives of American Mainline
          Churches,* edited by Joseph H. Fichter. New York: Rose of Sharon Press.
Wallace, Anthony F. C.
  1956   "Revitalization Movements," *American Anthropologist* 58:264-81.
Wilken, Robert L.
  1984   *The Christians as the Romans Saw Them*. New Haven: Yale University
          Press.
Wilson, Bryan
  1961   *Sects and Society*. Berkeley: University of California Press.
  1975   *Magic and the Millennium*. St. Albines, England: Paladin.

CHAPTER THREE

Factors in the Failure of the New Religious Movements

Bryan R. Wilson

The application of the concepts of failure and success to religion is a problematic exercise. Since religion is a matter of faith, its goals might be expressed in transcendental or metaphysical terms. Such goals are regularly represented as supramundane. What, it might be asked, does it profit a religious movement if it "shall gain the whole world and lose [its] own soul?" The attainment of Nirvana by all the world's Theravada Buddhists, and hence the extinction of Buddhism, could be seen as success. Just as the Christian Church exists for people *in this world,* so does Buddhism, its doctrines and organization. In Buddhism, as in Christianity, ultimate success comes when the world passes away. Christian religion is for man under the relative natural law, in the period between the fall and the resurrection: it is a social phenomenon with transcendent goals. The sociologist is concerned primarily with the limited goals of social organizations even though he may not totally ignore religion's own ultimate goals and expectations.

Those expectations are sometimes expressed in terms that do admit empirical appraisal, however. Does a religious movement fail when the prophecies it endorses fail? Have the Shakers—now reduced to a mere handful of believers—failed, since Christ has not come, sickness has not been eliminated, and the sin of sexuality is perhaps even more rampant than when Mother Ann Lee first pronounced against it? Or has the world, in some way, become a better place for their having been?—which is the way that they themselves explain away apparent failure. To take religious groups seriously, we must take their prophecies, their own criteria of self-appraisal, and even their rationalizations into account. Nor can we simply assume that growth means success and that decline means failure. Not all movements seek unconditional or unlimited growth, and those that do may pay for it at the cost of abandoning pristine teachings and organization. Even virtually extinct sects are sometimes accounted a success: a historian of the Muggletonians, a sect that arose in England in 1652 and now has one member remaining, has written: "Theirs is a success story, not in terms of a mass movement, but in terms of longevity. In those terms it is incontestably a success story; the more so when one realizes the astonishingly low level of interest shown by Muggleton himself, and by those who came after him, in the business of recruiting new members."[1]

It is sociological—one might say commonsensical—criteria that inform this paper, and one might begin by assessing the extent to which religious movements fail in the matter of not achieving their own purposes (or in wrongly forecasting God's). Yet such is the subjectivity of the product of religion that even objectively stated goals—"to save the world"; "to redeem the race"; "to 'clear' the planet"; "to gain eternal life"; "to eradicate sin"—are often unavailable to empirical investigation. Religious leaders rationalize their experience. While some movements do not seek to recruit, such growth is—except for highly ossified sects—rarely eschewed totally. When growth does occur, the movement's mission may be interpreted in qualitative rather than quantitative terms: the mere possibility of one sheep recovered may be worth leaving the ninety-and-nine at risk. For the sociologist, however, numbers, endurance, maintenance of commitment, persistence or attainment of goals become necessary indicators of relative success or failure, even allowing that performance may also be appraised in terms of the criteria that a movement has itself set forth about its social goals.

Among these sociological criteria, an analytical distinction may be posited between exogenous and endogenous factors, even though this distinction may not always be easily recognized empirically. The endogenous factors deserve greater attention, and I review five in which, on historic evidence, failure has occurred: ideology; leadership; organization; constituency; and institutionalization. These categories bear considerable convergence with the criteria suggested by Stark, although I omit the issue of maintenance of "medium tension." Tension with the world or the church is implicit in any new (hence deviant) religious movement, and, as Dean Kelley has suggested, "Strong organizations are strict"[2]; but just what constitutes "medium tension" may be discernible only retrospectively, and an item of this kind might bring one close to tautology.

---

[1]William Lamont in Christopher Hill, Barry Reay, and William Lamont, *The World of the Muggletonians* (London: Temple Smith, 1983) 114.

[2]Dean Kelley, *Why Conservative Churches Are Growing* (New York: Harper & Row, 1972, rpt.:Macon GA: Mercer University Press, 1986) 95.

IDEOLOGY

The failure of ideological pronouncements to find confirmation is an obvious Achilles heel of any religious movement. For many propositions, there are defense mechanisms: prophecies are postponed to another sphere of existence, or they are taken as having an essentially symbolic significance. What does it mean to tell people, "Blessed are the poor in Spirit for they shall inherit the earth"? After 2,000 years that prediction is manifestly still untrue, and the literal words are later regarded as poetic utterances rather than literal promises. The promise that "the peacemakers shall see God" is presumably for a life hereafter, and as such an untestable proposition. These elements of ideology are largely rhetorical—as little heeded, even by the devout, as the injunctions to "take no thought for the morrow, what ye shall eat and what ye shall drink." A movement may then survive even though its ideological and rhetorical promises should fail. Even where prophetic utterance has been amplified by specific time-bound calculations, there is abundant, and abundantly celebrated, evidence that ideological falsity does not occasion organizational failure, in the sense that people continue to believe.

The study by Festinger and his associates might not in itself be adequate to prove this point, so local was the sect he studied, and so few its votaries.[3] One might equally not be altogether persuaded by the application of that thesis to early Christianity itself. John Gager, who has made this application, argues that cognitive dissonance was perhaps in itself a fillip to the success of the early Christians; in having themselves been proved wrong concerning the imminence of the Second Coming, they were all the more eager to get others to espouse that belief, so vindicating themselves.[4] The causes for the expansion of early Christianity remain contentious, however; and, while Gager's thesis is ingenious and plausible, it remains a speculative hypothesis—one offering a radically divergent appraisal of failure from that of Stark.

There is considerably better evidence for Gager's point in more recent movements, and perhaps most dramatically in the case of Seventh-Day Adventism. The Adventists, already disappointed by the predictions of the Second Coming for 1843, became a denomination committed to adventism only after that failure, and only after a secondary elaboration of its causes and the injunction to preach the hitherto unheeded requirements of Scripture: namely, that the Sabbath be observed on the seventh day and that the dietetic prohi-

---

[3]Leon Festinger, Henry W. Riecken, and Stanley Schachter, *When Prophecy Fails: A Social and Psychological Study of a Modern Group That Predicted the Destruction of the World* (New York: Harper & Row, 1956).

[4]John G. Gager, *Kingdom and Community* (Englewood Cliffs NJ: Prentice Hall, 1975).

bitions of the Old Testament be honored. Adventism as a denominational persuasion developed out of failure. The Jehovah's Witnesses, less dramatically perhaps, are also a testimony to the capacity of true believers to ignore evidences of failure: after setting 1914 as the occasion of the Advent, Witnesses have come to believe, despite lack of physical evidence, that the Second Coming did indeed occur then. And later, despite strong expectations that 1975 was the last possible date for the manifestation of Christ, they have found justification for the continued delay by revising the basic dateline from which their calculations proceed.

The Southcottians, in Britain, may also have been expected to abandon hope once the prodigious swelling in the belly of their prophetess turned out not to be the man-child she had predicted but only an acute case of dropsy, which killed her. Yet successors arose to continue the prophetic tradition, and Joanna Southcott, far from being discredited, was recognized by continuing later Christian Israelite adherents in the succession of God-anointed prophets.

The failure of ideological promise, then, may not in itself cause a movement to decline: indeed, the opposite has been argued. Even the falsification of categorical and specific prophecy may be irrelevant to a movement's continuance, growth, and wider distribution. On the historical evidence—and other cases could certainly be cited—we must look for structural rather than ideological deficiencies when failure occurs. This can be said while allowing that ideology often prescribes (or powerfully influences) organizational structure. To give two examples: (1) on theological grounds (and in deference to the transcendent charisma claimed for Jesus), the charismatic claims made for the leaders of Christian sects are relatively weak; (2) the theology of Christian movements often incorporates biblical specifications for church organization and ecclesiology that are taken to be mandatory for the sect and may even constitute its specific *raison d'être*.[5]

LEADERSHIP

Economists regard as a principal factor in the limitation of growth of a firm the incapacity of management and the consequent failure of control and communication. We might relate the failure of religious movements to limitations of management or leadership. Not all religious movements neatly approximate the Weberian idea-types of leadership, but those that do so may enjoy greater stability than those that do not.

---

[5]For a study in the area of interplay of doctrine and organization, which Stark considers has not received sufficiently close attention, see Bryan R. Wilson, ed., *Patterns of Sectarianism: Organization and Ideology in Social and Religious Movements* (London: Heinemann, 1967).

Many Christian sects in the past have been exemplars and expositors of a democratic tradition and have rejected any of the strong forms of leadership, favoring unanimity, consensus, and brotherhood as the ideal attributes of polity. Such movements have often fallen prey to competition and rivalry for informal status among stronger personalities. Not infrequently, factually powerful if theoretically nonexistent, informal leaders have emerged—their position depending on the subtle operation of consent, which might suffer disruption on a wide variety of counts, from differences in ideology to purely organizational arrangements. In these movements, nothing more profound than personality differences and jealousies appears to be the most frequent cause of such struggles, however wrapped up the issues may be in a tissue of ideological controversy. Such movements tend to be schismatic, and schism is, in itself, widely acknowledged to constitute failure in Christian communities. One might say that, objectively speaking, it amounts to failure for all religious leaders.

Outside radical Protestantism, democracy is a rarely encountered polity in new religious movements. Charismatic leadership, in a strong or somewhat diluted form, is widely prevalent. In the strong instances, we find the messiah, the uniquely endowed guru, or the special vehicle transmitting to mankind a message from beyond. Such figures are much more at risk in the modern world than has usually been the case in time past. The speed and ubiquity of communications, the degree of public exposure, the exaggerated style of debunking and symbolic deflowering in which the media compete are all very much at enmity with charismatic claims. Whereas a leader like Mrs. Eddy could remove and insulate herself from the outside world, admitting only selected visitors now and then, and teach an occasional very special class in the principles of Christian Science, the modern charismatic leader finds it more difficult to escape overexposure. Like Ron Hubbard, he may take to the high seas, remaining so far out of sight that he is presumed dead. Like Bhagwan Rajneesh, he may take a vow of silence, which at least partly insulates him from journalistic questioners. Like Moses Berg, of the Family of Love, he may prefer to communicate in writing to his following. Yet, charisma depends on some exposure; it needs signs and cannot persist purely and merely as myth. Here and there, now and then, at least, the leader must be seen or heard—all the more so in movements that emphasize his personal qualities on which the very prospect of salvation rests, albeit less so where the leader produces a set of principles for others to follow, as in Scientology.

Yet, in all cases, whatever the claims to be the supernature of the charismatic leader, his charisma must maintain its anthropomorphic quality, even if the leader is literally also supposed to be God. Christianity, eager to proclaim its founder to be God, has always had to remember that he was also man, and his humanity has had to be constantly acknowledged even by those most committed to his deity. But the problems of Christology are merely a paradigm case—much refined by protracted polemics and sophisticated rhetoric—of the problems inherent in all charisma. Without such reiterations and exemplifications of the humanity of the deity, the nature of authority must change, as it does when the leader is removed from the scene. The occasions for the public appearance of the charismatic leader are in themselves necessarily stage-managed. The leader presents himself, not on the terms of the public, nor even of his followers, but on his own terms and at his own times. Exposure is a risk. A charismatic leader may capitalize on the claims made for him; he need never explain himself. His followers will rationalize his idiosyncrasies and aberrations. Nonetheless, outsiders may seize on just these vulnerabilities to discredit charismatic claims. The role of the charismatic leader is unstructured: there is no job description; no set pattern; few, if any, models; and uncertain expectations. Yet, this very uncertainty renders such a man vulnerable as it simultaneously confers on him the widest area of autonomy and discretion.

The public's readiness to see charisma deflated is the simple counterpoise of unbelief to the commitment of its votaries. This readiness has undoubtedly grown in modern society, in which the charismatic manifestations are increasingly confined to the fringes, in which there is dependence on systems and not on persons, in which objectively tested routine procedures and forward planning are relied upon rather than the exceptional competences of individuals. The charismatic becomes the bizarre: few men believe that social problems can be solved by the collective will, let alone by the supposed extraordinary willpower of one gifted individual. Thus, the charismatic leader becomes the object of public ridicule.

The image of the charismatic leader depends on a mythology of origins; on the incidence of portents and signs; on exceptional experiences; on his having had the opportunity to assimilate past wisdom; on hearsay stories of stamina, energy, untutored insight, and untrained exceptional skills. Above all, he must be above normal human failings and beyond the need of such therapeutic or miraculous powers that he is supposed to possess and that he applies to others. With such an image, the charismatic leader is always at risk. He may not suffer ill health; nor may he, in any common way, indulge in the pleasures of the senses. Yet, one after another of the leaders of new movements, in being exposed to public view, has been found wanting by the media. Contrary to expectations, Maharaj Ji married; Mr. Moon has been indicted for tax evasion; Mrs. Eddy wore spectacles; Father Divine died; L. Ron Hubbard did not get a university degree—all in defiance of the things claimed for them or by them. Such items, seized on by journalists, discredit charismatic claimants in the eyes of the general public and ultimately may tarnish the image even for some followers. Charisma is difficult to prove, and claims to it are easy to refute. Since so many new religious movements depend on such claims, their easy deflation is a factor in their failure.

ORGANIZATION

A characteristic difficulty of new movements, encountered long before the problems of institutionalization begin, is the accommodation of organizational procedures to the transcendental, mystical, and spiritual elements of the movement's message. The problem is not merely one of the routinization of charisma, although that may become a part of it; rather, it is the conjoining of modern, rational methods with the inspirational and charismatic. The problem is particularly acute for new movements and a factor that may occasion their failure. For older and established bodies—in which spiritual power is only symbolically expected, in which ritual has regulated emotion into orderly rhythms—these problems are very much less evident (although they have their analogue in the accommodation of tradition to modern rational planning). New movements, which reject traditional religious forms, are free to adopt up-to-date modern techniques in the dissemination of their message. Such techniques, however, are impersonal, uninfused with spirituality, and unsacralized by long usage or traditional encrustations of sanctity. They carry the full imprint of secular purposes and pursuits and sit uneasily with claims of charismatic power and religious concern.

The media quickly detect and exploit the divergence between the spiritual message and the practical organization of new religious movements, finding scandal in what, on reflection, must of necessity be brought into some relationship if a movement is to operate at all. Traditional religious bodies are also quick to criticize these apparent discrepancies of high spiritual proclamations and mundane and material arrangements, even though the difference between their situation and that of new movements lies only in the long-established legitimation of their own way of proceeding: in the antique respectability of their forms, nomenclature, property, and role-designations. The new movements are quickly accused of being "rackets"; and financial arrangements and unconventional attitudes to sex relations (whether more lax than those of the normative standards of the wider society, as in the case of the Family of Love and the Rajneesh movement, or more austere, as in the case of the Unification Church and Krishna Consciousness) are publicized as evidences of duplicity, ulterior purpose, and corruption. The media forget that the churches themselves are necessarily administrators of extensive corporate wealth, including endowments, shareholding in industries of all kinds, landownership, and government stock; that they have often had a dubious reputation as landlords; and that their financial arrangements operate to strictly economic criteria rather than, shall we say, in accordance with such prescriptions of the Scriptures as "Consider the lilies of the field."

When the ginseng factories and shops and the fishing industry of the Unification Church are singled out as evidence of undisclosed economic interests in the exploitation of workers, the press forgets that the Roman Catholic and Eastern Orthodox churches—long before there was a press to complain—had thousands of voluntary workers who were controlled in the minutiae of their everyday lives and committed to a condition of celibacy and dissociation of the sexes for a far longer period than that required in the Unification Church or the International Society for Krishna Consciousness. Yet, new movements lack both the legitimation of tradition and the assumption of moral excellence of the old churches, which appropriate to themselves the position of moral arbiters of the doings of others. The churches raise funds by regular collections—that most ubiquitous of religious practices—by public appeals, by the sale of various products, and even by begging for worthless items that others might then be persuaded to pay for. Fund-raising from the general public is not an invention of the new movements; the Salvationists and the Seventh-Day Adventists have an established tradition, and before their bid for freewill giving, the older churches exerted compulsory tithes on the God-fearing and the godless alike. Yet, for such activities, condoned as legitimate and even desirable in established movements, the new movements are condemned, and this promotes a hostile public image that may reduce a movement's acceptability and so its prospects of success.

The balance between practical and devotional or worshipful activities often differs between old and new religions. In movements with a strong intellectual commitment—for example, Jehovah's Witnesses and the Unification Church—much more attention is given to practical activities than to devotions. The Witnesses spend their time, even when corporately engaged, largely in learning techniques for evangelization and in the purely intellectual exposition of their beliefs. Not much time is spent in praise or worship. The Moonies assemble less often and with less regularity for specifically worshipful activity than do conventional churches, and their occasions together combine the social and the devotional. They spend much more time in fund-raising, witnessing, and home church activities, or in the movement's economic subsidiaries.

Such a different division of corporately spent time also elicits the criticism of those used to more conventional and compartmentalized religiosity. The "fanaticism" of these sectarians is condemned, and the poverty of their liturgical forms is advanced almost as a proof that they are "not really religions at all." Conversely, groups in which strictly devotional activity is emphasized—and the Krishna Consciousness movement is a convenient example—and where hours are spent in chanting are regarded as engaging in a worthless and meaningless activity, as being impractical and almost self-hypnotized. If Krishna devotees are regarded as manifesting almost atavistic superstition, it is practical efficiency, the development of computerized procedures in the promotion of religious causes, that engenders more suspicion. The explicit association of spiritual perceptions and technological jargon in Scientology is in itself an affront to those for whom religion and tradition are necessarily inextricably mixed, and for whom the patina of age is readily seen as the halo of sanctity. This conjunction of religious goals and technological means, which helps the *Watchtower* to be the magazine of perhaps the widest circulation in the Third World, is mistrusted just because, for the public at large, efficiency and religiosity are not associated with each other. Clearly, in itself such efficiency is not a factor of failure for a new religion; yet it can be so represented as an incongruity, as an item that proves the case, for those who want to promote that failure.

Although new movements adopt the techniques current in contemporary society, from careful accounting to the use of computers, they are not as efficient as modern business corporations. While they meet condemnation because they utilize the impersonal, rational, electronic devices so much identified with the faceless, secular society and often thought to be so incongruous to religion, they often suffer from lack of trained personnel to make fullest use of such equipment. New movements recruit religious devotees to man their administrative posts and such people often cannot make up with religious zeal what they lack in technical competence. The Divine Light Mission appears, from published accounts, to have disrupted its own efficiency by this mixture of rational techniques and irrational dispositions of personnel.[6] New movements tend to regard too rigorous a commitment to efficiency, particularly where personnel (as distinct from equipment) are concerned, as in some way inimical to spirituality. Amateur enthusiasm is matched with professional technology, and while a new movement is condemned for its commercialism and its concern for profitability, it simultaneously suffers from an inadequately trained staff. Older movements do, in practice, go further in training their personnel, even if, for traditional reasons, they have not legitimized their functions nor felt able to acquire all the accoutrements of modern business enterprise.[7]

---

[6]See Jeanne Messer, "Guru Maharaj Ji and the Divine Light Mission," in Charles Y. Glock and Robert N. Bellah, eds., *The New Religious Consciousness* (Berkeley: University of California Press, 1975) 52-72, esp. 68.

[7]For a discussion of the problems, see Paul M. Harrison, *Authority and Power in the Free Church Tradition* (Princeton: Princeton University Press, 1959).

CONSTITUENCY

In pluralistic societies, new religious movements have shown a strong tendency to recruit from one particular constituency, and the appeal of a movement to one such constituency may undermine its appeal to other sections of society. At times, the focus of that appeal might be clearly predicated in a movement's teachings. It is not surprising that Christian Science, Theosophy, and Vedanta, emerging when they did and couched in the intellectual literary forms that they embraced, attracted something of a leisure class: middle-aged, increasingly functionless, relatively well-to-do women. Once a movement becomes typecast in this way, the likelihood of recruiting effectively and widely outside the class that already predominates may well be limited. That impediment arises, on the one hand, from the perception of those inside about who are suitable as likely recruits and from the lines of social communication that they enjoy, facilitating the recruitment of more of the same kind and prejudicing much recruitment from those who differ. On the other hand, the impediment also arises from the perception of outsiders of "what sort of people" the adherents are. The new religious movements of recent times have appealed very largely to middle-class youth. Any distinctive self-perception or social image will produce its effect, but in this case the effect is further enhanced by the particular character of the young as a constituency.

A movement with a highly disproportionate membership of one sex, age group, social class, ethnic group, or ecologically based constituency, but particularly composed from one age group or one sex, has maintenance problems. The age-based sect becomes a feature of a stage in the life cycle of adherents, having as its primary source of further recruitment only the preconversion friends of its votaries or those of their generation. When adherents age, they drop out as sect experience becomes less congruous, or, within sects recruiting the middle-aged and elderly, they die. The mood and tone of the movement, being especially congenial to one age group, becomes somewhat less than congenial to others. The movement, resting on a narrow social base, has limited viability socially, no matter what measure of internal coherence its homogenous constituency confers upon it. In the longer run, such a movement, depending on the recurrent socialization of a similar age-group, has a much more limited sense of continuity than a movement that encompasses whole families of all generations. It is, of course, true that a movement with a constituency that requires constant renewal by conversions and that embraces people who are likely, on average, to remain for a relatively short time (that is, young people dropping in and dropping out or, in other movements, older people joining but then dying) can trade on the short-term enthusiasm of neophytes. But, when turnover is high, certain features of stability may be difficult to attain.

Not all movements seek to be encompassing of all sections of society, of course, and many are ideologically committed in ways that cannot possibly accommodate the ordinary family and all its extra-religious day-to-day mundane preoccupations: property, educating the young, mortgages, pensions, hire-purchase agreements, and the like. There are movements that do not seek to proselytize, or do so in very discreet and restricted ways—the Exclusive Brethren, the Zoroastrians, even the Quakers and the Unitarians, for example—none of which can, therefore, be said to have failed because they have not gained or sought mass adherence. But these are all movements embracing whole families and successive generations. Many new movements do not embrace whole families, and many are unlikely to enjoy the natural recruitment of the next and subsequent generations. In failing to do so, they put at risk their own appearance as "normal." To gather one age group or one sex into a body that proclaims itself as a way of salvation is to impair credibility. The public at large, particularly in societies that encourage equal opportunity and nondiscrimination, expects even salvation to be equally available.

The intrinsic problems of a specific age-based constituency are most evident, since it is the case that affects a number of new movements, in the disproportionate recruitment of the young. The more total the allegiance claimed by a new movement, the more threatening it appears when it recruits particularly the young. Religious movements are perhaps most successful in recruiting those without secure social roles (middle-aged women in the early twentieth century, young people today), since these groups can most easily adopt life-styles and new commitments, and can even transform their whole way of life. Movements that demand total commitment are generally perceived as directed most specifically at the young (although it must not be overlooked that movements such as Transcendental Meditation and Scientology that, at least initially and perhaps generally for most of their clientele, require only segmentary involvement also have total roles in their organizational and teaching echelons). Total commitment with the abandonment of all earlier associations and relationships generally entails that the young give up normal preparation for later life roles, and this requirement stimulates vigorous opposition. Society as we know it, and as the vast majority of people have a stake in it, makes indispensable the training of the young for the assumption of work roles in the system. Education, which is a peculiarly sacrosanct area of modern society, is challenged and disrupted by the new religions, and these allegations by parents have been perhaps the most effective arguments in law courts and with governments. If the Moonies and the Krishna Consciousness movement were recruiting mainly post-menopausal women, public reaction would be quite different. Clearly, persecution and public pressure are not direct causes of failure in new movements, but a tarnished image is in itself a handicap to success.

INSTITUTIONALIZATION

Finally, among these endogenous factors, we must mention the general problem of institutionalization of procedures that is a process familiar enough to all students of sectarianism. H. Richard Niebuhr made the socialization of the second generation his primary argument in enunciating the dictum that the sect became a denomination in the transmission from one generation to the next; and while, as a generalization that thesis is easily falsified, nonetheless, the process is a crucial one for all movements that expect to establish a stable commitment from continuing families. New religious movements in our own time, however, are not usually marked by the recruitment of whole families. Movement appeal is more highly individuated; if families come into being, they do so usually only after individuals have been converted. But there is no automatic assumption that the progeny of such families will necessarily become committed to the movement. The processes of institutionalization thus come to rest on other bases than those provided by transmission of a religious style and culture through the vehicle of the family. Yet no other agency is equally stable and continuous, unless it be a totally bureaucratic, routinized system. As we have seen, such devices are not easily accommodated to the transmission of a personal, affective, ethical culture. We have yet to see how new religious movements adapt to this challenge. The possibility of continually recruiting new adherents from the wider society faces the difficulty of sustaining the novelty appeal of the movement's ideology and simultaneously of explaining, or explaining away, the failure to achieve high rates of internal recruitment.

The dominant modes adopted by new movements are, on the one hand, the communal and, on the other, the therapeutic. The principal difficulty for religious communitarianism is that of establishing stable patterns of life in artificial communities, which have called themselves out from the wider society on the basis of shared ideology and strength of fellow feeling. All the evidence we have suggests that such communities, as they were known in the eighteenth and nineteenth centuries, were more likely to persist if they were religious than if they were secular, but even religious communitarian groups did not have a good record of long survival, a few exceptions such as the Shakers notwithstanding. Unlike monasteries of old, such movements are unsupported either by the religious ideology of the secular society or the goodwill of the population at large. They exist as somewhat embattled enclaves, lacking the stability of lifelong commitment and permanent vows as well-legitimated and sanctified devices for eliciting and sustaining commitment. The therapeutic movements are vulnerable because their hold on the clientele is itself so narrow. The basic client-practitioner relationship of all such movements makes difficult the creation of a solid core of support that will withstand outside onslaught and internal attrition of interest. If the therapy is purchased, then the customer has a right to become discontented, apathetic, or too busy to bother further. The therapeutic movements depend on marketability of product, and that product faces increasing difficulty as therapeutic styles and the diagnoses of ailments change over time.

SOME EXTERNAL CONSIDERATIONS

Some of the foregoing items necessarily allude to exogenous factors—the reaction to new movements of the media and the general public, for instance—that have their own impact on purely internal elements of a movement's ideology, organization, or life-style. The important exogenous factors in the relative success or failure of a movement include the extent of hostile reaction by the media, the public, and authorities; confusion of movements in the pubic mind; the transitoriness and changeability of the contemporary *Zeitgeist;* and the decline of stable relationships in modern society.

Before turning briefly to these factors, one must recognize the incidence of adventitious items that may, at times, have significant impact on particular movements. Although the illustrative cases relate to more conventional Christian sects, analogous items might operate at times for particular new religious movements. The occurrence of two World Wars was undoubtedly of importance for religious groups that had espoused conscientious objection to military service as one of their principles. Such groups suddenly found it necessary either to reinforce or to abandon positions that hitherto (at least in Britain where conscription was unknown until 1917) had been theoretical. Conscription imposed on all young sectarian men a crisis of conscience and so reinforced sect solidarity by leading the weak to disfellowship themselves (by accepting conscription) and the strong to intensify their sect identity and to reinforce their long-term commitment. It is perhaps not coincidental that this matter brought sects and the state into some measure of confrontation, there being no similar impact from an external development that gave confirmation of the wisdom of their teaching; confirmation could be ignored, confrontation could not. For example, contemporary dietetic wisdom is largely confirmatory of the position generally advocated in the last century by Seventh-Day Adventists—the preference for cereals and fruit; the sparing use of sugar, meat, and synthetic substances; and abstinence from tobacco and alcohol—but that movement has not benefited particularly from the shift in public opinion, any more than have Christian Science and Mormonism, which have also condemned tobacco and alcohol. The impact of conscription on, for example, the Christadelphians was to establish more firmly the boundaries of the sect, to create internal cohesion, to give the sect a very practical goal to pursue and a persistent and recurrent cause to fight, as each individual member had to establish his religious *bona fides* in the courts. Of course, the obverse of this internal cohesion was to bring the sect into a measure of opposition to the state and to incur public opprobrium. Whether one counts such an episode as a factor in success or failure depends on the expectations that one entertains about the prospects of a religious movement.

While adventitious items of the kind already referred to may provoke public hostility, they relate to one particular issue and may be differentiated from the creation of a climate of hostility that opposes a movement *tout court*. The escalation of a type of moral panic about new religious movements begins with specific incidents and leads to general indictments. Rumor, innuendo, and the confessions of disaffected members produce a climate of opposition. Sustained press campaigns, calls for government action, and the creation of anticult groups may be factors in the failure of new religious movements that seek to convert outsiders, who are progressively alienated by such publicity. Counter-publicity and litigation are dubious and expensive weapons for a new movement to employ, as both the Scientologists and the Unification Church have discovered; being a subject of controversy is in itself a potential source of negative public reaction, and a new movement may by initiating legislation further damage its own image with the public, even if it wins in court.

The proliferation of contemporaneous new religious movements has led to confusion of one with another, arising both from public ignorance and from fear, which induces unwillingness to acquire too close a knowledge of such things. Guilt by association produces a general negative public reaction towards all new religions, even though these movements are associated with one another only in the minds of outsiders who—ignorantly, like the press, or with greater sophistication, as among academics—seek to propound some general theories concerning the whole range of similar phenomena.

The very number of new movements indicates, in at least a general way, some commonality of circumstances in the general background against which they have arisen. It cannot be said without qualification that the number of movements leads to a type of competition within an available area of recruitment, since divergent elements among them may be significant in their specific appeal; and yet, for those arising to market therapeutic techniques or those dealing with the occult, there may be a certain competitive factor that may lead to differential success and failure as there certainly is among the various "human potential" movements. There may be a tendency for movements working in one area to outbid one another, to adopt styles that exaggerate certain features of the existing social ethos in either a positive sense (that is, hedonism) or a negative sense (asceticism and alienation). Broadly, the Japanese new religions endorse hedonistic values—very evident in Sekai Kyusei Kyo (The Church of World Messianity), Perfect Liberty Kyodan, and to some extent Soka Gakkai—and so do the Rajneesh Movement, Scientology, and Transcendental Meditation. In contrast, distrust of contemporary hedonism is evident in the Krishna Consciousness movement and the Unification Church. In the hedonistic culture of contemporary society, some new movements may be tempted to vie with others in promises of gratification. It is difficult empirically to establish that the sheer profusion of movements has been a factor in the failure of any one of them, but such a development is theoretically plausible, and to some extent the emphasis in the appeal of many movements may have been influenced by the activities of others, particularly for those members drawn from the "cultic milieu."[8]

The new movements have individually divergent relationships with contemporary culture in their acceptance or rejection of its various facets. Yet all the movements operate within that cultural context and bear in some degree its imprint, even if their main thrust is in opposition to it. Even if a movement's ideas are largely condemnatory of contemporary society and its materialism, hedonism, the demand for instinctual gratification, the spontaneity of expression, and the rejection of inhibitions, nonetheless, to communicate with its audience, a movement tends to go some way in conceding to some of these values. Certainly, in its own organization, it may embrace the latest techniques of modern organization and communication. Sometimes its clientele is partly recruited after intensive exposure to extreme forms of contemporary values—as with the recruitment of ex-hippies by various charismatic groups, the Family of Love, and Krishna Consciousness. But the imprint of a particular cultural climate may entail the possibility of becoming irrelevant as the cultural context undergoes change. If movements become frozen in certain postures, this may eventually cause failure. On the other hand, insofar as they embrace change, they also risk being held up to ridicule for volatility, expediency, and opportunism.

To avoid failure, a movement must at least retain members (even if it abandons active proselytizing). Yet, movements recruiting young people—at a stage in their lives when they have forged no permanent identity, no stable roles, no permanent relationships other than those inherited by birth—are particularly vulnerable not only to the lack of experience of permanent commitment among their clientele, but also to the fact that in contemporary society abiding relationships are much less the norm than they were. We may see this in the increase of divorce and the presumed greater transitoriness of marriage; in the growing disposition for people to move house; in the growing frequency with which priests and religious, supposedly bound for life, abandon their orders; and in the Christian mission field, which is no longer peopled by individuals who have undertaken a lifetime's obligation but by those on limited, perhaps only three-year

---

[8]The "cultic milieu" is a concept developed by Colin Campbell, in "The Cult, the Cultic Milieu, and Secularization," *A Sociological Yearbook of Religion in Britain* 5 (1972): 119-36.

contracts. In part, modern culture—with its emphasis on individual autonomy, cultural pluralism, changes of personal style, the right to one's own choices and changes of mind—militates against the espousal of permanent, stable, enduring values and relationships of the kind that have characterized successful religion in the past. These contemporary features obviously affect all religions in the Western society, old and new; but for new movements, which depend so much more on young recruits unsocialized in the more persisting values of the past— the values of persistence—the prospect of failure by virtue of unstable commitment may well be even more powerful than for movements that have acquired an established form and *modus vivendi,* no matter how archaic it appears to have become.

· CHAPTER FOUR ·

How New Is New?
The Flowering of the
"New" Religious Consciousness
since 1965

J. Gordon Melton

When the history of the 1970s and 1980s is written, future historians will undoubtedly see it as the time of the great religious transition—the time in which we as people realized that the American experiment in freedom was producing a previously unimagined religious pluralism. These decades forced a vision of a time in which the dominance of Christianity in this country (which will remain for the foreseeable future) could be destroyed and replaced by a chaos of religious forms.

The fact of the matter is that during the last two decades we have witnessed the proliferation of alternatives to mainline Christianity in the appearance of several hundred religions that have immigrated to these shores from Asia and the Middle East. They have been joined by new Christian variations that have become controversial because of their practices (speaking in tongues, faith healing, and so forth) or doctrinal heresy (denial of the divinity of Jesus).

American religion experienced a major shift in power and position during the 1970s. While the nation's population grew, major liberal Protestant denominations experienced an unprecedented membership loss. But where did these members go? They did not go to the ''new'' religions and alternative faiths. The overwhelming majority went to conservative evangelical Christian Churches whose prominent growth marks another significant shift in American religious life.[1]

In light of the mass movements in Church memberships, the alternative religions represent a relatively minor phenomenon. Using the broadest definition, the alternative faiths are limited to less than 500 groups.[2] Many of these groups have less than 100 members, most have less than 1,000. Only a few such as the Unification Church, the International Society for Krishna Consciousness, the Divine Light Mission, and the Church Universal and Triumphant can count their members in the thousands. Very few—the Black Muslims, the Neo-pagans, the Association for Research and Enlightenment (the Edgar Cayce group), and a few older movements such as Christian Science—can count members in the tens of thousands.

If not yet growing appreciably in numbers, the alternative religions have moved out of the narrow cultural and ethnic niches to which they were largely confined and now claim a position in middle America. Their attraction of members still in their childbearing years means that they can expect continued expansion from children who will grow up within the group itself. Before the end of the century, the surviving groups will no longer have to rely entirely on new converts for growth.

THE ALTERNATIVE RELIGIOUS TRADITION IN AMERICA

In order to understand the current blossoming of alternative religions, a brief historical background is necessary. Such a necessity was suggested by the very hypothesis that generated the popular misnomer "new religions." The idea of a *new religious consciousness,* a perspective that the prominent alternative religions share and that suddenly burst into popularity during the late 1960s, is a widely held scholarly assumption. In examining the content of this new religious consciousness, however, students of America's alternative religions quickly realized that what has been called the *new* religious consciousness is identical in every respect with the *old* occult-theosophical teachings. That identity further suggests that the blossoming of the alternative religions in the 1970s is not so much a new event in Western culture as

---

[1]Compare the figures in the various editions of the *Yearbook of American Churches* along with the statistics in Douglas W. Johnson, Paul R. Ricard, and Bernard Quinn, *Churches and Church Membership in the United States* (Washington: Glenmary Research Center, 1971) and Bernard Quinn et al., *Churches and Church Membership in the United States* (Washington: Glenmary Research Center, 1980).

[2]This information is derived from the files of the Institute for the Study of American Religion and the *Directory of Religious Bodies in the United States* (New York: Garland, 1978).

the continuation of the flowering of occult mysticism and Eastern thought that began in the nineteenth century.[3]

The emergence of the alternative religious tradition in the West is fittingly symbolized by the 1893 World's Parliament of Religions in which for the first time representatives of all the major world religions (and not a few minor ones) gathered for a six-week meeting for dialogue around a multiplicity of issues and a sharing of belief systems. Out of this meeting several alternative religions were formed. Swami Vivekananda, possibly the single most electrifying speaker at the Parliament, organized the first American Hindu group: the Vendanta Society. Buddhist Anagarika Dharmapala talked philosopher-editor Paul Carus into organizing the first American Buddhist group that sought members from among the general population, the Maha Bodhi Samaj. A few days after the Parliament, Dharmapala admitted the first Westerner into the Maha Bodhi Samaj at a Theosophical Society meeting.[4]

The Theosophical Society, which brought Annie Besant, possibly the second most charismatic speaker at the Parliament, held its last united gathering during those weeks. Soon after the Parliament ended, the American section under William Q. Judge bolted from the European and Indian branches and took most of the members with it. Judge died within a year of the schism, and the American Theosophists further divided. The four theosophical bodies present by 1900 continued to divide and became the source for most of the occult bodies that appeared in the twentieth century.

The 1890s saw the first stable Spiritualist organization, the National Spiritualist Association of Churches (1893), and the numerous metaphysical-New Thought groups that had spread across the United States in the last half of the nineteenth century formed their first national organization, the International Divine Science Association. Its biannual conventions held between 1892 and 1899 led to the national New Thought Convention at Hartford, Connecticut, in 1899. That convention culminated in the formation of the International New Thought Alliance in 1914.

By the end of the decade, alternative religion had a broad national base with national organizations representative of the major Eastern faiths, Spiritualism, the occult, and New Thought. Once established, these organizations grew steadily. Spiritualism, for example, often thought of as having its heyday in the nineteenth century, experienced a growth in the twentieth cen-

---

[3]Cf. Carl Raschke, *The Interruption of Eternity, Modern Gnosticism and the Origins of the New Religious Consciousness* (Chicago: Nelson-Hall, 1980).

[4]Cf. Rick Fields, *How the Swans Came to the Lake* (Boulder CO: Shambhala, 1981).

tury hardly imagined possible by the nineteenth-century lecturers and local associations.

This first flowering of alternative religion in the 1890s did not happen without preparation. It built upon the long history of the two Swedenborgian Churches, Mesmerism, Spiritualism and psychical research, and P. P. Quimby's metaphysical students. Also not to be forgotten, in a country that could boast of only thirty-five percent of its citizens as church members, was the continuing popularity of folk magic in rural America and the introduction and spread of African magical religion (Voodoo) in Louisiana.

And lest we come away with the notion that this alterative religious community grew among people alienated from the mainstream of American culture, let us take note of the center of the alternative religious community in the 1880s: Boston and its environs.[5] This community was built around the prestigious Lowell Institute, which opened its hall to the dissemination of a variety of new ideas, and the faculties of Harvard and Boston Universities. Most prominent among its leaders were the two sons of a devout Swedenborgian, William and Henry James. The former founded the American Society for Psychical Research in 1884 and brought many of America's intellectual elites, such as Charles Sanders Pierce and Josiah Royce, into it. Brother Henry was one of a number of Boston intellectuals with more than a passing interest in Buddhism, an interest sparked by a set of lectures given in 1877 at the Lowell Institute by Harvard zoologist Edward Moore upon his return from Japan.

Around the James brothers could be found a growing following for Eastern religion. The Unitarian Church forged an alignment with several Hindu groups and brought the first Hindu teachers to America. Remembering the Transcendentalists' role in the Unitarian action, Protap Chundar Mozoomdar, the first of these gurus, went directly to Concord upon his arrival in America in 1883.[6] Emerson's widow opened her living room for his first lecture. Also, during this decade, two Harvard professors, William S. Bigelow and Ernest Fenollosa, traveled to Japan where they were formally received into the Tendai Buddhist sect. Fenollosa had a major role in the Oriental movement in American art due both to his purchases of Oriental art works and the books he wrote about his discoveries.

Boston was, of course, home to Christian Science (founded in 1875) and the major students of Phineas P. Quimby—Annette and Horatio Dresser and Warren Felt Evans. Rev. Charles Cullis, the unknown fountainhead of the

----

[5]Ibid.

[6]Suresh Chunder Bose, *The Life of Protap Chunder Mozoomdar* (Calcutta: Nababidhan Trust, 1940).

orthodox Christian healing movement, served a Boston parish in the 1880s. His work was continued by two students of William James, Elwood Worshester and Samuel McComb, who combined Cullis's interest in healing and James's in psychical research to begin the Emmanuel Movement: the first successful healing movement to spread through the mainline churches. It survives today as the International Order of St. Luke the Physician.[7]

The Boston community also produced America's first astrological superstar, Evangeline Adams (from the prominent political family).[8] She became interested in astrology only after a prior adoption of an Eastern (Hindu) religious perspective given to her by Dr. J. Heber Smith. Smith, a nationally known diagnostician on Boston University's medical faculty, integrated astrology into his professional work. The growing astrological community included astronomer Joseph G. Dalton, who compiled one of the first American-produced ephemerides, and Helen Taylor Craig, author of *The Stars and Your Destiny,* an early astrological best-seller.

The development of an alternative religious community that could be said to have given its allegiance to what would recently be called the "new religious consciousness" did not end with the flowering in Boston or the institutionalization of the community in the 1890s. It grew steadily throughout the twentieth century. The Boston community illustrates how strongly Eastern religion, the occult, and New Thought metaphysics interacted with each other. Occult groups, by far the strongest segment of the community on a national level, became the avenue for introducing Eastern religion and thought to America. A basic idea grew within the occult community: true occult wisdom was to be found in the East. Prominent American advocates of Eastern thought arose at the turn of the century. New Thought leader William Walker Atkinson authored several New Thought classics but is best remembered for the volumes he penned under the pseudonym Yogi Ramacharaka. L. W. de Laurence, founder of the occult publishing company that bears his name, began his occult life as a "Hindoo" guru.

As Eastern teachers followed Vivekananda to America, they sought out occult publishers such as the *New York Magazine of Mysteries,* the Yogi Publication Society, Samuel Weiser, and the Theosophical Publishing Company to spread their message. The Theosophical Society provided the major force for the spread of Eastern thought. From its presses rolled the first books advocating (as opposed to merely examining) Eastern thought. Blavatsky standardized the term "reincarnation," which had, until she became a pop-

---

[7]Sanford Gifford, *The Emmanuel Movement, Medical Psychotherapy and the Battle over Lay-Treatment, 1906-1912* (published by the author, 1974).

[8]Evangeline Adams, *The Bowl of Heaven* (New York: Blue Ribbon Books, 1926).

ular writer and patron of occult authors, described a belief called by many names: transmigration, rebirth, metempsychosis, and so forth.

The steady growth of the alternative community was interrupted in the early part of the century by a series of Asian exclusion acts that cut immigration and denied potential citizenship to Asians already in America. The acts had two effects on the religious community. First, they cut off the trickle of Eastern teachers coming to the United States, thus effectively limiting the spread of Hinduism and Buddhism. Buddhist teachers allowed into the country largely confined their activities to serving the Japanese-speaking groups on the West Coast. The few swamis who came established small Hindu movements: Baba Premanand Bharati (the Krishna Samaj); Yogi Hare Rama (the Benares League); Sri Deva Ram Sukul (Hindu Yoga Society); Swami Bhagwan Bissessar (Yogessar); Srimath Swami Omkar (Sri Mariya Ashrama); Kedar Nath Das Gupta (Dharma Mandala); American-born guru Pierre Bernard (American Order of Tantricks); and Pandit Acharya (Yoga Research Institute).

The small amount of Buddhist work (primarily Zen) begun among Caucasians was completely disrupted by the internment of all the teachers during World War II.

Second, the exclusion of Asian teachers shifted the burden of spreading Asian wisdom to occult teachers. After World War II, Eastern thought was filtered through (and more or less distorted by) the likes of Manley Palmer Hall, Alice Bailey, Baird T. Spaulding, and Edwin Dingle. Possibly more important than their individual teachings, however, occultists as a group hammered home the central idea, "The East is the true home of spiritual knowledge and occult wisdom."

Most occultists would satisfy their yearnings for the true wisdom by sitting in occult groups and reading occult books. A few, not satisfied with secondhand knowledge, made pilgrimages to the East and discovered teachers such as Meher Baba and Ramana Maharshi. A few pilgrims returned home to begin Eastern religious groups. Growth was slow. Personal contact between Eastern teachers and potential Western disciples was infrequent. Travel was difficult, time-consuming, and expensive. Nevertheless, new Hindu and Buddhist groups emerged and grew in the West, further preparing it for the blossoming to come in the late 1960s.

The lengthy history of the new religious consciousness in America prior to the mid-1960s established a foundation for the rapid spread of alternative religions in the late 1960s and 1970s. After World War II, the further growth of the Asian religions in the West was abetted by a series of events in Asia. First, after Japan's surrender, America sanctioned religious freedom. The new freedom resulted in the rapid spread of many suppressed religious groups and the founding of many more.

Several hundred emerged within a decade. Second, in 1948 India attained its independence. As full members of the British Commonwealth, Indians had a freedom to move, and they spread throughout the British Isles and Western Europe. Among the travelers were swamis, gurus, and avatars. Third, the Chinese Revolution sent numerous refugees into Hong Kong. Among the refugees were religious leaders fleeing atheistic rule. This mass movement led directly to the crucial event that, building upon both Asian and American history, triggered the contemporary blossoming of alternative religions in the United States.

In 1965 President Lyndon B. Johnson quietly rescinded the Oriental Exclusion Act for the purpose of allowing the Hong Kong refugees to enter the United States. The consequences have been staggering. Johnson's action placed Asian immigration quotas upon a par with those of Western Europe. For the first time in half a century, Eastern teachers were free to migrate to America. The growth of the so-called new religions (primarily the old religions of Asia newly arrived in the West) can be traced to the movement of Eastern teachers to take up residency in the United States beginning in 1965:

> 1965 Swami Bhaktivedanta (ISKCON)
>   Sant Keshavadas (Temple of Cosmic Wisdom)
>   Thera Bode Vinita (Buddhist Vihara Society)
> 1968 Yogi Bhajan (Sikh Dharma)
> 1969 Tarthang Tulku (Tibetan Nyingmapa)
> 1970 Swami Rama (Himalayan Institute)
> 1971 Swami Satchidananda (Integral Yoga Institute)
>   Gurudev Chitrabhanu (Meditation International Center)
>   Maharaj Ji (Divine Light Mission)
> 1972 Sun Myung Moon (Unification Church)
>   Vesant Paranjpe (Fivcfold Path)

Once the significant legal blockade to the growth of Asian religion was removed, changes that had occurred in the previous half century came to the fore to actively promote the growth of both Asian and occult religions. Three changes stand out as particularly important: the new stance of Asian religion, the awareness of Westerners about Eastern religion, and several developments in the scientific community.

ASIAN RELIGION'S NEW STANCE

Between 1917 and 1965 Asian religion changed, at least in one important aspect. It was motivated by *a new missionary spirit*. Very like the change that came over Christianity in the move from the eighteenth to the nineteenth century, a dormant zeal to spread their faith emerged among Hindus and Buddhists, who set out to return the compliment paid Asia by the Christian missionaries in the previous century.

Prior to the restrictions on Indian migration, only three swamis had been enthused enough to begin a Western Hindu thrust, and only Vivekananda's work survived. His efforts were complemented in the 1920s by the arrival of Swami Yogananda and the few other gurus who slipped through the meager quotas allowed for India. Only Vivekananda's and Yogananada's efforts found even miniscule support in their homeland. This lack of interest among Indians in converting Westerners is no better illustrated than in the case of Sikhism. Prior to 1968 thousands of Sikhs crossed the Canadian-American border illegally and settled on the West Coast as agricultural workers. Being predominantly male and unable to bring potential wives from the Punjab, they intermarried with the local population, primarily Mexican-Americans. However, until Yogi Bhajan appeared in 1968, fresh from the Punjab with a definite mission to evangelize the West, no orthodox Sikh teacher had tried to proselytize among the non-Punjabi population.

Buddhism actually began a missionary attempt in the 1890s, but that move was *not* initiated by Asians. It resulted from the zeal of a Western convert, Col. Henry S. Olcott, the president of the Theosophical Society. Olcott's major ally was Anagarika Dharmapala, whom he encouraged to come to the World's Parliament of Religions and to start the Maha Bodhi Samaj in America. But Olcott generated little response from other Buddhists, particularly the Japanese. It took Soyen Shaku, who had also addressed the Parliament, a decade to convince his supporters that Westerners were ready and, more importantly, fit to receive the treasures of Buddhism. He was able to start and solidify a small Zen movement in California before the axe fell cutting off further immigration.

In recent decades, even Japanese Buddhism has absorbed the missionary spirit. The Soto Zen sect set up an English-language guest department to receive foreign students and train potential leaders. The Reformed Zen Church, headed by Jiyu Kennett-roshi, is a direct result. After years of work in Japan, Kennett-roshi established a Soto mission as an outpost of the department in California. The sect also began to send to America roshis who were proficient in English. The first came in 1959 to assume leadership of the old Soto temple in San Francisco. Without any prior response from the English-speaking community to build upon, Suzuki-roshi built the San Francisco Zen Center, now one of the largest Zen communities in America, within two years.

The Hindu response to the new open-door policy has included an increase in the number of gurus receiving guidance to make the West the site of their labors. We could multiply the examples, but the conclusion would be the same: the United States and the West are experiencing a large-scale movement of both people and religion from East to West, a movement with the potential to reshape the Western religious scene as significantly as nineteenth-century Christianity reshaped Africa and the Orient.

WESTERN RESPONSE

The new missionary zeal in the East encountered a public situation greatly different from that Vivekananda and Soyen Shaku had experienced in 1893. The American public had, by 1965, been prepared for the spread of Eastern ideas both in the multiplication of academic courses in Eastern religion and the proliferation of books and other forms of information on Eastern teachings. No better measure of the growth of openness to Eastern ideas can be found than in the spread of the belief in reincarnation. In the 1880s, when the Theosophical Society began to champion the idea in the West, few supporters could be found. By the turn of the century, reincarnation had strong non-Theosophical advocates, and in the 1920s it split non-Theosophical groups such as the Spiritualists and New Thought. By 1980 twenty-three percent of the American public professed belief.

The spread of Zen, the first form of Buddhism to receive a popular response in America, can be traced directly to the appearance of English-language materials. Early in this century, D. T. Suzuki translated a variety of Buddhist texts into English. These translations and others such as those in Dwight Goddard's *A Buddhist Bible* (1932), however, were not of the quality or type to attract a popular audience. Still they did provide material for a small group of highly motivated people, among them Alan Watts. In 1956 Watts published *The Spirit of Zen,* a popular treatment of Suzuki's Zen that found a ready public audience for a popular movement—Beat Zen.

The more successful gurus, upon initiation of work in the West, would either come with a preexisting supply of books or quickly move to print popular inexpensive editions—the first step in a movement to audiovisuals, which are now widely employed by those groups wealthy enough to produce them.

SCIENCE INTO RELIGION

Three significant developments within the scientific community have played a crucial role in the blossoming of the alternative religions since 1965. First, in the 1930s parapsychology was born and for many superseded psychical research (which played a role in the flowering of alternative religion in the 1890s). Founder J. B. Rhine wanted to add a new methodology to the study of paranormal experience, and the resulting efforts had some unplanned consequences, not the least being the granting of a previously denied legitimacy to occult religions. The symbol of that new level of acceptance was the full recognition of the Parapsychological Association as a member of the American Association for the Advancement of Science.

Second, another scientific revolution began in 1938 when a Swiss chemist synthesized what became known as LSD. His later discovery of its mind-altering effects and the spread of the chemical through the scientific community after World War II set up a religious revival when several of the scientists turned from research to evangelism. The popular discovery of consciousness-altering chemicals and their widespread availability, coupled with the identification of psychedelic experiences with religious experiences, seem to have strengthened the turn to religion as an aftereffect of their imbibement.

The mainline churches, as a whole, opposed the use of psychedelic substances on moral grounds while the alternative religions have tended to accept them (The Farm), tolerate them (most groups), or provide members with what they believe to be a better ecstasy (Hare Krishna, Jesus People).

Third, a revolution in psychiatry and psychology has provided a new openness to alternative religions. The twentieth-century critique of Freud and Watson produced a number of alternative psychological systems, many of which have found a level of acceptance among professionals. Some of these systems took insights directly from the occult and, in turn, became legitimizing agents and tools of familiarization for alternative religions. The most prominent example, of course, is the work of C. G. Jung, who became an accomplished student of the occult and whose thought, especially his concept of archetypes, gave a theoretical underpinning to modern Neo-Paganism and magic. Lesser known is Robert Assagioli, an Italian psychiatrist who absorbed Theosophy and especially its revisionist presentation produced by Alice Bailey. His thought and the professionals who practice his system, psychosynthesis, have become thoroughly intertwined with Bailey's Arcane School and its offshoots.

On a broader scale, humanistic psychology took a positive turn toward religion and religious experience. In connection with parapsychology, it began to explore "peak" experiences and altered states of consciousness. Joined by Asian-trained psychologists, it gave birth to the human potentials movement whose role as a bridge between more traditional psychology and alternative religions has been frequently noted.

IN CONCLUSION

The groups popularly called "new religions" did not suddenly burst upon the American public in the late 1960s. Alternative religions that participate in the theosophical-occult-Eastern worldview popularly called the "New Religious Consciousness" have been part of the American scene for at least a century and a half and have steadily grown in force and size and influence since their first appearing in Swedenborgianism, Transcendentalism, and Spiritualism. Their dramatic blossoming in the 1970s can best be seen as the continuation of the growing presence of alternative religions within Western culture as a whole.

The prime resource for alternative religions has been the traditional religions of Asia. Transcendentalism grew as a response to the first translations of Hindu and Sufi writings into English. The burst of alternative religion begun in the 1890s was spurred by the dissemination of popular literature on Eastern religion but slowed by the Asian exclusion acts. During the twentieth century, numerous trends that challenged dominant religious perspectives and favored the occult-Eastern worldview appeared. These trends included the development of a missionary zeal by Eastern religion, the spread of information about Eastern religion in the West, and the emergence of parapsychology, psychedelic drugs, and humanistic psychology. These trends would have converged with the alternative religious community in any case and produced a spurt of growth.

The 1965 recision of the Oriental Exclusion Act helped to hasten the convergence and magnified the effect. With the greatly increased access to the American public, Asian teachers flocked to America (and the West as a whole) and turned what might have become merely another small spurt of growth in alternative religions into a major increase in American religious pluralism.

As noted above, the new and alternative religions are still far from reaching a point that they can seriously challenge the power of mainline churches or Evangelical Christianity. They have, however, grown to the point that they can, if allowed to continue without significant legal obstacle, provide an alternative that can and will gain the increasing allegiance of middle America.

DIAGNOSTIC ELEMENTS

CHAPTER FIVE

Science and Religion: The Case of Scientology

William Sims Bainbridge

A third of a century after its founding, Scientology has achieved moderate but still uncertain success. Its degree of tension with the environment is variable, both because its relations with the outside continually change and because it is a set of nested secret societies, those at the core being more deviant than those open to new recruits. While its psychological therapy techniques are well designed to build strong social bonds among members, it has not proven good at spreading rapidly through family and friendship networks. Scientology's greatest departure from Stark's model of success is that it has no discernible cultural continuity with the Judeo-Christian tradition.

However, Scientology claims cultural continuity with science, Christianity's modern rival in defining reality. It is a "technological religion" (Braddeson, 1969:100), for example using electronic E-Meters in pastoral counseling. Here, I shall consider two great strengths: Scientology's roots in the popular science fiction subculture and its fortuitous harmony with contemporary scientific cosmology.

SCIENCE FICTION

Scientology leader David Aden told me the "extreme popularity" of science fiction may affect religion: "In some ways, *Star Wars*, *E.T.*, and even *Close Encounters of the Third Kind* all have religious or quasi-religious overtones or messages. The Jedi were members of a *religion*, not merely a military force; E.T.'s mental connection with the boy postulates or may imply some kind of spiritual kinship; and the final scene of *Close Encounters* has religious overtones." In *Star Wars*, Obi-Wan Kenobi says, "The Force is what gives the Jedi his power. It's an energy field created by all living things. It surrounds us and penetrates us. It binds the galaxy together." Yet Han Solo initially rejects The Force as "Hokey religion " (Lucas, 1977:49, 78).

Science fiction is both propaganda for science and a distorter of science in the popular mind. Where science sees a universe governed by chance and mechanism, science fiction imagines a galaxy filled with life and oriented toward human purposes. Thus, it functions rather like a new civil religion, legitimating anthropocentric attitudes and providing compensators for the alien sterility of the physical world. Although science fiction writers tend to reject conventional religious teachings, stories concerning religion are quite common. Their fans accept notions (like extrasensory perception) that might be regarded as supernatural, and they have contributed to the birth of several new religions, Scientology being the most prominent example (Bainbridge, 1982a).

In 1938, adventure author L. Ron Hubbard began writing for John W. Campbell's magazine *Astounding Science Fiction,* now called *Analog.* Hubbard's 1982 novel, *Battlefield Earth,* is dedicated to Campbell, Robert A. Heinlein, and E. E. Van Vogt. Campbell was the leading force of the "Golden Age" of science fiction, and Hubbard's "dear friend" Heinlein was the most highly regarded author. Van Vogt shaped the early development of Dianetics and Scientology through a novel, *The World of Null-A,* based on General Semantics: a pseudoscience that sought to cure personal and social ills through linguistic therapy, invented by Alfred Korzybski (1948, 1950; cf. Gardner, 1957:274, 281).

In 1950, Hubbard lectured on "General Dianetics." Hubbard (1968c:154) criticized Korzybski's ideas but cited this earlier cultic entrepreneur as an intellectual mentor (cf. Wallis, 1977:36). Van Vogt considered establishing a Church of General Semantics, and it was apparently through his imaginary future world of null-A that it became a template for Scientology. Van Vogt (1961) saw a close connection between the linguistic therapy of Korzybski and Hubbard's theory of engram memories, but many similarities are apparent to the disinterested observer as well.

The hero of Van Vogt's novel is Gilbert Gosseyn—"go sane," the opposite of "go crazy"—a pawn in a cosmic chess game. In 2560, the story goes, an elite, angelic, prepotent corps of General Semanticists rules the United States. To become a member of this group, a man must study the philosophy of null-A and then submit to a month-long examination by The Games Machine. The characteristics required to win are those attributed to the state of "clear" in Scientology.

At times of danger, Semanticist supermen achieve "cortical-thalmaic pause," a willed disconnection of the lower centers of the brain rather like "release" from the "reactive mind" in Dianetics. Gosseyn's adventure involves wheels within wheels of conspiracy, and at the end he learns he has been the puppet of a mysterious man who turns out to be—himself. Not only does Scientology postulate nested mysteries (Hubbard, 1970), but it uses many psychological procedures to transform a Scientologist into a puppet master of himself, working the psychic strings from "a few feet behind his head" (Hubbard, 1968a:77).

Today many Scientologists assert their religion offers spirituality rather than status and power, but when I studied it in 1970 for six months by joining, Scientology was an elaborate game played for compensatory prestige (Bainbridge, 1971: Bainbridge and Stark, 1979, 1980). According to Hubbard, "Life can best be understood by likening it to a game" (Hubbard, 1956:45) and "The highest activity is playing a game" (Hubbard, 1965:103). The E-Meter lie detector used in Scientology is far simpler than Van Vogt's Game Machine, but similarly is used to authenticate high status and confer honor.

Scientology was a system of status achievement alternative to science and the universities, even at one time offering a doctorate degree (Hubbard, 1968b:12). Hubbard asserted Dianetics was a science (Hubbard 1951b), yet it first appeared in Campbell's fiction magazine, and Campbell contributed an essay on the scientific method to the first Dianetics book (Hubbard, 1950a, 1950b). While science fiction fans were the first converts to Dianetics (Gardner, 1957:265), a controversy immediately swirled around it in the subculture (Hubbard, 1951a; Sturgeon, 1951; del Rey, 1951) and they generally do not accept Scientology today.

We can quantify the relationship between Hubbard and science fiction with survey data from two sources. From March 1938 through October 1976, *Astounding Science Fiction* conducted a monthly readership poll called "The Analytical Laboratory." Readers ranked the stories in an issue from best-liked to least; then the editor calculated the average point score and relative standing of each story. Although there are several problems with the huge dataset represented by the 464 published polls, it proved possible to translate the scores into a universal ranking system, using regression formulae (Bainbridge, 1980).

Based on pilot survey research (Bainbridge and Dalzeil, 1978a, 1978b), I administered two long questionnaires at the 1978 "Iguanacon" World Science Fiction Convention—which drew about 4,000 authors, editors, artists, critics, and diehard fans from all over the world, representing the heart of the science fiction subculture. The main questionnaire (N = 595) focused on authors and types of literature, while the other (N = 379) emphasized movies and television. Both charted the ideological structure of science fiction (Bainbridge, 1982b) and included questions about L. Ron Hubbard. Table 1 presents statistics on the popularity of 30 authors, all those who were rated at least ten times by the Analytical Laboratory and also were included in the main Iguanacon survey.

Table 1 gives the authors in order of decreasing popularity in the Analytical Laboratory, and while the datasets were formulated differently, one can chart changes in popularity over the years by comparing them. In Hubbard's science fiction days, *Astounding* was the central publication of the field, so its poll represents the subculture well. Because I was interested in popularities of authors as they were known to readers, I did not include the stories an author wrote under pseudonyms. Hubbard published in *Astounding* using the names Frederick Englehardt, Rene Lafayette, and Kurt von Rachen (Day,

TABLE 1

	ASTOUNDING-ANALOG ANALYTICAL LABORATORY			1978 WORLD SF CONVENTION "IGUANACON" SURVEY		
AUTHOR	FICTION ITEMS	MEAN DATE	POINT RANK	MEAN SCORE	PERCENT LOVING	PERCENT FAMILIAR
Robert A. Heinlein	25	1947	145	5.05	52.6	97.1
E. E. "Doc" Smith	13	1944	190	3.48	18.1	68.7
Jerry Pournelle	11	1973	265	3.96	18.7	76.3
A. E. Van Vogt	59	1944	298	4.10	18.1	81.5
Harry Harrison	32	1966	316	4.21	18.4	76.0
Frank Herbert	28	1963	329	4.42	26.3	87.6
Poul Anderson	67	1960	332	4.37	38.0	37.1
Hal Clement	29	1953	340	4.18	19.2	71.9
Jack Williamson	19	1944	343	4.13	13.8	64.5
Clifford D. Simak	39	1949	350	4.54	25.6	79.5
Isaac Asimov	45	1950	351	5.08	48.2	97.3
Raymond F. Jones	31	1949	378	3.15	2.6	25.7
James Blish	12	1956	380	4.37	16.2	86.1
Gordon R. Dickson	43	1965	387	4.64	30.7	79.5
James H. Schmitz	39	1964	390	4.43	31.1	43.2
Eric Frank Russell	45	1951	397	4.11	19.8	45.9
Randall Garrett	32	1961	405	4.03	15.8	40.5
Walter M. Miller, Jr.	10	1952	410	4.35	22.0	41.3
Mack Reynolds	48	1964	428	3.47	10.9	55.6
Murray Leinster	40	1953	432	4.10	15.0	59.5
Lester del Rey	24	1944	433	4.03	12.7	79.5
Lewis Padgett	35	1945	434	4.46	29.6	38.0
Fritz Leiber	14	1946	439	4.85	38.5	85.0
L. Ron Hubbard	23	1944	441	2.15	3.6	46.4
Theodore Sturgeon	23	1945	457	4.69	31.8	86.6
L. Sprague de Camp	27	1946	460	4.41	22.5	79.2
Katherine MacLean	10	1959	472	3.78	8.9	30.1
Robert Silverberg	15	1961	480	4.52	23.6	84.7
Algis Budrys	22	1957	636	3.89	11.0	53.6
A. Bertram Chandler	19	1952	647	3.81	10.7	45.4

POPULARITIES OF LEADING SCIENCE FICTION AUTHORS

1952; McGhan, 1976), as well as his own, but here we are concerned with the public perception of him as revealed through the ratings of stories widely known to be his.

The first two columns in Table 1 report the number of stories and novel episodes published under the author's name during the years of the Analytical Laboratory and the mean year of their appearance, which for Hubbard's twenty-three items was 1944. The third column gives the estimated rank for the typical story by the author out of a thousand *Astounding* stories taken at random. The details of this index are explained in the original article. Low numbers mean high rank, and a story of perfectly average popularity would receive a score of 500. Hubbard's score of 441 means his typical story was received with slightly more than average enthusiasm. But he was rated much lower than his associate A. E. Van Vogt, who had exactly the same mean year of publication and thus was facing exactly the same competition.

The main Iguanacon questionnaire asked respondents to rate 138 authors and 62 kinds of literature on a standard 7-point preference scale, from "0" (do not like) to "6" (like very much). Five editions of this questionnaire presented the items in different random orders to guard against spurious results from accidents of placement. The fourth column in Table 1 gives the mean preference rating on the 0 to 6 scale, while the fifth gives the percent of those rating the author who awarded him the top score of 6, indicating that they love his works. The final column gives the percent of 595 familiar with each writer, a measure of popular recognition within the science fiction subculture.

Among all 53 authors with ten or more items in the Analytical Laboratory, Hubbard stands 30th in popularity, and among the 30 in this table, he stands 24th. Thus he was regarded in his day as a passable, familiar author but not one of the very best. The subculture wishes it could forget him today. His mean Iguanacon score of 2.15 is the lowest in the list, a full point lower than the second lowest, Raymond F. Jones. The percentage giving him a "6" score is much lower than any of the others except Jones. While his popularity has dropped steeply among the core members of the science fiction subculture, the authors flanking him in the list, Leiber and Sturgeon, have risen near the top over the same years.

For deeper correlational analysis of the Iguanacon data, we need to focus on respondents who are especially valid representatives of their subculture. The questionnaire included 140 supposed author names, two of which were bogus—a trap to catch dishonest, frivolous, or inattentive respondents. Four hundred and nine respondents avoided rating these fake authors yet did rate 50 or more of the real ones, thus proving themselves reliable experts. Hubbard's mean rating in this group was 2.14, and fully 217 of the 409 expressed an opinion about him. Only Richard S. Shaver ranked lower, with 1.19.

For more than a decade, Shaver caused great controversy in science fiction with a series of stories about a sinister race of "dero" gnomes living under the earth (Palmer, 1958; Shaver, 1958; Steichart, 1958). The subculture was offended by Shaver's vehement claim that the poorly written stories were true and that the world faced imminent invasion from underground. In the 1970s, Erich von Daeniken achieved somewhat more success with stories of the same kind (Bainbridge, 1978). Raymond A. Palmer—Shaver's editor, promoter, and defender—got the third lowest Iguanacon mean score, 2.22. Table 2 lists all authors correlated with Hubbard above .19 (achieved by Heinlein), significant beyond the .01 level.

By far the strongest correlations are with Shaver ($r = .46$) and Palmer ($r = .44$). Apparently, respondents feel that what Hubbard has been doing with

TABLE 2

AUTHORS ASSOCIATED WITH HUBBARD IN IGUANACON SURVEY DATA					(N = 409)
		CORRELATION (r) WITH PREFERENCE FOR:			
AUTHOR	MEAN RATING	L. RON HUBBARD	JOHN W. CAMPBELL	A. E. VAN VOGT	ROBERT A. HEINLEIN
Richard S. Shaver	1.19	.46	.22	.29	.18
Raymond A. Palmer	2.22	.44	.27	.36	.06
Jack Williamson	4.17	.37	.33	.38	.22
Richard Wilson	3.33	.36	.05	− .08	.04
Raymond F. Jones	3.23	.35	.26	.22	.01
Otis Adelbert Kline	2.67	.32	.19	.21	.32
E. E. "Doc" Smith	3.40	.28	.30	.33	.20
Mack Reynolds	3.46	.27	.26	.31	.27
Eric Frank Russell	4.14	.27	.37	.21	.20
Donald A. Wollheim	3.47	.26	.36	.22	.23
Murray Leinster	4.06	.25	.33	.40	.26
John W. Campbell, Jr.	3.91	.24	---	.23	.23
A. E. Van Vogt	4.06	.23	.23	---	.24
Arthur C. Clarke	4.92	.23	.28	.24	.32
Lin Carter	2.63	.22	.20	.35	.20
Edmond Hamilton	3.98	.22	.27	.28	.10
Philip Jose Farmer	4.67	.22	.08	.14	.17
Jerry Pournelle	3.95	.22	.28	.30	.24
Stanley G. Weinbaum	4.03	.22	.28	.20	.10
Robert E. Howard	3.36	.21	.10	.11	.16
Hal Clement	4.18	.20	.25	.30	.20
Ben Bova	3.71	.20	.22	.34	.18
Robert A. Heinlein	5.07	.19	.23	.24	---

Scientology is similar to what Shaver and Palmer did: advertising science fiction dreams as if they were solid facts. In the 1930s, there were vain attempts to mobilize science fiction on behalf of such causes as communism and technocracy (Bainbridge, 1976), and the subculture developed a powerful consensus that SF should stay out of world affairs and not seek to make the fiction real.

The list of twenty-three authors in Table 2 includes Hubbard's editor, John W. Campbell; Campbell's successor at *Astounding-Analog,* Ben Bova; and Hubbard's associates, Heinlein and Van Vogt. The most popular novel by Raymond F. Jones, *The Alien,* involves the medical transformation of the hero into a superman, a theme very close to that of Scientology. Many authors on the list are classic writers of Hubbard's period or before, including some—like Williamson, Smith, Leinster, Clarke, and Heinlein—who are among the most respected. Most of them wrote for *Astounding.* For comparison, I have included columns for Campbell, Van Vogt and Heinlein. The rough correspondence of most coefficients across the rows suggests that Hubbard represents the group of authors he worked among and shows that respondents' preferences are based on real knowledge.

The hypothesis that science fiction fans reject Hubbard because he has founded a new "occult" religion receives little support from the data. Out of the 62 types of literature included in the main questionnaire, the pair with the lowest mean scores are "occult literature" (2.05) and "the holy Bible" (2.17). In their personal lives, these fans appear extremely secular and irreligious, yet my surveys find them especially likely to believe in extrasensory perception, and many of the most popular authors have written about religion (Farmer, 1977; cf. Ash, 1977). Preference for Hubbard does not correlate with preference for "occult literature" ($r = .04$) or "the holy Bible" ($r = .05$) among the 409 good respondents, nor are these two literatures associated ($r = .05$).

In the movie and television questionnaire, however, Hubbard is significantly associated with two pseudoscience television programs, "In Search Of" ($r = .26$) and "Project UFO" ($r = .20$), as is Shaver (Bainbridge, 1979). Respondents consider Scientology to be pseudoscience rather than religion, and they do not like it. However, part of Hubbard's unpopularity may stem from the kind of fiction he wrote, a possibility examined through correlations linking him with various types of literature in Table 3.

Here I have included Hubbard's three associates and a fifth author, Harlan Ellison, who represents the opposite end of the field. In the 1960s, Ellison led the New Wave movement against the literary and political values of Campbell's *Astounding.* Hubbard's associates wrote classic science fiction from the early days, often based on discoveries in the physical sciences. Hubbard's correlations are lower than those of Campbell, Van Vogt, and Heinlein but in the same direction, while Ellison's ideological opposition comes out in his negative if small coefficients. Three items state what Ellison stands for in science fiction: avant-garde fiction that experiments with new styles, that often is based on the social sciences, and that takes a political stance critical of our society. Like his associates, Hubbard is unsupportive of the New Wave.

The next five phrases describe the style and human content of Hubbard's fiction, characteristics often stronger in his writing than in that of his associates and unknown in Ellison's work. Hubbard wrote much about war and barbarians, sometimes both at once, and in such tales the main character had better be brave and aggressive. But the main character also has to be generally "superior," and the stories must provide rational explanations for every-

TABLE 3

AUTHORS DESCRIBED THROUGH IGUANACON SURVEY DATA				
(N = 409)				
	CORRELATION (r) WITH PREFERENCE FOR:			
LITERATURE TYPE	L. RON HUBBARD	JOHN W. CAMPBELL	A. E. VAN VOGT	ROBERT A. HEINLEIN	HARLAN ELLISON
Classic science fiction from the early days of SF	.19	.39	.31	.24	−.03
Fiction based on the physical sciences	.14	.22	.30	.24	−.11
Fiction based on the social sciences	.01	.11	.12	−.04	.28
Avant-garde fiction that experiments with new styles	.08	.02	.04	−.04	.40
Fiction that is critical of our society	.06	.08	.12	−.08	.25
Stories in which there is a rational explanation for everything	.22	.19	.18	.09	−.06
Stories in which the main character is brave and aggressive	.22	.24	.17	.19	.02
Stories about barbarians	.21	.03	.17	.10	.01
Stories about war	.21	.15	.18	.24	−.08
Stories in which the main character is a superior person	.19	.17	.11	.16	.00
Stories in which the main character is sensitive and introspective	.01	.12	.01	−.05	.25
Fiction that deeply probes personal relationships and feelings	−.15	.04	−.03	−.05	.33

thing that happens. There is no premium in Hubbard's stories for being sensitive and introspective, and we see a negative correlation with fiction that deeply probes personal relationships and feelings.

For example, *Final Blackout,* originally published in *Astounding* and considered "Hubbard's masterpiece" (Tuck, 1974:233), concerns a man known only as "the lieutenant" whose main virtue is the capacity for remorseless killing in a war that has no redeeming social value. Hubbard's chilling story "Fear" follows a murderer who has repressed memory of his crime; he descends into psychosis because he makes the mistake of introspecting.

The science fiction subculture does not remember Hubbard fondly, but it gave him a deep reservoir of alternative culture from which to draw in creating his new scientific and technological religion. Scientology can appropriate many of science fiction's ideas about the spiritual meaning of science and the mystical implications of advanced technology. Other new religions are postulated frequently in the fiction, and there is every reason to expect that it will give birth to a flourishing new faith every generation or two.

THE ANTHROPIC PRINCIPLE

Recent developments in astrophysics and scientific cosmology, especially the application of quantum theory principles to the origin of the universe, provide the basis for a radical new perspective of such sweeping implications that it is hard to believe it will much longer remain unknown to the general public. The labors of many physicists and mathematicians contribute to the new perspective, although few of them are willing to give public support to its most radical versions.

For the very first time, science challenges religion's role in explaining the origins of the universe. Until very recently, physics and allied sciences either left ultimate questions for religion to answer or denied that these were problems capable of rational solution. By temperament and professional commitment, many scientists were atheists. But all their science really demanded of them was agnosticism. Then the job of science was to explain the form and behavior of material things, but now it seeks also to explain the very existence of the universe.

Why is there something rather than nothing? Why is the world the way it is? Why are phenomena lawful? What is our place in the universe? The new answers offered for these questions are entirely incompatible with the Judeo-Christian-Islamic tradition, but they seem quite compatible with the root beliefs of Scientology.

Popular writers of a mystical bent have interpreted indeterminacies in mathematical logic and quantum theory in ways favorable to Eastern religions, such as Taoism and Zen (Capra, 1975; Zukav, 1979; Hofstadter, 1979).

Social historians have long argued that Western science arose on the theological assumptions of a single God who created a lawful universe (Westfall, 1958; Merton, 1970; cf. Gale, 1976), but some popularizers of science want us to believe that Einstein, Heisenberg, and Goedel have established complete relativism, indeterminacy, and undecidability as the facts from which only mystical conclusions can be drawn.

The universe is no less lawful today than a century ago. But now some of the laws are statistical in nature, and others, like the law of conservation of mass and energy, are limited in application. Mass and energy can come into being spontaneously, without cause or creator, according to quantum theory and empirical observation. This does not render the universe chaotic on the large scale because the duration and magnitude of these quantum events are very small. But we must rethink ordinary ideas of existence and causality enshrined in Western religion and traditional science.

The mystical writers on science argue that the rational Western mind cannot comprehend the universe that is unfolding, yet it was Western scientists who provided the theories and observations, not Taoists and Zen Buddhists. The new perspective is not Eastern, partly because it is more Humanist than Christianity rather than less, but also because it postulates a lawful, rationally intelligible universe. Indeed, the best starting point for a discussion relevant to the sociology of religion is the familiar Argument from Design, a rational attempt to prove the existence of God. The idea is Western, but not new.

In the tenth book of *The Laws,* Plato rests the Argument from Design on observations of astronomical regularity. How do we know the gods exist? "Why, to begin with, think of the earth, and sun, and planets, and everything! And the wonderful and beautiful order of the seasons with its distinctions of years and months!" (Plato, 1934:275).

An excellent modern discussion was provided by Harvard biochemist Lawrence Henderson (1913, 1917), who was an accomplished sociologist as well and the mentor of my mentor, George Homans. While he did not name God, Henderson found great evidence of "teleology" in the fact that the environment was so highly ordered and fit for the evolution of life. In a detailed chemical analysis, Henderson argued that the properties of hydrogen, oxygen, and carbon—and other elements of the natural environment—were so improbably well suited for life that it was beyond him how any "mechanism" could explain them, leaving only the possibility of teleology.

As a youngster I recall pondering the Argument from Design and being unimpressed, confident that my adolescent mind knew enough science to refute it. Sure, this world seems suited for life, but what about all the others? Natives of Pluto and Mercury do not conclude the universe is too well designed to be an accident. Of course not, because on such hellhole planets, life cannot evolve.

Thus, it seemed to me the goodness of the environment was a mere selection effect—only in good places does intelligence evolve and ask how things could be so incredibly good—the result not of teleology but of a cosmic lottery. But now I realize the Argument from Design is not defeated by such logic because it remains surprising that universal laws make life and consciousness possible anywhere.

Plato saw the Argument from Design as a mere prelude to a thesis about the unmoved mover, which we find antiquated today. But in reporting the theory of an opponent, presumably Democritus (cf. Gomperz, 1901), he anticipated the modern Western alternative to teleology:

> Fire and water, earth and air . . . all owe their being to nature and chance, none of them to art; they, in turn, are the agents, and the absolutely soulless agents, in the production of the bodies of the next rank, the earth, sun, moon, and stars. They drifted casually, each in virtue of their several tendencies; as they came together in certain fitting and convenient dispositions—hot with cold, dry with moist, soft with hard, and so on in all the inevitable casual combinations which arise from the blending of contraries—thus, and on this wise, they gave birth to the whole heavens and all their contents, and, in due course, to all animals and plants, when once all the seasons of the year had been produced from those same causes; not . . . by the agency of mind, or any god, or art, but . . . by nature and chance (Plato, 1934:277).

Today not only the concept of the atom of Democritus, but also his model of the world as stochasticism constrained by law has risen to dominate physics, astronomy, and many other sciences. Einstein denied that pure chance can replace determinism as the explanation for events—God does not play dice. And it was partly this faith that caused him so quickly to fall behind the march of physics as it developed a consistent, empirically supported model of the world based on quantum theory (Clark, 1971; cf. Heisenberg, 1969).

While some popular twentieth-century writers have found the fingerprints of God on biological forms (Bergson, 1911; Toulmin, 1982), others have discerned a less personal teleological principle in the operations of chance and necessity (Monod, 1971; Eigen and Winkler, 1981). A conception of the universe as a set of chance events operating under a system of natural laws still leaves room for the Lawgiver. After we have extrapolated backward from Hubble's discovery that the universe is expanding, and we have postulated a Big Bang, it is still possible to imagine a Voice before that saying, "Let there be light!"

The new perspective abolishes the Lawgiver because it views natural laws as nothing more than Big Chances. As a lad, I feared the possibility that existence was stochastic. Cosmic monkeys punching randomly on God's abandoned typewriter have written the story of my life and world. Even if everything makes sense right up to the present instant, the fact that it was pure chance means that the next time a monkey's finger touches a key, gibberish is the most probable result.

A theory of pure chance unrestrained by law is unacceptable to the human mind if only because it is so terrifying. To live confidently, we must feel that trustworthy laws underlie our world. A cosmology must offer a sense of security to mortals if it is to be at all popular. The views of Democritus were not widely popular, and Christianity found the philosophy of Plato much more compatible with its faith.

A stochastic universe need not be a blooming, buzzing confusion if certain large random events associated with its origin establish overarching, invariable principles that ever after operate as the framework within which small chance events and causally determined events occur. God does not roll dice; the dice roll themselves.

Imagine the set of all possible dice, an infinite number of all possible shapes, defined by the random intersection of an infinite number of planes in space. Select two dice at random, again and again. Eventually, you will select two dice that are cubes, like the ordinary dice of many games. Let them roll, several times. In this analogy, a pair of cubic dice represents the natural laws of this universe, and a roll of lucky seven represents the evolution of life on earth.

Seven is a fairly likely roll for cubic dice, less so if you had selected icosahedral dice, and far less so if the dice you selected had a billion faces. In a universe where the laws are analogous to billion-sided dice, stable material forms may be impossible, let alone sentient life. But in a universe such as ours, the chance selection (as it were) of appropriate dice has given us natural laws suitable for a coherent game.

J. Richard Gott (1982) has published a detailed mathematical model of how our entire universe could have come into being spontaneously, requiring no cause or creator, a quantum event simply on a much larger scale than those routinely observed by nuclear physicists. While the theory postulates initial conditions prior to the chance event producing the universe, the trend in this field is to eliminate such background assumptions altogether.

But what about the Argument from Design? Does it not seem implausible that one roll of the indeterminant universal dice would just happen to produce a coherent environment capable of producing intelligent life? The new perspective answers that there was an infinite number of rolls of every possible set of dice, not just one. The quantum accident theory of the origin assumes that similar events occur without limit, with somewhat different conditions randomly imposed each time. Thus, universes are born in large numbers every second with every conceivable set of natural laws.

Also, a new model of the early history of the universe—the so-called "inflationary universe theory" of Alan H. Guth (1981)—seems ready to fill the gap between a random quantum event generating the universe and the lawful Big Bang that gave it its present form. Guth postulates that each universe is like a froth of many bubbles, our own bubble being larger than the part of the universe we observe, over 30 billion light years across. At the beginning of a period of rapid inflation, all the contents of our vast bubble were in causal contact, influencing each other—thus producing a shared set of physical constants, such as the speed of light, the ratio of the mass of an electron to that of a proton, the gravitational constant, and the extreme evenness across the sky of the 3-degree background radiation detected by radio telescopes.

These theories are new and undergoing rapid modification. But it appears that there are two points in cosmic history at which different universes or sub-universes proliferate. In our dice metaphor, Gott's spontaneous appearance of our universe is like the accidental selection of a pair of cubic dice out of the set of all possible shapes. Guth's concept that ours is but one favorably arranged bubble in a form of world-bubbles is like saying that when the cubic dice were rolled many times, in our case they came up lucky seven.

A set of "universes" is called a *world ensemble*. Estimates of the number of universes and world-bubbles are very high, so the probability that one will be suited for the evolution of intelligent observers is also high. When such observers ask themselves why their universe is well-ordered and exhibits such fitness for life, the proper answer may be not that a God made it for them but a supra-Darwinian process of natural selection from the ensemble has automatically ensured that only in a fit and ordered universe would the question ever get asked. Paul Davies has been an active propagandist for this interpretation:

> The only systematic attempt (outside religion) to explain the extraordinarily contrived appearance of the physical world has developed out of a radical departure from traditional scientific thinking. Called the *anthropic principle,* the idea is to relate basic world features to our own existence as observers. The principle has its origins with great physicists such as Boltzmann, and in recent years has been restated by a number of eminent scientists, including Brandon Carter, Robert Dicke, Freeman Dyson, Stephen Hawking, Martin Rees and John Wheeler. Some of these scientists go so far as to claim that our existence can be used as a biological selection effect, allowing one to actually explain the otherwise mysterious numerical values of the fundamental physical constants. (Davies, 1982:viii)

The typical exposition of the anthropic principle begins like the Argument from Design, detailing the remarkable coincidences of physical facts in a surprisingly ordered universe that make life possible (Carr and Rees, 1979; Davies, 1982). Stephen Hawking calculated that a decrease of one millionth in the early expansion rate of the universe would have led to a recollapse before life could evolve. John Leslie (1982:145) commented, "Nowadays, when the God hypothesis is unpopular, many dislike the notion that Life balances on a razor edge; Hawking's estimate thus suggests to them only that Hawking is wrong. But minds could change when it was seen that an Ensemble could do much the work God used to do."

One version of the anthropic principle considers that we were not so much lucky as creative. Rationally based on some interpretations of quantum theory, this approach argues that, in a sense, we *create* the universe by observing it (Wheeler, 1980). If one shifts the terms of this argument slightly in the direction of religion, then Man takes the role formerly played by God. Thus the new cosmological theories are incidentally creating the cultural background for new brands of solipsism, some of which may take the social form of religions.

Davies (1983a:874) reports, "Many of the weird and abstract concepts thrown up by the new physics have struck deep chords with those of a mystical persuasion. Much to the bewilderment of the profession, cults have grown up around quantum physics, black holes and the theory of relativity." This reaction in popular culture is likely to increase now that nontechnical books and articles on the anthropic principle and related subjects have begun to appear (Davies, 1980, 1983b; Gale, 1981; Corwin, 1983; MacRobert, 1983; Overbye, 1983; Smith, 1983).

Anthropic interpretations of quantum cosmology do assert a relativistic conception of existence, one that in the popular mind may easily evolve into a radical subjectivism, that in turn becomes solipsism, that in turn becomes the belief that humans are capable of supernatural power over the world of their experience. If the theory is transformed in this way as it becomes more widely known, then it will no longer be true to the conceptions of the scientists who invented, it, not even to Wheeler's extreme view that the universe is a "self-exciting circuit" brought into being by our perception of it. Quantum cosmology is compatible with the proposition that we are helpless leaves blown by irresistible winds of universal law and offers no hope for help from the beyond. But people will probably not understand it that way.

Some critics will object that the theory fails to explain the objective existence of the universe and that an underlying principle—perhaps God—is still needed as the ground of all being. Not so. In a sense, quantum cosmology suggests we are in error to say that the universe exists with respect to any objective frame of reference. According to the conception of Edward P. Tryon (1973), gravity is negative energy, and the total gravity of the universe exactly balances the positive energy (including all the matter). Thus, the net result of adding together everything in the universe is zero. With reference to ánything outside the universe, therefore, the universe does not exist.

The problem may be that we misunderstand ourselves when we speak of existence. The desire for a sense of ultimate security drives us to postulate an objectivity or a deity beyond the world of our immediate experience. It might seem the only alternatives to objectivism are a mushy mysticism in which all the world is illusion (maya) or an infantile, wish-fulfillment egocentrism. But hardheaded schools of philosophy, very close to the scientific approach to the sociology of religion followed by Rodney Stark and myself, avoid postulating an external objectivity.

It was pragmatist William James who wrote, "The true . . . is only the expedient in the way of thinking" (James, 1963:98). *Truth* and *existence* are concepts having meaning only in reference to what conceivably can be observed. In life we experience objects and phenomena as real and communicate about them in language that habitually imputes objective qualities to them. Our speech modifies nouns with adjectives, and it is a short step to the assumption that the adjectives name properties of entities identified by the nouns. It is not mysticism to note that our ordinary ways of thinking involve imprecise metaphors and the linguistic relics of ancient myths about the universe. The concept of objective existence may be among them.

In behaviorist psychology, using language like that of B. F. Skinner (1938), one could define existence as follows: "For a thing to exist means that it is capable of acting as a reinforcer of behavior." In the terms of behavioral sociology, represented by the thinking of George Homans (1974), one might put it like this: "A thing exists if it could, even in the slightest degree, reward a person." One can see immediately how lunch could exist, in these formulations, but even a distant star can constitute a minor reinforcer or reward in the life of an astronomer. It would be a mistake to interpret this to mean that Zeus exists because a statue of Zeus may be pleasurable to behold or because faith in Zeus could encourage a Greek warrior. Here it is a statue and a faith that are capable of reinforcing behavior or rewarding a person, not the god himself.

The Stark-Bainbridge theory of religion is not narrowly behaviorist because it gives major roles to cognition and culture. (Stark and Bainbridge, 1980, 1984, Forthcoming). But our definition of existence would be similar: "A thing exists if some explanation incorporating it, evaluated through the rewards it achieves or costs it avoids, proves more valuable than any explanation not incorporating it." All of these unmystical, positivist, utilitarian definitions of existence understand the concept in terms of a relationship to potential observers, rather than in terms of an objective frame of reference.

What kinds of religion will be best able to exploit the new discoveries and theories? Certainly Epicureanism was well designed for such a universe, intellectually based as it was on the atomic theory of Democritus. But real Ep-icureans, in the classic rather than gastronomic sense, are hard to find these days. While it is possible to argue that the same philosophic tradition con-tributed to Christianity, Marxists have seemed more interested in Democritus and Epicurus than have Christians (DeWitt, 1954; Marx, 1841).

If God did not create the universe, then in what sense is He truly God? A being from the beyond that shares the same stochastic origins as we, even if extremely powerful and benevolent, would be more of an extraterrestrial big brother than a father, deserving respect more than devotion and having no special claims on our faith and loyalty. God-oriented religions may remain popular, perhaps in part as compensators for the world given us by the sci-entists or despite science in a world uninterested in astrophysics. But reli-gions without God are possible.

Scientologists are free to believe in God, or not, as they choose. While Hubbard's theories postulate an Eighth Dynamic of survival that might be in-terpreted as the Deity, other interpretations are also possible. In at least two of his books he reports that auditing research has failed to discover a godlike world mind or a single original being (Hubbard, 1953:25, 1955:123). Quite in line with solipsistic interpretations of the anthropic principle, he frequently suggests that humans can create universe and truth by the sheer act of per-ceiving or defining (Hubbard, 1952, 1956:71-83, 1968a:20, 1968c:65,69,94).

The concept of World Ensemble is like the *multiple universes* postulate of science fiction. Scientology believes humans sequentially inhabit various different worlds over numerous incarnations. Hubbard has often been de-scribed as a nuclear physicist (Hubbard, 1952, 1953, 1957), so it would be quite comfortable for Scientologists to appropriate the latest thinking in quan-tum physics to their religion.

Thus, Scientology harmonizes with current developments in cosmology, and Hubbard's religion could gain strength by adding to the new scientific perspective on existence the hope and human meaning that only a transcen-dent creed can give. Both Scientology and the anthropic principle make Man, not God, the center of existence. In an age of religious transformation, we can predict that many people will join Scientology or other techno-scientific religions, seeking to be God rather than to find Him.

CONCLUSION

Scientology faces many challenges, including a tendency toward schism. The recent rumors of Hubbard's death, rejected by a California court, only underscore the problem any new religion suffers when the founder's stew-ardship ends. Among Scientology's strengths are its several links to science and technology and thus to the crucial cultural forces of our century. Born in science fiction, it can draw on this storehouse of novel ideas and on the vast popularity that this literature has recently achieved. While the new cosmological ideas of world ensemble and anthropic principle have as yet achieved little popularity, they provide a profound basis for development of Scientological doctrines in directions that would make them highly respectable and attractive to intellectual elites.

While it is impossible to predict the fate of Scientology as a particular religious organization, we must suspect that some religion very much like Scientology will be a major force in the future of our civilization.

REFERENCES

Ash, Brian
    1977   "Fringe Cults." In *The Visual Encyclopedia of Science Fiction,* edited by Brian Ash, 333-42. New York: Harmony.
Bainbridge, William Sims
    1971   "The Scientology Game." Master's thesis, Boston University.
    1976   *The Spaceflight Revolution.* New York: Wiley-Interscience.
    1978   "Chariots of the Gullible," *The Skeptical Inquirer* 3:2:33-48.
    1979   "In Search of Delusion," *The Skeptical Inquirer* 4:1:33-39.
    1980   "The Analytical Laboratory, 1938-1976," *Analog* 100:1:121-34.
    1982a   "Religions for a Galactic Civilization." In *Science Fiction and Space Futures,* edited by Eugene M. Emme, 187-201. San Diego: American Astronautical Society.
    1982b   "Women In Science Fiction," *Sex Roles* 8:1081-93.
Bainbridge, William Sims, and Murray Dalziel
    1978a   "New Maps of Science Fiction." In *Analog Yearbook,* ed. Ben Bova, 277-99. New York: Baronet.
    1978b   "The Shape of Science Fiction," *Science-Fiction Studies* 5:164-71.
Bainbridge, William Sims, and Rodney Stark
    1979   "Cult Formation: Three Compatible Models," *Sociological Analysis* 40:283-95.
    1980   "Scientology: To Be Perfectly Clear," *Sociological Analysis* 41:128-36.
Bergson, Henri
    1911   *Creative Evolution.* New York: Holt.
Braddeson, Walter
    1969   *Scientology for the Millions.* Los Angeles: Sherbourne.
Capra, Fritjof
    1975   *The Tao of Physics.* New York: Bantam.
Carr, B. J., and M. J. Rees
    1979   "The Anthropic Principle and the Structure of the Physical World," *Nature,* 278:605-12.
Clark, Ronald W.
    1971   *Einstein: The Life and Times.* New York: Avon.

Corwin, Mike
    1983   "From Chaos to Consciousness," *Astronomy* 11:2:15-22.

Davies, Paul C. W.
    1980   *Other Worlds.* New York: Simon and Schuster.

    1982   *The Accidental Universe.* New York: Cambridge University Press.

    1983a   "God and the New Physics," *New Scientist* 98:872-74.

    1983b   *God and the New Physics.* New York: Simon and Schuster.

Day, Donald B.
    1952   *Index to the Science-Fiction Magazines, 1926-1950.* Portland OR: Perri Press.

Del Rey, Lester
    1951   "Superman—C.O.D." *Marvel Science Stories* 3:3:116-19.

DeWitt, Norman Wentworth
    1954   *St. Paul and Epicurus.* Minneapolis: University of Minnesota Press.

Eigen, Manfred, and Ruthild Winkler
    1981   *Laws of the Game.* New York: Harper and Row.

Farmer, Philip Jose
    1977   "Religion and Myths." In *The Visual Encyclopedia of Science Fiction,* edited by Brian Ash, 222-36. New York: Harmony.

Gale, George
    1976   "On What God Chose: Perfection and God's Freedom," *Studia Leibnitiana* 8:1:69-87.

    1981   "The Anthropic Principle," *Scientific American* 245:6:154-71.

Gardner, Martin
    1957   *Fads and Fallacies in the Name of Science.* New York: Dover.

Gomperz, Theodor
    1901   *Greek Thinkers.* Vol. 1. London: Murray.

Gott, J. Richard
    1982   "Creation of Open Universes from de Sitter Space," *Nature* 295:304-307.

Guth, Alan H.
    1981   "Inflationary Universe: A Possible Solution to the Horizon and Flatness Problems," *Physical Review* D23:347-56.

Heisenberg, Werner
    1969   *Der Teil und das Ganze.* Munich: Piper.

Henderson, Lawrence J.
    1913   *The Fitness of the Environment.* New York: Macmillan.

    1917   *The Order of Nature.* Cambridge: Harvard University Press.

Hofstadter, Douglas R.
    1979   *Goedel, Escher, Bach: An Eternal Golden Braid.* New York: Basic Books.

Houmans, George C.
1974   *Social Behavior: Its Elementary Forms.* New York: Harcourt Brace Jovanovich.

Hubbard, L. Ron
1950a   "Dianetics: The Evolution of a Science," *Astounding Science Fiction* 45:3:43-87.

1950b   *Dianetics, the Modern Science of Mental Health.* New York: Paperback Library.

1951a   "Homo Superior, Here We Come!" *Marvel Science Stories* 3:3:111:13.

1951b   *Science of Survival.* Los Angeles: Publications World Wide.

1952   *Scientology 8-80.* Silver Springs MD: Distribution Center.

1953   *Scientology 8-8008.* Edinburgh: Publications Organization World Wide.

1955   *The Creation of Human Ability.* London: Scientology.

1956   *The Fundamentals of Thought.* Edinburgh: Publications Organization World Wide.

1957   *All About Radiation.* Edinburgh: Publications Organization World Wide.

1965   *A New Slant on Life.* Los Angeles: The American Saint Hill Organization.

1968a   *Level I PABS.* Edinburgh: Publications Organization World Wide.

1968b   *Level 0 PABS.* Edinburgh: Publications Organization World Wide.

1968c   *The Phoenix Lectures.* Edinburgh: Publications Organization World Wide.

1970   Tape recorded lecture prepared for the Grand National Convention of the Twentieth Anniversary of Dianetics and Total Freedom, weekend of 3-5 July.

James, William
1968   *Pragmatism and Other Essays.* New York: Washington Square.

Korzybski, Alfred
1948   *Science and Sanity.* Lakeville CT: International Non-Aristotelian Library.

1950   *Manhood of Humanity.* Lakeville CT: International Non-Aristotelian Library.

Leslie, John
1982   "Anthropic Principle, World Ensemble, Design," *American Philosophical Quarterly* 19:141-51.

Lucas, George
1977   "Star Wars—Episode IV: A New Hope." In *The Art of Star Wars,* ed. Carol Titelman, 9-135. New York: Ballantine.

MacRobert, Alan
1983   "Beyond the Big Bang," *Sky and Telescope* 65:211-13.

Marx, Karl
1841   *Differenz der Demokritischen und Epikureischen Naturphilosophie.* Jena, DDR: Friedrich-Schiller-Universität.

McGhan, Barry
  1976   *Science Fiction and Fantasy Pseudonyms.* Dearborn MI: Misfit Press.
Merton, Robert K.
  1970   *Science, Technology and Society in Seventeenth-Century England.* New
          York: Harper & Row.
Monod, Jacques
  1971   *Chance and Necessity.* New York: Random House.
Overbye, Dennis
  1983   "The Universe According to Guth," *Discover* 4:6:93-99.
Palmer, Raymond A.
  1958   "The Facts Behind the Mystery," *Fantastic* 7:7:81-90.
Plato
  1934   *The Laws of Plato.* Translated and edited by A. E. Taylor. London: Dent.
Shaver, Richard S.
  1958   "The Shaver Mystery—A Defense," *Fantastic* 7:7:91-103.
Skinner, B. F.
  1938   *The Behavior of Organisms.* New York: Appleton-Century.
Smith, David H.
  1983   "The Inflationary Universe Lives?" *Sky and Telescope* 65:207-10.
Stark, Rodney, and William Sims Bainbridge
  1980   "Towards a Theory of Religion: Religious Commitment," *Journal for
          the Scientific Study of Religion* 19:114-28.
  1984   *The Future of Religion.* Berkeley: University of California Press.
  Forthcoming   *A Theory of Religion.*
Steichert, A. J.
  1958   "The Shaver Mystery—Dangerous Nonsense," *Fantastic* 7:7:105-10.
Sturgeon, Theodore
  1951   "How to Avoid a Hole in the Head," *Marvel Science Stories* 3:3:114-
          16.
Toulmin, Stephen
  1982   *The Return to Cosmology.* Berkeley: University of California Press.
Tryon, Edward P.
  1973   "Is the Universe a Vacuum Fluctuation?" *Nature* 246.
Tuck, Donald H.
  1974   *The Encyclopedia of Science Fiction and Fantasy.* Chicago: Advent.
Van Vogt, A. E.
  1948   *The World of Null-A.* New York: Ace.
  1961   "Predisposition and the Power of Hidden Words," *Journal of the Di-
          anetic Sciences* 1:1:1-18.
Wallis, Roy
  1977   *The Road to Total Freedom.* New York: Columbia University Press.

Westfall, Richard S.
   1958   *Science and Religion in Seventeenth-Century England.* New Haven: Yale University Press.
Wheeler, John Archibald
   1980   ''Beyond the Black Hole.'' In *Some Strangeness in the Proportion,* ed. Harry Woolf, 341-75. Reading MA: Addison-Wesley.
Zukav, Gary
   1979   *The Dancing Wu Li Masters.* New York: Bantam.

· CHAPTER SIX ·

Hostages to Fortune:
Thoughts on the Future
of Scientology
and the Children of God

Roy Wallis

The new religions of the postwar Western world may be seen as differing responses, for different constituencies, to the problems posed by rationalization. Unlike earlier forms of new religious movements, often a response to the circumstances of oppression and deprivation, the latest wave of movements has found support primarily among the relatively comfortable classes, recruiting particularly among young adults of middle- and lower-middle-class backgrounds. I have argued in a number of recent accounts (Wallis, 1978; 1979a; 1982a; 1984) that two major types of movement can be identified: the *world-affirming* type, exemplified in large measure by a movement such as Scientology; and the *world-rejecting* type, exemplified by a movement such as the Children of God. World-affirming movements offer beliefs and practices for succeeding in society as it is, while world-rejecting movements postulate a complete transformation of society for some divinely ordained alternative.

The first step to any informed guess as to the future prospects of new religious movements is an understanding of their appeal. What has been the source of their success to date? What trends are discernible, if any? And what past parallels are there that might provide some clue to what the future holds?

THE SUCCESS OF SCIENTOLOGY

Rodney Stark argues that successful new religions retain cultural continuity with conventional faiths of their society of origin. While displaying little continuity with the conventional *religious* faith of the West, Scientology developed a style drawing upon the cultural characteristics of Western science, technology, and psychotherapy—focuses of faith for many Westerners. Moreover, Scientology clearly addresses widely prevailing cultural themes. An achievement-oriented society has various effects on those participating in the "rat race." Since achievement is a goal in itself, there are no clear criteria for when *enough* has been achieved. A pervasive sense of *incompleteness, inadequacy,* of *unfulfilled potential* is a consequence. Second, achievement requires deferral of gratification; self-discipline and control; repression of spontaneity, impulse, and emotion. Those who sacrifice these responses to the world in the interest of achievement may find that though they secure material and professional success, their personal lives are cramped by convention, role-playing, and inability to express freely those instinctual aspects of the self so long repressed. Third, rationalization increases impersonality, mediation of relationships, and contractually based and role-articulated interaction—depriving many people of an enduring sense of intimacy. The world-affirming new religious movements have emerged primarily as a response to these difficulties. Some, such as the Human Potential Movement, are broad and multifaceted, offering a wide range of ideas and techniques designed to ameliorate these problems. Others, such as Scientology, are more specific in the area of the market to which they seek to appeal. Scientology's theory and practice address particularly issues of unfulfilled potential. Although clients may unburden themselves in the course of auditing (the name for the movement's practice), liberation from the constraint of social convention is little part of its purpose—Scientology is a thoroughly "uptight" enterprise. And intimacy, although it may emerge from prolonged involvement in Scientology activities, is not greatly encouraged. Ron Hubbard has always had a profound suspicion of "Second Dynamic"—or sexual—involvements, and Scientology activities are not structured in such a way as to maximize opportunities for intimacy.

PARALLELS WITH CHRISTIAN SCIENCE AND A POSSIBLE FUTURE

Scientology appears to have a number of parallels with an earlier movement in this area of the religious market, namely Christian Science (Wallis, 1979b). Both movements offer their services in a market with many competitive suppliers. They successfully negotiated the transition from being one among many suppliers of a therapeutic method to being unique purveyors of a religious philosophy. Both developed effective central control around the person of the leader, and both created impressive centralized bureaucratic structures that could continue to dominate the movement after the leader's death (although, of course, that has yet to be put to the test in the case of Scientology) and restrain fragmentation. Thus, in Stark's terms they succeeded in achieving effective mobilization, including strong governance and a high level of individual commitment.

Another parallel with Christian Science lies in the seminal character of Scientology. Despite strong central control, it has been prolific in the groups and movements generated by those who have had some contact with it but who are reluctant to observe the constraints that the organization and its leadership seek to impose upon practice—particularly in relation to synthesis with other ideas and techniques from beyond Scientology.

Apart from Mrs. Bill's Central and Universal Church of Christ, Scientist, some of the founders and members of groups and churches in the widely inclusive New Thought Movement had passed through Christian Science, often breaking with it because of its authoritarianism or because the practitioners saw possibilities of combining its beliefs and practices with other schools of thought not permitted by Mrs. Eddy's church[1] (Wallis, 1974: 318). Ideas and practices from Christian Science thereby became diffused far beyond the institutional structure of the church through such groups as The Unity School of Christianity, the Church of Absolute Science, and the following of Emma Curtis Hopkins (Braden, 1969: 399), as well as a range of popularizing literature.

Similarly, Scientology has been the progenitor of many groups and practices. The Process, Amprinistics, Abilitism, and Dianology were early schismatic offshoots (Wallis, 1976: 151-52), often rather short-lived. Re-evaluation Counseling seems to owe much in theory and practice to early Dianetics and has given rise in its turn to Co-Counselling International, a still more democratically organized form of that practice. Est (Erhard Seminars Training) has been a singularly successful synthetic derivation, which has itself gone on to generate new movements, transmitting aspects of Scientology thought or practice far from the domain of Ron Hubbard. Scientology influence on Abilitism was carried into its later form of the Anubhava School of Enlight-

---

[1]Charles Braden is of two minds about the importance of Christian Science for the New Thought Movement. Although he lists a number of people influenced by, or involved with, Christian Science, he says "The author's extended questionnaire study of the religious backgrounds of several hundred leaders of such groups as Unity, Religious Science, Divine Science, etc., revealed that almost none of these leaders had come out of Christian Science " (Braden, 1969:399). In his volume on New Thought, however, he says that a number of Mrs. Eddy's "trusted lieutenants, reacting against her authoritarian possessiveness, broke with her and became the teachers of men and women who later founded movements of considerable extent and influence that have collectively been considered as New Thought groups." (Braden, 1963: 138) In addition to the groups and leaders mentioned in the text, there is also the case of Ernest Holmes (see Holmes, 1970: 84-89 and passim).

enment, which promoted the Enlightenment Intensive—a method based on a Scientology practice that has become very widely popular throughout the Human Potential Movement. Other groups and movements, such as the Rajneesh Movement, have adopted and adapted the technique (now called the Rajneesh Insight Intensive), with no awareness of its Scientological origins. Scientology was at least one inspiration of other occult movements such as Eckankar.[2] Doubtless other schisms and syntheses will occur on the death of Hubbard. Already, as in the case of Christian Science, a body of popularizing literature has begun to spread some of the concepts and beliefs of Scientology far from the controlling hand of their source.

The case of Christian Science is suggestive in a further respect, however. Although the movement grew steadily until shortly after Mrs. Eddy's death, numbers of churches and practitioners began to show a slower rate of growth in most parts thereafter and even to decline, the more rapidly since the Second World War. Christian Science was a wealthy movement, appealing to a middle-class and even upper-class following. It was able to invest this wealth in impressive church buildings and publishing, and thus still maintains a significant architectural presence in many western cities and publishes widely, while its membership declines towards negligible numbers to fill the church seats available for them.

Christian Science addressed and purported to provide solutions to problems that by no means have disappeared in the years since Mrs. Eddy's death. Disease and suffering remain widely prevalent. However, the cultural style of the remedy offered by Christian Science no longer resonates so readily with the ethos of the times. Its metaphysics, and the nineteenth-century style of their articulation, carry little contemporary conviction.

I would hazard the guess that in the capitalist West, problems of achievement are similarly likely to remain prominent. What is more in doubt is whether the manner in which Scientology offers to resolve them can long survive the death of its founder. Autocratic founders like Mrs. Eddy or Ron Hubbard establish such powerful institutional structures to implement their control that these inhibit innovation thereafter, a consequence made the more likely by the tendency to crush independent thought in immediate subordinates. Thus, the movement's style tends shortly to become outdated. My guess would be that Scientology will follow Christian Science in this respect. In fifty years' time the quasi-naval uniforms and gold braid of the elite "Sea Organization" may well seem quaint and curious (even more than they do now); the metaphysical form of Scientology notions—and the language in

---

[2]See Festinger et al. (1956) and Wallis (1979c) for two small but famous flying saucer groups, the leaders of which were influenced by Dianetics.

which they are articulated, the presuppositions upon which they draw—will seem old-fashioned, out of touch with the current idiom. In his contribution to this volume Bainbridge argues that its incorporation of scientific language and thought forms is one reason for Scientology's success in the contemporary world. In contrast, I would argue that nothing dates faster than yesterday's science and scientific terminology because of the rapidity with which it undergoes change. Scientology, like Christian Science, will probably remain institutionally and economically strong, while membership declines due to the perceived irrelevance of its formulations.

The other fairly predictable development from Scientology is accommodation with the surrounding society and state. It is, after all, the most common outcome of all for religious movements that survive their initial phase of fervor. Evidence is not readily available for the impact of state hostility directed against the movement (although I attempt to assess this impact at an earlier period in Wallis, 1976: 190-224). It is difficult to believe that exposure of the role of Scientology officials and members in conspiracies to steal documents, breaking and entering, spying, covert and criminal acts against critics, journalists, legal personnel, and so on, could have left its enrollment economy entirely unscathed. Thus, in Rodney Stark's terms, this may mark the fact that Scientology has moved beyond the optimum level of tension with the surrounding environment to a point where its deviance was already affecting recruitment. The eagerness of the movement's leadership to disassociate themselves from those convicted for such acts, and to proclaim a purging of the unrighteous, further suggests that the publicity was having an effect on income, and they recognized it was time to de-escalate the conflict. The extent to which the policy and practice of the movement have been fundamentally affected, however, or to which this is just one more public relations exercise is hard to determine. However, it is unlikely that the heirs of the now aged Hubbard will continue to fight the war (see L. Ron Hubbard, "The War," in Wallis, 1976: 263-64) with quite the personal zeal that animated him.

Thus I would suggest that a likely pattern of development for Scientology is one of successful institutionalization and social accommodation, accompanied by increasing obsolescence of its cultural style and declining membership hidden by an impressive architectural and publishing facade.

THE SUCCESS OF THE CHILDREN OF GOD

World-affirming movements, I have argued, are a response to enduring conditions of capitalist society. On the other hand, world-rejecting movements have tended to be a response to the circumstances of *social marginalization*. They are born characteristically from the anxiety, despair, and deprivation of those who find themselves socially marginalized. The world-rejecting movements of the 1960s, however, did not draw upon the poor and dispossessed but upon a constituency that had turned against the materialism and impersonality of corporate capitalist society and that had migrated to its margins and interstices in rebellion or indifference. There they had sought to change society or to found an alternative way of life.

But their attempts to recreate the world by secular means through drugs, politics, and the commune movement had largely foundered in exploitation, violence, entropy, and disorganization. From the resulting disillusionment and unrequited idealism, many world-rejecting new religions drew recruits. In some cases they represented the fulfillment of radical youthful ideals. A convert to the Children of God illustrates this pattern of "migration to the margins" prior to recruitment. Born in 1950 to a wealthy Lima (Peru) business family, he comments that:

> I was sent to the best schools in Lima. . . . Most of the time we were given what we wanted. . . . After I finished High School . . . my father decided it would be best if I went to the United States to get trained in Business Administration so that one day I could take over his business. . . . (At the University of Texas) I met some people involved in smoking marijuana which got me started in that world. . . . I started to experiment heavily with drugs. . . . But by 1972 I had become disillusioned with what was becoming of the Youth Revolution in the States. . . . By this time I had met a very young and pretty high society girl. . . . Together we got into dealing drugs, which proved to be very profitable, and we became very rich in just a short time. (*Family Education Book of the Month*, no. 1 [May 1982]: 19-20)

Subsequently he and his wife decided to abandon this materialistic life-style, to live a simple life in the Peruvian Andes, and to order their lives according to the Bible. They found this difficult to accomplish on their own. On meeting the Children of God, they were greatly impressed by the members' success at living a biblically oriented life and by the "spirit of love" in the Home, and they joined up.

Such stories are quite typical of large numbers of young people attracted to movements of a more world-rejecting cast in the 1960s, but their recruitment was facilitated by another factor. A number of world-rejecting movements possessed clear cultural continuities with the counterculture, and since secular change efforts had failed, many young people were open to the idea— sometimes encouraged by the drug experience—that a supernatural realm existed and that salvation was now likely to come only from that direction. Robert Ellwood, in his discussion of the Jesus People, argues that at this time, "what was needed was a religion for a situation of failure" (1973: 18). But equally significant was the fact that the youth culture's vision of creating a functioning, meaningful, loving, sharing society appeared to have been realized in the communalism of the Children of God, the Unification Church, and other such movements. Since the way of life seemed so successful, many young people were prepared to take the movement's beliefs on trust. It seemed to offer much that the dropouts and hippies had been trying to achieve: a stable, warm community; a rejection of worldly materialism, competition and achievement; a structured setting for the experience of ecstasy or mystical insight. Not all who joined, of course, had experienced the hippie culture, but all identified with its aspirations for a more idealistic, spiritual, and caring way of life, in the context of more personal and loving social relationships. An example from my research on the Children of God will make the point. Lydia became a nun after completing high school:

> But even after taking final vows, inside I felt there was something wrong, and I began to feel more and more disillusioned, empty, without direction and mostly just lonely and looking for real love. . . . Finally in the fall of 1971 I made the decision that I simply had to leave. . . . But after 3 or 4 months I realized I was lonelier than ever. . . . On that life-changing Saturday in March I rode my bicycle to the park and was relaxing under a tree watching the people when I noticed a tall young man with a guitar. . . . He . . . walked straight over to me and without saying a word began singing a song, looking intently into my eyes. . . . The song and the love so touched me that tears came to my eyes. . . . "How long you been [sic] waiting for somebody to love you? How long you been waiting for someone to show you the way . . . ?" I soon found myself surrounded by about 5 more young men all smiling down at me with the same radiant look of love shining on their faces. I was so taken by the love and totally new spirit of these boys that when they invited me to come home and eat supper with them I readily agreed. (*Family Education Book of the Month*, No. 1, May 1982: 280-83)

The Children of God—although emerging in a context in which conventional faiths had, in Stark's terms, been weakened by secularization—drew upon the enduring tradition of conservative evangelicalism and fundamentalism in American Christianity, resonating with the sometimes long-since abandoned strain of conventional faith in the childhood of many rebellious American and European young people.

Following Stark's model, the Children of God effectively mobilized a high level of individual commitment among its followers who were prepared to devote their lives and possessions entirely to its cause. The prophetic leadership of Moses David ensured strong governance. By migrating frequently, particularly in the face of heightened local opposition, the movement was able to maintain a reasonably "favorable ecology."

PRESENT TRENDS,
THE LESSONS FROM PARALLEL CASES,
AND A POSSIBLE FUTURE

But movements born into historically particular circumstances may be rendered precarious as those circumstances change. Those world-rejecting movements that emerged in the 1960s largely developed out of the specific historical conditions of the disintegration of the counterculture and depended upon the existence of a substantial constituency of young people sufficiently alienated from their society to be prepared to seek such drastic alternatives to it. The economic recession of the 1970s gradually eroded the bases for such a constituency just as the economic expansion of the early 1960s had generated it.

The recession of the 1970s created a more precarious job market. Economic contraction was incompatible with a widespread sense of social progress and experimentation. Fewer young people were prepared to jeopardize their occupational future by embarking upon any countercultural digression from the established paths of entry into adult life. The hippie as a social type had largely disappeared, and young people in general were more concerned with ensuring their job prospects than with pursuing social ideals. As the economic order of their society became more precarious, fewer young people wished to abandon it, even temporarily.

The disappearance of the constituency for many of the youthful world-rejecting movements has been reflected in two ways. First, there has been a tendency for them to stagnate numerically. Second, they have been forced to adapt in the face of their changed circumstances. In order to locate a new constituency, these movements have often felt a need to change their style and their methods of proselytization in a manner that would de-emphasize some of their more overtly world-rejecting features. Even initially extreme world-rejecting movements, such as Krishna Consciousness and the Children of God, have modified their public presentation in ways that would gain them greater access to less marginal sectors of society.

The Children of God were in their earliest years, from 1968-1971, even more radically world-rejecting than they were to become subsequently. (This might even constitute a challenge to Stark's contention that movements succeed to the extent to which they maintain a *medium* level of tension. It might be argued that they succeeded in their early years precisely because they maintained a very high level of tension with their environment, but the difficulty of applying any metric to these terms limits their utility.) In the first period, they regarded virtually everyone outside their movement as a servant of Satan. Thereafter, their attitude softened somewhat. There were "other sheep" outside the Children of God; one could be an "Associate" or a

"Friend" of the movement without submitting entirely to its way of life. Even such slight compromises with the world as these provoked some followers to abandon the movement (Wallis, 1979d). Later, the Children of God moved away from street proselytization of young dropouts to witnessing in expensive bars, discos, and hotels to middle-aged businessmen and other relatively comfortable social groups to be found in such milieux. Later they focused, too, on witnessing door-to-door in order to reach young married couples with children and the elderly, for whom they might also provide a regular "Church of Love" in their homes, a Bible Study group, or a Sunday or vacation Bible club for the neighborhood children. The Children of God acknowledged readily enough in interviews that one reason for this change in style was the disappearance of the "dropout" as a potential recruit, or at least "dropouts" of the caliber of those so prevalent in the late 1960s and early 1970s. In recent years the movement has begun to secure the bulk of its new following in the underdeveloped world and to substitute their own very high birth rate for the gradual decline in youthful Westerners.

The world-rejecting new religions vary considerably in the degree to which they have embraced the emergence of stable institutional structures and patterns of activity. Those for whom tradition has been a major source of legitimation—as in ISKCON—have accepted institutionalization readily enough. Others have not met this prospect with equanimity. In the Children of God, institutionalization threatened the charismatic autocracy of Moses David who, therefore, constantly undermined attempts to establish any enduring administrative structure and procedures or to fix the beliefs of the movement into an unchanging creed (Wallis, 1982b). Consequently, there has been a peculiar volatility and liability in the movement's behavior—a pattern of constant and relatively unpredictable change, with few firm structures or acknowledged routines to provide an enduring framework on the leader's death. Combined with the tendency to force into rebellion and defection all leadership cadre not prepared totally to subordinate themselves to Moses David, the result of this history is likely to be severe fragmentation and disintegration on his death. The elimination of effective alternative independently minded leadership has depleted the movement's resources for adapting to the founder's death in an innovative way, and what survives fragmentation is likely to return to old patterns and practices, preserving itself in introversionist withdrawal rather than developing newer and more effective forms.

Moreover, of course, like all millenarian movements, the Children of God face the problems of prophetic failure or postponed hope should the new dispensation not materialize and Christ return in 1993 (as Mo has predicted). Prophetic failure has led to disintegration or demise in many chiliastic movements, and as Bryan Wilson (1970: 94) observes, "The expectation of social transformation is not easily sustained over a long period, when the awaited advent fails to occur. Consequently, revolutionist sects [as he refers to this type] are often of relatively brief duration.'' Or if they manage to survive and institutionalize, it is at the cost of their revolutionist or millenarian character.

No particular single contemporary example is as peculiarly apposite for the Children of God as Christian Science is for Scientology, but Norman Cohn's (1970) study of medieval millenarian movements and Bryan Wilson's (1973) of such movements in the Third World bear eloquent testimony to the transience and propensity for disintegration of millennial movements. Such millennialist sects have institutionalized and survived, of course, notably the Jehovah's Witnesses and the Christadelphians. But in neither case did the founder advance such extreme charismatic claims as does Moses David, and both movements had become fairly well institutionalized before the founder's death—around local ecclesias in the case of the Christadelphians, and the Watchtower Society and its publications in the case of the Witnesses. Beliefs and practices were subject to a relatively slow rate of change, not to constant modification as in the Children of God. Hence at the founder's death, followers might disagree on certain points of doctrine or practice, but they were not thrown into chaos and uncertainty as seems all too likely on the death of Mo.

REFERENCES

Braden, Charles
    1963   *Spirits in Rebellion: The Rise and Development of New Thought.* Dallas: Southern Methodist University Press.
    1969   *Christian Science Today.* Dallas: Southern Methodist University Press (originally published 1958).

Carey, Sean
    1983   ''The Hare Krishna Movement and Hindus in Britain,'' *New Community* 10 (3):477-86.

Cohn, Norman
    1970   *The Pursuit of the Millennium.* London: Paladin (originally published 1957).

Ellwood, Robert S.
    1973   *One Way: The Jesus Movement and Its Meaning.* Englewood Cliffs NJ: Prentice-Hall.

Festinger, Leon, Henry W. Reicken, and Stanley Schachter
    1956   *When Prophecy Fails: A Social and Psychological Study of a Modern Group That Predicted the Destruction of the World.* New York: Harper & Row.

Holmes, Fenwicke
    1970   *Ernest Holmes: His Life and Times.* New York: Dodd and Mead.

Wallis, Roy

1974   "Ideology, Authority and the Development of Cultic Movements," *Social Research* 41:299-327.

1976   *The Road to Total Freedom: A Sociological Analysis of Scientology.* London: Heinemann (New York: Columbia University Press, 1977).

1978   The Rebirth of the Gods? Inaugural Lecture. Belfast: The Queen's University.

1979a   "The Elementary Forms of the New Religious Life," *Annual Review of the Social Sciences of Religion* 3:191-211.

1979b   "Coping with Institutional Fragility: An Analysis of Christian Science and Scientology," ch. 2 in *Salvation and Protest.* London: Frances Pinter (New York: St. Martin's Press).

1979c   "Reflections on *When Prophecy Fails,*" ch. 3 in ibid.

1979d   "Millennialism and Community: Observations on the Children of God," ch. 4 in ibid.

1982a   "The New Religions as Social Indicators." In *New Religious Movements: A Perspective for Understanding Society,* edited by Eileen Barker. New York: Edwin Mellen.

1982b   "Charisma, Commitment and Control in a New Religious Movement." In *Mellennialism and Charisma,* edited by Roy Wallis. Belfast: The Queen's University.

1984   *The Elementary Forms of the New Religious Life.* London: Routledge and Kegan Paul.

Wilson, Bryan

1970   *Religious Sects.* London: Weidenfeld and Nicolson.

1973   *Magic and the Millennium.* London: Heinemann.

· CHAPTER SEVEN ·

Social Movement Culture and the Unification Church

John Lofland

Social movement organizations (MOs in the scholarly jargon) generate cultures that vary along a continuum of "richness" at one extreme and "poverty" at the other. We often gropingly and intuitively contrast movement cultures in such terms as elevating versus constricting, compassionate versus spiteful, generous versus hard-eyed, humorous versus humorless, complex versus simple, flexible versus rigid. On the "richness" side, *some few* MOs appear to create quite vibrant, multihued, upbeat, complex, outward-extending cultural lives that imbue their members with a liveliness and vibrancy. Others, by contrast, display stunted, simple, and emotionally narrowing cultures.

My purpose here is to advance the comparative analysis of social movement organizations in such cultural-contrast terms. The initial need is, obviously, a relevant scheme in terms of which to compare MOs, and devising one is my primary task in this chapter. I suggest three master clusters of movement culture variation: elaboration, expressiveness, and compassion. The first concerns the sheer quantitative dimension of culture, asking how much of it there is and to what range of matters it is applied. The second strives to elucidate qualitative variation in the degree to which a culture links personal, emotional experience to collective life by means of shared, expressive symbols. The third assesses cultural substance in terms of the character of its mandated and sustained social relations, a "character" that ranges along the continuum of being more or less compassionate. To the degree a movement's culture is elaborate, expressive, and compassionate, it is "rich." "Poverty" is the reverse.

Degree of "cultural richness" relates to a movement's probability of success—as success is formulated in Rodney Stark's seven-variable model—in several ways, three of which may be stated briefly as orientation prior to elaboration at appropriate points below. First, cultural richness—especially expressiveness—is associated with a strong degree of *cultural continuity,* Stark's first variable. *De novo* religious schemes experience greater difficulty connecting with the personal experiences of potential members than do cognitive systems with strong elements of familiarity.

Second, richer movement cultures contain more possibilities for furnishing rationales that legitimize effective organizational structures. Stark addresses this as the problem of *effective mobilization* in his third proposition, observing that a great many new religions lack a cognitive apparatus that is supportive of coordinated collective action—an indispensable requisite of movement success. Elaborated and expressive movement cultures, in particular, are more likely to furnish conceptual resources that are supportive of collective action.

Third, cultural richness (especially elaboration and expressiveness) fosters *cultural continuity* (Stark's first variable), but it is at the same time likely also to promote *secularization,* ideological and behavioral accommodation to the parent society (the seventh variable proposed by Stark). What the movement gains on the first score is, as time goes on, taken away on the seventh score. This may be thought of as a *dilemma of cultural richness.* Richness promotes continuity *and* secularization. The delicate task of all would-be successful movements is that of maximizing the former while at the same time maintaining control of the latter, a possibly impossible feat.

I will use the strategy of ''key-case comparison'' in explicating the richness-poverty continuum, focusing on a specific MO that furnishes some instructive contrasts when set in comparative perspective. This strategy is to be distinguished from ''full-array comparison'' where all the relevant types, or at least instances of all the key types of cases, are systematically compared point for point. The key case I will use is that of the Unification Church (UC).

I. CULTURAL ELABORATION

Heuristically, we may envision what we would expect to find in an MO with the most quantitatively elaborate of cultures. In rudimentary Guttman fashion, the classes of these things may be ordered from those found in the least elaborate culture (a specification of ''minimum culture''), moving through and up to the least empirically frequent items found in the empirically less frequent but most elaborate MO cultures.

1. Distinctive Cognitive Orientation

Even the simplest MO has some sort of cognitive categories by means of which it is set off from other units, if only its very name. Beyond these are distinctive goals, approved behavior (norms), and named roles. The next category includes those concepts labeled ideology, theory, analysis, theology, ontology, history, science, and the like.

MO cultures vary in terms of the sheer number and systematic interrelation of the cognitive categories making up what we commonly label the "ideology." Despite the fact that classic writers on social movements imply otherwise, most MOs possess quite simple ideological "systems," "systems" so rudimentary that the very word system is too grandiose. I think, in particular, of the simplicity of the cognitive screens of the classic MOs making up much of the civil rights (for example, Bell, 1968), community protest (for example, Bailey, 1974) commune (for example Zablocki, 1980), and many other movements. Only MOs of the ultraleft, among political movements, begin to rival our key case, the Unification Church, in the complexity and range of cognitive categories. In some ways Blumer led us astray in his famous formulation of the "twofold character" of movement ideology: the "erudite and scholarly" versus the popular. The former "is developed by the intellectuals of the movement [and] . . . is likely to consist of elaborate treatises of an abstract and highly logical character" (Blumer, 1969:110). In actuality, almost no MOs generate such a twofold ideology, as do very few movements. It is the exception rather than the rule; this does not exclude the UC, which I think we must mark down as perhaps the most assiduous of ideological elaborators among contemporary MOs. In numerous publications, it undertakes, for example, to apply its principles to ever-new topics and to elaborate and reformulate its thought on topics it has already addressed.

2. Cognitive Elaborators

One important vehicle for the elaboration of cognition is a stratum of intellectuals charged with exactly that job. Again almost singularly among MOs (and most especially among those of comparable age and membership size), the UC has created a large (proportionate to its total membership) intellectual class whose job is culture creation. It is, moreover, culture creation of a "high" character in that it, to use the words of Blumer, "seeks to gain for its tenets a respectable and defensible position in [the] world of higher learning and higher intellectual values" (Blumer, 1969:110). The cognitive systems of dominant elites are studied for the purpose of taking account of their claims, formulating UC principles in response to them, and developing UC arguments that can counter these cultural elites. All of this has the broader aim of creating an ideology that intellectual and other elites of mainstream society must take seriously. No other current MO even begins to compete with the UC in such terms. Indeed, democratic socialist intellectual Stanley Aronowitz has lamented that the MOs of the American left not only fail to develop effective theory counter to the "ideological hegemony enjoyed by instrumentalist and positivist paradigms in American intellectual life," but also have a "profound contempt for and fear of theoretical work" associated with a fear of "elitism" (Aronowitz, 1983b:18-20).

3. Cultural Dramatization

Cultures vary in the degree to which they are physically dramatized.

(1) Salient forms of dramatization include dancing, singing, and playing musical instruments. MOs differ markedly in these practices. Most seem to engage in them relatively little and to reserve such performances for special occasions, such as rallies and marches, and often also call upon specialized and free-lance performers who are not MO members. The UC strides a different road. First, it has an array of its own singing, dancing, and musically performing troups. Unlike many MOs it does not shy away from professionalism and excellence in cultural performance. Second, musical and other performances by ordinary members in ordinary settings are encouraged, as are collective singing and dancing.

As a broader and comparative generalization, it seems to be the case that religious more than "political" or "ego" movements foster music, dance, and song. In this light, the UC is much like other religious movements, only more so.

(2) MOs differ in the degree to which they engage in expressive, collective assemblies and the adroitness and artfulness of the design and consummation of such assemblies. In my travels through diverse movement worlds, I have been impressed by the relative poverty of most MO expressive assemblies. Especially political MOs—being quite "instrumental"—seem almost embarrassed by suggestions that some of their gatherings might be more than, or other than, tightly focused intellectual analyses of the latest atrocities in the world (save for the practice of giving "parties" that are virtually identical in form and function to middle-class cocktail gatherings).

The UC, in contrast, mounts expressive assemblies frequently, elaborately, and diversely. First and most obvious are their religious worship services. Second, there is a series of sheer celebrations in their complex set of "Days." Third, openings of new installations call forth initiating celebrations. Fourth, conclusions of programs require farewell celebrations. The farewell banquets of some of their more elaborate conferences, such as those given for the International Conference on the Unity of the Sciences, are particularly impressive. And the UC is of course both famous and infamous for the weekend—the almost nonstop expressive assemblies it puts on for potential recruits at locations in Northern California and elsewhere.

(3) It is almost absurd even to mention painting, sculpture, musical composition, and literature in the context of movement organizations. Even the UC does little about such matters, but some nonetheless.

4. Cultural Dissemination

Almost all MOs have at least some primitive means of disseminating their views. Most commonly this is a "newsletter"—the primordial artifact of MO culture. The UC is unusual in striving to cover the gamut of ways in which it is possible to disseminate views: newspapers of several sorts, periodicals, videotapes, pamphlets, posters, books, and more. Most other MOs look anemic alongside the UC in this area. It has even formed a motion picture production company and fielded one major movie. One supposes that television shows and records are next.

5. Interculture Contact and Promotion

Historically, human cultures were generated in relative or virtually complete isolation from one another. Occasions of initial interculture contact were quite traumatic. An individual of a different culture coming onto an isolated culture was likely to be either venerated as a god or treated as subhuman. A human nonmember of one's culture was a possibility difficult or impossible to conceive (L. Lofland, 1973). As time went on, and cultures were increasingly in contact, such touchings were occasions for war and conquest. Only slowly have some humans come to accept the idea that cultures other than their own can be tolerated and perhaps appreciated and treated with respect rather than dominated and obliterated. Within current nation-states, diverse cultures still mostly accommodate by mutual avoidance. (Between nation states they of course still seek domination and obliteration.)

In a global system of ever-accelerating, intercultural contact, variation in the character of such contact becomes itself a topic of signal importance. Such culture as practiced by social movements, because they are promoters of social change, is even more important. And to the point at this moment, the quantitative elaboration of contact is a key variable.

Sadly, most MOs are not exceptions to the generalizations I have just made about intercultural contacts. Like other cultural groups, most MOs tend to look out over the social landscape with suspicion, fear, and hostility and quantitatively to restrict their contact with people unlike themselves, most particularly with people who are only in small ways unlike themselves. This is marvelously ironic in the case of movement organizations because—as movements—they are, by definition, in the business of trying to convince other people of the wisdom of certain social changes. The irony is that MO members preach heavily to the converted, as it is conventionally phrased, except on specially staged occasions, which are commonly marches and rallies where—let it be noted—the speech is public but the persons immediately present are the already believing. Occasions of face-to-face contact with the unbelieving, rare as they are, tend to have an intemperate quality, one extreme form of which has been frozen and displayed for our inspection in the concept of "mau-mauing" (Wolfe, 1971).

Both quantitatively and qualitatively, the UC furnishes us dramatic contrasts with this more common MO pattern. Confining our attention for the moment to the quantitative, like many religious MOs, the UC is conversionist and proselytizing. A significant portion of member energy is invested in making contacts with potential members and presenting the UC point of view. Member for member it may be the most intensively proselytizing of MOs in the current world. Combined with its wide range of other intercultural contacts, members probably likely spend much less time, proportionately, in contact with their "own kind" than do members of other MOs.

Beyond efforts to encounter individuals in public places and to entice people to attend revivalist-like assemblies, there are the large-scale, long-running, and unique efforts to make face-to-face contact with various categories of intellectuals and other leaders in societies around the world. Holding aside the moral objections some people have to these efforts, we need only to view them from a comparative MO perspective to appreciate their quite astonishing quantitative and qualitative nature. Imagine the National Organization for Women staging conferences to which they invite the editors of *Hustler* and *Playboy,* and vice versa; imagine the Southern Christian Leadership Conference staging conferences to which they invite members of the Ku Klux Klan, and vice versa; imagine the Campaign for Nuclear Disarmament staging conferences to which they invite the United States Joint Chiefs of Staff, and vice versa. The face-to-face contacts of diverse perspectives contrived and achieved by the UC are not as dramatic as these, but they move in that direction and would go even further if the people the UC invited who are in sharp contrast to UC views did not so frequently decline their invitations.

Whatever objections one may have to the UC (and they have serious faults that I will address), such objections ought not be allowed to obscure the singular project of interculture contact in which they have been engaged. In the early eighties they were staging several dozen such conferences each year, involving several thousand intellectuals and others in locations around the world, and on which they were spending several millions of dollars each year.

But beyond such *episodes* of interaction with outsiders (which themselves lead to *relationships* with outsiders), the UC has created numerous specialized organizations that they perceive as implementing their views and to which they recruit persons supportive of the specialized aims of the particular organizations. Similar to "broad left" and "popular front" umbrella organizations for which some political MOs have a penchant, the UC creations address diverse matters. And even beyond this are the interculture contacts generated by UC programs in which only UC members are active, but the nature of the task means daily contact with outsiders, as in the Home Church program and their worldwide missionary teams (now claimed to be present in 133 countries), and in their medical teams.

This rather elaborate culture and organization of external contact bodes favorably in terms of Stark's sixth proposition, which suggests that in order to be successful a new religious movement must maintain a permeable "outer social surface" (as well as dense internal ties). Of course, contact alone is not sufficient to produce conversions and hence rapid growth, but it is obviously a precondition. Ironically, however, the UC does not as yet seem to make all that many conversions through these multitudinous contacts.

Most MOs restrict their cultural lives to the five classes of matters I have now mentioned: cognition, specialized creators of cognition, dramatization, dissemination, and intercultural contact and promotion. Even within these categories, most MOs tend not to be especially elaborate in their efforts. The UC stands out from the crowd, as it were, in its assiduousness at all these levels.

6. Cultural Economics

The great divide between culturally primitive MOs and those that are truly elaborate is between economic endeavors necessary to field and sustain acitivites of the types I have just listed and those that go beyond them. As I have suggested, very few MOs cross this divide. The UC is of special interest for, among other reasons, it does venture across and into what we may call cultural economics (and into an even higher level). It seems to be striving, in fact, to establish much the same array of economic institutions that we find in total advanced societies, for the UC has already become involved in such areas as manufacturing, real estate, agriculture, banking, restaurants, travel agencies, hospitals, newspapers, printing, and office services.

7. Domestic Culture

Finally, highest and most venturesome for MOs, efforts may be made to propound detailed cultural practices for the domestic lives of members. Perhaps because of the sheer intimacy of this "private sphere," as one hears it termed, few MOs, especially classic political MOs, say much about it; that is, develop much cultural symbolism pertaining to it and strive to pattern actual domestic arrangements on that symbolism. The several waves of commune formation in American history have, of course, dwelled on this, and it is becoming increasingly central to the feminist and religious-right movement in America.

In recent years the UC, too, has both actively elaborated ideas about proper domestic life and full-tilt reorganized its members in America from brother-sister communes to husband-wife nuclear families of a special type that are still in the process of emergence. Against the backdrop of several occasions of its quite spectacular mass marriages (cf. the cultural dramatization discussed above), an ethic of the centrality of the nuclear family and of childbearing has been fostered.

The categories of culture I have so far explained and the UC materials I have reported are directed to two generalizations: one, MO cultures differ quite manifestly in the degree of their elaboration; two, in comparative MO perspective, UC culture is, taken in composite, quite elaborate.

II. CULTURAL EXPRESSIVENESS

In addition to sheer elaboration or complexity, cultures, including MO cultures, vary in the extent to which their cognitive categories carry what Selznick and Selznick have called "expressive meaning," or "expressive symbolism," and "symbolic value." For them, "The mark of culture . . . is that the ordinary objects and forms of group experience have symbolic value" (Selznick and Selznick, 1964:667).

In order to understand the phenomenon of "expressive symbolism" or "symbolic value," we need first to step back, so to speak, and to reappreciate the existential human situation that gives rise to what Selznick and Selznick call the "primordial culture-creating act." The existential situation of humans is, in their view, one of impersonality, an environment of objects that has no direct and personal relations to humans. However, the special, "minded" quality of humans renders such an environment objectionable and unacceptable. Humans react against impersonality in the "primordial culture-creating act that is "the transformation of an impersonal setting into a personal one" (Selznick and Selznick, 1964:658). Such an act

> is an effort to make the world rich with personal significance, to place the inner self upon the stage, to transform narrow instrumental roles into vehicles of psychic fulfillment. It implicates the self and strives to invest the environment with subjective relevance and meaning. In an older tradition we might have referred to this investment as "the objectification of spirit" (Selznick and Selznick, 1964:659).

> The product of [the culture-creating act] is a world of [expressive] symbols. Culture is created when, in the struggle against alienation, [humans] . . . transform the instrumental and the impersonal, the physical and the organic, into a realm of evocative, expressive, person-centered meanings (Selznick and Selznick, 1964:660).

In Selznick and Selznick's view, symbolic expressiveness is something in terms of which cultures can vary. The possibility of such variation is the reason they label their theory of culture a "normative" one, for they do not "shrink from identifying some cultures as attenuated, some symbols as emptied out, some experiences as truncated or distorted." And in contrast, other cultures may have "subtle and rich symbolic system[s]" (Selznick and Selznick, 1964:660). Or as Gary Fine points out about as seemingly mundane and inconsequential "idiocultures" as those of little league baseball teams: some— the more successful ones, he reports—"develop . . . a robust culture of baseball-related items" (Fine, 1979:736).

1. Bringing this to bear on MOs and holding aside the question of sheer cultural elaboration that I have just discussed, we may entertain the possibility that some MOs cultivate and sustain much richer symbolic lives than others.

It is useful to distinguish two sources of this variation. First, MOs vary in the degree to which they appropriate existing expressive symbols into their own schemes and use them internally to enrich the cultural lives of their members. Many reactive and rejecting political movements of our time seem to do this very little and appear even self-consciously to avoid the powerful expressive symbols of the encompassing culture. The UC is decidedly the reverse. Its culture embraces many of the most evocative of Western cultural symbols and values: God, faith, the family, spirituality, love, perfection, progress toward an earthly kingdom of God, self-discipline, and anticommunism, among others. Consider the closing words of the UC promotional videotape "People of the Quest." The Unification Church reaffirms the importance of classic spiritual values:

> — the value of man as a divine creation;
> — the value of the family as the most important building block of a good society;
> — the value of community service to establish a healthy nation;
> — the value of a nation's living for the benefit of the world before its own interests;
> — and above all, the value and law of love as the altar, purpose and cornerstore of all relationships (Unification Church, 1983).

The very last words of this program are those of the Rev. Moon himself, and they are spoken by him: "We have one primary goal, the age-old quest for a peaceful world centered on God." After Rev. Moon says this, he and Mrs. Moon are shown singing to one another and kissing.

What I speak of as the willingness to incorporate received, traditional, and expressive symbols into the UC scheme can otherwise be conceived as a relatively high degree of *cultural continuity,* the first variable in Rodney Stark's model of factors affecting the success of religious movements. Like the other movements Stark describes, the UC sees itself as building on and completing Christianity rather than striking out *de novo.* This approach seems to have worked well for the Mormons and Muslims especially and could function in the same fashion for the UC. This is a tricky matter, however. The UC *stratum* of "cultural elaborators" (described above in section I.2.) is, among other tasks, busily working out ways in which many elements of UC ideology can be shown to have quite respectable antecedents in Christian thought. That enterprise increases cultural continuity certainly, but carried too far and too thoroughly, it becomes a potent force for *secularization*—the seventh consideration in Stark's formulation. It is a new shoal on which the UC could founder. The movement's problem, therefore, is one of steering between too much continuity (secularization) on the one side and over-allegiance to its distinctive views on the other side.

Second, MOs are differentially creative of their own internal symbolism. Here too the UCers have been busy and are still in the process of gathering a rich array of distinctive modes of making experience meaningful and personal. Their world abounds in such cultural concepts as these: True Parents, True Father, spiritual children, the Family, the three blessings, the four-fold foundation, restoration, indemnity, central persons, MFTs, the blessing, holy salt, spirit world, heart, and many others.

2. Associated with but distinguishable from evocativeness is the degree to which a culture embodies conceptions of the ideal that are highly valued and striven for. In positing ideals, the expressive symbols reach beyond the realities of the moment and call people to larger visions and elevating motives, motives to which they are encouraged to subscribe. Some theorists of culture claim, indeed, that culture is only about valued ideals; all else is merely reactive or instrumental behavior and not properly called culture. In reality, I think, this matter is a variable, and social organizations differ strikingly in the clarity and force with which they conceive and act to actualize ideals of social and other arrangements and performances.

Almost by definition, one would expect movement organizations to be highly idealistic and optimistic and, further, that these qualities be manifest in cheerfulness. Sadly, this is not my experience of many MOs. Commonly, there is a thorough critique of the present, which implies an ideal, but this critique does not go on to show much optimism about attaining ideals or cheerfulness about living toward them. To the extent one can construe ideals, they are often of a fairly narrow and self- or categorically interested kind rather than attuned to broad conceptions of common human values. In being so symbolically restricted and dolefully demeaned, however, perhaps most MOs are being but rational; often there is scant objective ground for optimism and cheerfulness.

Numerous observers have noticed how very different is the expressive symbolism, idealism, and therefore cheerfulness of UC members. Justified or not, UC cultural values are enormously idealistic and optimistic, and members exhibit a distinct kind of positive attitude as a result. As phrased by a longtime and close observer of the UC:

> In relation to our situation of crises, the Unification movement believes itself to be inspired by a faith which points the way to a future which will see the Kingdom—or, in their language, "a God-centered world"—realized in the order of space and time. Thus, rather than viewing our cultural situation as a scenario of despair, the Unificationists see a scenario of hope (Bryant, 1982:12).

3. Such optimism and idealism is founded on extremely broad and ultimately justifying conceptions. The UC uses legitimizing symbols much broader than those employed in many other MOs. The address of Rev. Moon to the class graduating from the UC seminary in 1983 capsulizes several of these "cosmic-scale" symbols:

> People in the world tend to see things primarily from a self-centered perspective. However, members of the Unification Church learn to view everything from a higher and larger dimension. For example: money, power, knowledge—even salvation—are regarded from a worldly viewpoint as benefitting the individual, or at most the family. How rare it is to find a person who puts even the welfare of the nation above that of the family! But for us the entire cosmos, both spiritual and physical, takes priority over the individual, the family, and even the nation.
>
> Goals such as liberation, freedom, and happiness are generally sought for the sake of a few people rather than the human family as a whole. But unlike the rest of the world, we strive toward liberation, freedom and happiness not only for all of mankind, but even for God. Anyone who overlooks this difference fails to understand our true nature (Moon, 1983).

In addition, the expressive symbol of "love," particularly in the sense of giving oneself for the benefit of others, is a key cultural ideal. In comparative perspective, this symbol is almost quaint and even embarrassing, most especially among political MOs. It has of course figured to a degree in some Gandhian-inspired movements, such as segments of the American civil rights efforts of the sixties and the peace movement. But, on the whole, most other MOs honor quite different central symbols, such as justice and freedom.

III. CULTURAL COMPASSION

Elaboration and expressiveness are formal rather than substantive dimensions of cultural variation. They speak to features of the architecture of culture rather than to the materials of its construction.

I want third and finally, therefore, to take up the question of content and focus on the kind of substance having to do with the degree of civility and humaneness with which MO members treat one another and outsiders. We do not find it difficult to speak of the cultures of societies as being, for example, more warlike, or aggressive, or gentle, or militaristic, or exploitive than cultures of other societies. In the same fashion, perhaps it is possible to compare MOs in such terms.

Reversing the Guttman-like logic I used in speaking of cultural elaboration and therefore beginning with the "strongest" state, we may conceive three levels of *compassion* in MOs.

1. In most extreme form, the values of an MO counsel and justify physical violence as an instrument of movement policy and as a strategy of member control. Few if any MOs are so indiscriminately belligerent, but some move in that direction. Most seem, empirically, only to encourage and justify "defensive" violence against outsiders and to prohibit all internal violence. In comparative perspective, the UC seems rather similar to most other movements in this respect. In particular, it manufactures parts for weapons of state warfare, elects to support governments that employ violence as an instrument of policy, and supports the rightist administration of the United States of America—a government that is flauntingly proud of its macho lack of compassion.

2. MOs differ in their promotion and practice of psychic and interactional violence. At a second level, then, abusiveness of the human self and social order may not entail physical violence but may assault the integrity of persons and social interaction.

(1) One central form of this type of violence is propagation of dehumanizing and demeaning stereotypes of outsiders by such methods as scapegoating, vilification, and inferiorization. All movements seek to overcome some sort of evil, of course, but evil can be conceptualized as residing in arrangements and acts rather than in the character of persons. The more compassionate movement culture lodges evil in the former rather than the latter.

(2) Stereotyping and person-based forms of psychic violence can also be practiced against subsets of one's own members in such forms as scapegoating purges and arbitrary categorizations of some members as inferior, using, for example, race, gender, or sexual preference criteria.

(3) Internal authority systems vary in terms of the degree to which the wishes of members are taken meaningfully into account and consent is achieved in the formulation of policy and its execution. At one extreme, self-appointed elites merely propagate and administer policy and rule by intimidation. At the other extreme, there is civil, consented, democratic governance.

(4) Members of all social organizations make mistakes, lie, default, and the like. Deviant behavior among members must therefore be managed, and that management can be more or less compassionate.

(5) The physical and mental states of some members invariably go awry. When they do, one easy option is to expel or otherwise "ease out" such problems, forcing other social organizations to pick up the burden. "We are like an army," a leader can declare, and the mentally and physically ill can be left behind.

The materials available to me regarding these five aspects of interactional and psychic violence in the UC are sketchy and contradictory. Unlike elaboration and expressiveness and some other facets of compassion, these are less "on the surface" of any movement organization, including the UC. They are part of the "internal life" or even the "underlife" of any movement, and I must assume that the UC does not differ from other MOs in having an internal life and an underlife that are shielded from observation. Also, the reliable reports that we have so far on the UC have dealt with the matters just mentioned in highly incomplete and contradictory ways.

(6) Finally, but certainly not exhaustive of the topic of psychic and interaction violence, there is the matter of everyday interactional violence versus compassion in contacts with outsiders. I have already made reference to the quantitative aspect of UC contact with outsiders—reporting that there appears to be a great deal of it, comparatively speaking. Qualitatively, the interactional persona of the model UC member does seem to lean heavily to the compassionate side. This cultural persona is especially striking as practiced by the students and graduates of the UC Seminary, a cadre numbering in the hundreds. Among this elite, leadership is provided by some forty seminary graduates who are (in the early eighties) advanced Ph.D. students in divinity and religious studies programs of leading American universities.

This seminary elite carries the main interactional burden of the many conferences and organizations I mentioned. As one would predict, they are frequently subject to unfriendly inquiry about and commentary on the UC in such face-to-face settings, especially in those where the object is to present UC ideas *per se*. In this last instance, the Ph.D. elite is subjected to severe criticism all day long, day in and day out, for up to seven-day periods several times a year. One can well ask, how many organizations of *any* kind are prepared to place (or do place) any of their members in such a difficult position? But that too aside, my interest here is UC member behavior under such stress (as well as in the cultural persona enacted by other members in intercultural contacts).

For whatever reasons, people who attend UC-sponsored conferences, especially those presenting the UC doctrines, are prone to publish articles about the experience, and these are useful sources in forming judgments about UC interactional style with outsiders. The half a dozen or so of these I have read (along with numerous verbal reports to me from other attendees) always take severe issue with the content of UC ideology but are uniformly impressed with UCers "as people." Praiseworthy qualities often mentioned include member openness to criticism of their doctrines, friendliness, and helpfulness. The Ph.D. student elite is subject to searching criticism of UC theology, but they remain ever "cool," even cordial, and engagingly civil in the face of abrasive and hostile commentary. The diversity of personalities one sees acting in this way (and not simply the Ph.D.-earning elite) clues us to the existence of cultural patterning as distinct from converging personality dispositions. Indeed, the cultural personas displayed by UCers—their distinct order of civility and geniality—are rather like the classic hallmarks of the "cultured person" (Selznick and Selznick, 1964:652). Beyond this, observers often mention qualities of "warmth" and "caring." One observer was so emotionally moved by such impressions that he has described his response in the famous conversion words of John Wesley: "My heart was strangely warmed" (Quebedeaux, 1983).

3. A cultural scheme may be quite compassionate in the physical, psychological, and interactional senses I have reviewed but still define the movement's situation in a way that stresses the practical necessity of (if not the cultural idealness of) a significant measure of duplicity in its dealings with outsiders. Perhaps the best-known instance of this is the so-called "entryist" strategy sanctified by V. I. Lenin for the purpose of infiltrating worker organizations in revolutionary Russia and since employed as a model by numerous Leninist/Trotskyist parties. In entryism, members of a given MO mute or conceal their "true" political affiliations and beliefs for the purpose of acquiring power and influence in a target association. Phrased more abstractly, some MOs develop exoteric as distinct from esoteric doctrines, tenets, actions, and aims. The former are framed for public consumption and understanding, the latter directed only to the initiated.

I assess all such forms of double-dealing with the world to be less than compassionate. In must be said that the UC has practiced duplicity in several ways over the years, although it has dropped some forms of it under public pressure. But that historical record of double-dealing is still backdrop to the present, and suspicions must of course linger that there may still be secret and unsavory aims, beliefs, plans, and programs of action.

IV. GENERALIZATIONS AND IMPLICATIONS

I have drawn attention to movement organizations as culture-creating-and-bearing social organizations and suggested that these cultures vary in terms of their quantitative elaboration, qualitative expressiveness, and human compassionateness. Along the way I have made particular reference to the Unification Church in comparative movement-culture perspective.

The point of all concepts, distinctions, and identified variations is, of course, enlightening generalizations, perspectives, and answers to questions.

The following are among those I trust we can fruitfully draw from the fore-going.

1. Cultural Richness and Poverty. I hope there is now an empirical and not simply a normative sense in which we can say that some movements are culturally richer than others. Most, indeed, are quite modest affairs in the cultural senses I have elaborated, and we can say, therefore, they offer their members relatively little in such ways.

2. The Richness of Political and Religious Movement Cultures. In the spectrum of MOs, religious ones may, on the whole, foster more robust cultures than political ones. Tentatively assuming this generalization to be true, how might we account for it? Several factors are candidates. First, religious institutions and movements historically antedate political movements. In the struggle to differentiate the two, cultural poverty or starkness was one obvious and easy-to-manipulate differentiator. Politics got stuck, as it were, with the constricted side of the differentiating dialectic. Second, we still live in the shadow of the most culturally robust political movement of modern history: German National Socialism, an elaborate and expressive culture that was also so cruel and authoritarian—so lacking in compassion—that it has given political culture a bad name. In the minds of many, rich political culture is still construed as fascist at worst and authoritarian at best, and we cannot lightly dismiss the possibility that rich MO culture in fact always is.

But momentarily assuming that the link between fascism in particular and authoritarianism in general and rich political culture is historically accidental rather than necessary, one implication can be that political movements ought not be so bashful about constructing richer cultures. In so counseling, I do not suggest the willy-nilly appropriation of practices and forms found in other movements. We definitely do not need, for example, democratic socialist versions of the Nuremberg rallies, although a fundamental reevaluation of the nature of the "rally" and its features is absolutely in order and a topic of high priority in any effort to enrich political culture.

3. The Recruitment Dilemma of Culture. There is a recruitment dilemma to be confronted by efforts to enrich movement culture, perhaps *most especially* by democratic political movements.

To enrich culture is, in one way, to increase demands on members. Increased demands may restrict the breadth of possible recruitment (Aronowitz, 1983a:47). Therefore, the richer the movement culture, the more isolated and enclave-like the movement organization may become. And, isolation defeats the outreach and social change aims of the movement. The Democratic Socialists of America (DSA) and the various Leninist/Trotskyist groups illustrate the two contrasting and unsatisfactory solutions to this dilemma.

> The great attraction of the various Leninist organizations is that they insist upon a total commitment from the individual—personal sacrifice of time and

money in return for which the organization tries to deliver a coherent ideological and cultural community that meets a wide variety of needs. [The Marxist discourse of such groups as against the popular-democratic discourse of the DSA] constitutes a marker that provides the individual with the security of belonging to a culture. In contrast, the democratic left [as in the DSA] possesses a frail "we," not only because its politics tends, willingly, to leave the hard divisive ideological questions unanswered, but also because it makes membership a matter of paying a minimum annual dues that places little strain on most people (Aronowitz, 1983a:47-48).

The perilous path to blaze, therefore, is one that enriches culture in ways that are not too restrictive of recruitment and therefore productive of movement-isolation, but that is also not, on the other hand, authoritarian.

   4. Cultural Richness and MO Longevity. If cultural richness offers member satisfactions and other adaptive resources, we should expect that movements with richer cultures will be more successful (in several senses of that word) than movements that are culturally poorer.

   The most rudimentary meaning of movement "success" is sheer organizational survival for a given period of time, the criteria employed by Rosabeth Kanter (1972) in her comparative study of nineteenth century utopian colonies. And, indeed, if we scrutinize the specific items Kanter finds associated with such success, we find they consist importantly of the kind of beliefs and practices I have termed cultural elaboration and expressiveness.

   On the other hand and unhappily, many other of the correlates of longevity-success are *negatively* correlated with indicators of compassion! As Bruce Hackett has pointed out to me (in conversation), Kanter's findings suggest that in winning the battle of survival, utopian colonies lose the war for the more compassionate world that they were originally waging.

   5. Patterns of Cultural Elaboration, Expressiveness, and Compassion. As the form of incongruity we can read from Kanter's findings suggests, elaboration, expressiveness, and compassion do not always vary together. An elaborate culture is not necessarily a compassionate one, and so forth. This very lack of conjunction helps, in fact, to increase the precision with which we can perceive movements in comparative perspective.

   With regard to the case I have described—the Unification Church—it seems reasonable to say its cultural pattern as so far developed is relatively elaborate, quite richly expressive, and only moderately compassionate.

   6. Cultural Richness and Movement Success. The concept of movement culture focuses in a selective fashion on the seven variables Rodney Stark offers as affecting a movement's success in the sense of establishing itself as a major presence in a society. Mainly, the idea of movement culture expands our understanding of the first, third, and seventh variables in that model: cultural continuity, effective mobilization, and secularization. I have suggested that cultural richness fosters continuity, mobilization, *and* secularization. It has, therefore, a two-edged relation to success. What richness gives in continuity and mobilization, it takes away in secularization. Relative to the key case I have traced, managing this dilemma is one of the central problems facing the Unification Church.

REFERENCES

Aronowitz, Stanley
  1983a   "Remaking the American Left, Part One: Currents in American Radicalism," *Socialist Review* 67 (January-February): 9-51.

  1983b   "Remaking the American Left, Part Two: Socialism and Beyond," *Socialist Review* 69 (May-June): 7-42.

Bailey, Robert
  1974   *Radicals in Urban Politics: The Alinsky Approach.* Chicago: University of Chicago Press.

Bell, Inge Powell
  1968   *Core and Strategy of Non-violence.* New York: Random House.

Blumer, Herbert
  1969   "Collective Behavior." In *Principles of Sociology,* edited by A. M. Lee, 65-121. New York: Barnes and Noble.

Bryant, M. Darrol
  1983   "Towards Understanding the Unification Movement," paper presented at a Unification Church-sponsored conference entitled "Exploring Unification Theology," Funchal, Portugal, 2 August.

Fine, Gary
  1979   "Small Groups and Culture Creation: The Idioculture of Little League Baseball Teams," *American Sociological Review* 44 (October): 733-45.

Kanter, Rosabeth
  1972   *Commitment and Community.* Cambridge: Harvard University Press.

Lofland, Lyn H.
  1973   *A World of Strangers: Order and Action in Urban Public Space.* New York: Basic Books.

Moon, Sun M.
  1983   "Founder's Address," *Unification News* 2:7(July):13.

Quebedeaux, Richard
  1983   "Are You A Moonie?" Paper presented at a Unification Church-sponsored conference entitled "Exploring Unification Theology," Funchal, Portugal, 5 August.

Selznick, Gertrude, and Philip Selznick
  1964   "A Normative Theory of Culture," *American Sociological Review* 29 (October): 653-69.

Unification Church
  1983   "People of the Quest," a videotape, New York: Holy Spirit Association for the Unification of World Christianity.

Wolfe, Tom
  1971   *Radical Chic and Mau-Mauing the Flak Catchers*. New York: Bantam
          Books.
Zablocki, Benjamin
  1980   *Alienation and Charisma*. New York: The Free Press.

CHAPTER EIGHT

Dialectical Processes in the Development of Hare Krishna: Tension, Public Definition, and Strategy

E. Burke Rochford, Jr.

All new religions begin with the hope if not the expectation of successfully reaching their spiritual goals. While the criteria by which members judge success or failure may shift with the fortunes of the group, it is nevertheless clear that all religions—new or old—are guided by the hopes that members attach to their spiritual aims and purposes. Yet the potential success or failure of any religious movement hinges on more than the presence of a committed membership or other internal sources of stability such as effective leadership and organization. No religious movement develops within a social vacuum. Rather, it must constantly take into account and modify its course of action in light of the evaluations and responses of the larger society. Any new religion must forge a working relationship with the sociocultural environment in which it operates if it is to mobilize the resources (that is, people, power, and finances) crucial to its prospects for success (Snow, 1979; Turner and Killian, 1972; Zald and Ash, 1966).

This paper focuses on the development of the International Society for Krishna Consciousness (hereafter ISKCON), more popularly known as the Hare Krishna movement.[1] My discussion and analysis highlights the dialec-

---

[1] The Hare Krishna movement originated in India and was brought to this country by A. C. Bhaktivedanta Swami Prabhupada in 1965. ISKCON is dedicated to spreading Krishna Consciousness throughout the world and has communities and preaching centers on every continent. At its height in the mid-1970s ISKCON had

tical relationship between three processes that have influenced ISKCON's career in America over the past decade: sectarian tension, strategies of accommodation, and the movement's changing public definition. Beginning in the mid-1970s, ISKCON, along with several of the other new religions, was in a high state of tension with its environment. The anticult movement was at its peak in America, and ISKCON became a special target of public scrutiny and action because of its practices in airports and other public places (Rochford, 1984). Being seen by the public as more deviant than religious, and more threatening than respectable, ISKCON found that the legitimate lines of action available to it for purposes of mobilizing resources and expanding its influence in America were limited.

As the Stark model predicts, new religions in a high state of tension with their environment face significant obstacles in expanding their influence and reaching group goals. Reflecting this high state of tension, the general public and society's institutions (for example, legal and medical institutions) often define and respond to such groups as deviant and threatening rather than as legitimate religious enterprises. For a new religion to be in a high state of tension with its environment invites social control efforts directed toward outright suppression of the group. It was precisely such a scenario that helped undermine the Krishna movement's expansionary efforts in the late 1970s and that resulted in ISKCON's decline in America by the end of the decade (Rochford, forthcoming a).

In this paper I address the strategies of accommodation used by ISKCON to reduce the extreme level of tension so detrimental to the movement's development in America during the 1970s. ISKCON's leaders undertook a number of strategies aimed at fostering a more positive public image by attempting to shift the movement's beliefs and goals more into line with the dominant culture and its religious institutions. The overall purpose of these efforts was to convince the public that ISKCON was a legitimate *religious* movement and not a deviant and threatening group out to exploit the American public.

By pursuing a course of accommodation and adaptation, however, ISKCON unwittingly risked yet another threat to the movement's potential for success in America—secularization. While a high level of tension invites ac-

---

approximately 5,000 core members throughout the world. The aim of the Krishna devotee is to become self-realized by practicing the bhakti yoga process, which involves chanting Hare Krishna and living an austere life-style that requires avoiding meat, intoxicants, illicit sex, and gambling. The present study focuses on ISKCON in America. For a discussion of the movement's historical roots in India, see Judah (1974). For a more detailed history of the movement's growth and expansion in America and internationally, see Rochford (1982: Forthcoming).

tive suppression by society's institutions, rapid and extensive accommodation to the larger culture can equally undermine the prospects of a new religion. Secularization acts to rob a new religion of the uniqueness of its spiritual message and thereby deprives it of a basis for attracting new converts. As Bryan Wilson describes, sectarian movements face the delicate task of maintaining a moderate degree of tension with the larger society yet avoiding either too much tension or too little.

> The sect's desire to separate from the world and its concerns—and the values which express that separateness—results in certain distinct tensions for the organization and for its members. For each sect there must be a position of optimal tension, where any greater degree of hostility against the world portends direct conflict, and any less suggests accommodation to worldly values. . . . The means used by the sect to cope with these particular tensions is crucial for the persistence of sect organization. The sect may depart from the accepted moral rules of the wider society, but beyond a certain point the sect comes into conflict with even the democratic state in the pluralist society. . . . If the sect is to persist as an organization it must not only separate its members from the world, but must also maintain the dissimilarity of its own values from those of the secular society (1959:12).

Before turning to ISKCON's efforts to foster a more favorable public definition, I first want to address the issue of tension in more general terms.

SOURCES OF TENSION

By their nature sectarian religious movements are ideologically in a state of tension with the sociocultural environments in which they operate (Bainbridge and Stark, 1980; Johnson, 1963; Wilson, 1959). Sects reject the values and norms of the larger society while churches largely accommodate their beliefs to those of the dominant social order. In sum, the sect rejects society and in turn is rejected by it; the church is part of the society and in many ways simply reflects and reinforces the latter's values and goals.

While sects reject their social environment, the question remains whether such rejection necessarily implies *active* tension between the group and the host society. Several investigators of the church sect typology assume that rejection of the values and goals of society defines sectarian tension (Johnson, 1963; Wilson, 1959), but Bainbridge and Stark have recently questioned this presumed linkage. They state: ''Rejection blurs a relationship that is a two-way street. The sect not only rejects society—it, in turn, is rejected by society'' (1980). Some sectarian religious groups reject the beliefs of the dominant society yet remain in a relatively *low* state of tension with their environment. For example, some world-rejecting movements are in a low state of tension because they remain largely isolated and thus out of the public eye.

Some sects choose to retire to the countryside to fulfill their spiritual goals and thereby remain virtually uninvolved with the larger society (for example, the Amish, the Amana community). Other sectarian movements, while not isolated from the larger society, are nevertheless of little or no interest to the general public because they remain small and do not have conversionist aims that bring them into direct and constant contact with members of the public. Conversely, some religious groups such as the Church of Scientology are largely world affirming in their beliefs yet, because of their tactics and policies, elicit a significant negative reaction from the public and social control agents acting on its behalf (Wallis, 1975, 1983).

Rejection of the larger society's values and normative structure, by itself, is thus not an adequate basis for judging a religious movement's level of tension with its environment. Ideological differences, at most, speak only to the *potential* for active and consequential levels of tension. For a level of tension to influence the career of a new religion also requires some degree of exchange between the group and members of the larger society; ideological differences must be apparent to an interested public. There must be a dynamic process of give and take between the group and its environment if ideological differences are to lead to antagonism and tension. By acting on the society through proselytizing and attempting to mobilize resources, a religious movement reveals itself and thus opens up the possibilities for tension to arise.

Tension, then, does not directly result from a religious movement's sectarian beliefs. Beliefs are important only to the extent they are communicated to a public who evaluates and responds in some way toward them. As Turner and Killian (1972) have long argued, it is the role of the public to define a movement's relations to the larger society's value scheme. Social movements of all types are viewed as either respectable, peculiar, or threatening on the basis of the public's evaluation of their purposes. As such, tension is best viewed as a function of the public's perception and definition of a religious group. Likewise, as the public's definition undergoes change (for example, from peculiar to threatening), so too does its level of tension with the society (for example, from medium to high).[2]

---

[2]It is precisely such a change in public definition that resulted in ISKCON's increasing tension level with American society in the late 1970s. As I describe elsewhere (Rochford, Forthcoming a, Forthcoming b), ISKCON in the early part of its history in America was largely defined by the public as a peculiar religious movement. Three factors were influential in ISKCON's public definition undergoing change from peculiar to threatening: (1) the influence of the anticult movement grew in America during the mid- and late 1970s; (2) ISKCON's book distribution and solicitation practices in public places became a source of public controversy; and (3) Following on the heels of the Jonestown tragedy, one of ISKCON's leaders was arrested and charged with possessing a large cache of guns and ammunition. This event received national media attention.

As suggested in Table 1, the new religions collectively span the tension continuum from high to low. For purposes of illustration I have grouped a number of the new religions along the tension continuum on the basis of the public's definition and response. While the basis for judging the public's definition of the new religions included in Table 1 is admittedly intuitive, there can be little question that the Unification Church, Hare Krishna, the Children of God, and the Church of Scientology have been at the heart of the cult controversy in America over the past decade. These four groups have been the major targets of the anticult movement as well as the center of media attention regarding the new religions. Furthermore, these groups have been the major target of deprogramming efforts, legal action, and a variety of other measures meant to suppress their influence in America. As a result, these groups have been forced to rely largely on covert strategies to recruit new members and to mobilize other resources.

The new religions in the medium tension category (for example, the Divine Light Mission and the followers of Yogi Bhajan and Muktananda) have been defined by the public as more peculiar than threatening. Although viewed by the public as religious in nature, such groups have generally been ostracized because of their unconventional beliefs. These new religions have been

TABLE 1

TYPOLOGY OF NEW RELIGIONS AND THEIR RELATION TO SOCIETY*					
NEW RELIGIOUS MOVEMENT	PUBLIC DEFINITION	LEVEL OF TENSION WITH SOCIO-CULTURAL ENVIRONMENT	REJECTS DOMINANT VALUES AND GOALS	RESPONSE OF SOCIETY	RESULTING STRATEGIES OF ACTION AVAILABLE
Hare Krishna Unification Church Children of God Scientology	Threatening and Deviant (Pseudoreligion or Nonreligion)	High	Usually Yes	Suppression and Hegemony	Covert Means of Action
Divine Light Mission Sikh Foundation (Yogi Bhajan) Muktananda	Peculiar (Religious: Nonconventional)	Medium	Yes	Watchful Eye, Ostracism	Limited Access to Legitimate Means
Jesus Movement Transcendental Meditation	Respectable Nonfactional	Low	No	Limited Interest and Support	Access to Legitimate Means
Meher Baba Gurdjieff Sri Chinmoy	Factional but Relatively Unknown and Undefined	Low	Yes	Disinterest	Limited Access to Legitimate Means

* This typology of new religions borrows heavily from Turner and Killian's discussion (1972:257-59) of the ways in which a social movement's public definition affects both the type of opposition it confronts and the resulting means of action that are made available to it to pursue its goals and objectives.

granted only limited access to legitimate means by which to spread their influence and mobilize resources. As both Stark and Bryan Wilson suggest, these religious movements appear to be in a position of optimal tension with society—neither inviting suppression nor risking secularization.

In the low-tension category are two types of new religions: respectable nonfactional groups, such as various organizations comprising the larger Jesus movement, and new religions that, while factional and world rejecting, remain relatively unknown and therefore largely undefined by the public. The respectable nonfactional category also includes Transcendental Meditation, which—like the Jesus movement—more or less reaffirms dominant values. In an effort to capture a share of the religious marketplace in America, TM has for all intents and purposes largely abandoned its traditional religious beliefs and life-style (Johnston, 1980). As A. L. Basham argues, groups such as TM—and to a lesser degree the modern Ramakrishna movement—represent "streamlined forms of Hinduism" (Gelberg, 1983:166). As such, these groups have become largely secularized (see Bainbridge and Jackson, 1981 for a detailed discussion of TM's development as a religious movement). The second type of new religion in a low state of tension with its environment includes groups such as Meher Baba, Gurdjieff, Sri Chinmoy, and a host of others lesser known. While these groups are factional (that is, rejecting dominant values), and theoretically might well be expected to reach a medium to high state of tension with society, they remain largely unknown and undefined by the American public, and consequently in a low state of tension. Given these groups' lack of notoriety, they are generally able to maintain a degree of access to legitimate means of action.

A major difference between low-tension new religions that are respectable and those largely unknown to the public is that the former are subject to processes of secularization while the latter are not. Secularization by definition implies some degree of public acceptance of a religious group even if only as a tolerated adjunct to other religious institutions. Should these lesser known new religions become subject to public scrutiny, it is likely they would be defined as peculiar, or perhaps even threatening, and their level of tension with society would escalate accordingly. Their prospects for becoming secularized would thus be minimal.

TENSION AND ISKCON'S STRATEGIES OF ACCOMMODATION

By the end of the 1970s ISKCON was in a high state of tension with its environment in America. The public viewed the movement as largely deviant and threatening, thereby stripping it of its religious content and purposes. As a result, ISKCON faced decline, and its future was uncertain at best. In an effort to revitalize the movement, its leadership and members alike began seriously to consider the impact of the public on ISKCON's goal attainment and the very survival of the Krishna movement in America. If ISKCON was to fulfill its commitment to spreading Krishna Consciousness, it had to secure a more favorable public image. It had to convince the public that its purposes were fundamentally religious in nature and that the movement was not a deviant cult.

Complicating ISKCON's efforts to upgrade its public definition were its book distribution and solicitation (that is, sankirtana) efforts in airports and other public places. These contacts between ISKCON members and the public further added to the movement's already negative public image. While sankirtana largely supported ISKCON's communities throughout the seventies, this financial base had come at a considerable cost to the movement's public image. The public often saw the devotees' efforts as motivated more by financial greed than religion (Rochford, 1984). These contacts went a long way toward convincing members of the public that ISKCON was more a deviant and exploitive group than a truly spiritual movement. As a result, ISKCON's level of tension with society escalated.

To help defuse the conflict surrounding sankirtana, ISKCON sought to differentiate money-making from its missionary activities. The movement actively sought alternative sources of income so that its book distributors could concern themselves primarily with preaching when contacting persons in public settings. ISKCON's communities thus developed and expanded a variety of economic enterprises including: selling art work and candles, expanding the number of movement-owned vegetarian restaurants, and producing and selling various types of health food products such as natural candy (for example, "Bliss Bars") to natural food stores. In several communities devotees are becoming involved in the computer business, both selling computers and doing computer programming for local businesses. In addition, ISKCON's growing Indian congregation will likely become an increasingly significant source of income for the movement. Already in several American cities containing large populations of immigrants from India, ISKCON is receiving considerable financial support. For example, in Detroit, Indian adherents contributed $100,000 to the movement's book trust fund in 1982.

Beyond the movement's ongoing efforts to redirect the focus of sankirtana toward missionary activity are a number of other strategies of accommodation meant to alter in a positive manner the public's image of ISKCON. In the remainder of the paper I will discuss three of them: (1) aligning the movement's goals and values with the larger Hindu tradition; (2) taking up social welfare activities (for example, food programs for the poor and needy); and (3) building cultural and religious attractions directed toward introducing large numbers of people in America to Krishna Consciousness. These strategies are aimed at convincing the public of ISKCON's religious character and purpose—that while the movement's beliefs and life-style may be unconventional and peculiar to most Americans, they nevertheless are religious. Such a message is meant to lower the level of tension between the movement and society.

ALIGNING ISKCON WITH HINDUISM

The increasing involvement of Indian people in ISKCON promises to have the effect of increasing the movement's legitimacy in the eyes of the public. In the past, ISKCON has called on its Indian supporters to denounce the actions of the anticultists who have on occasion kidnapped ISKCON members and subjected them to psychological and physical harassment (that is, deprogramming). In addition, they have been called on to testify to the religious authenticity of the movement's beliefs, thereby undermining anticult claims that ISKCON is no more than a contemporary concoction meant to deceive and exploit America's young people. On still other occasions, Indian members have been asked to back claims that government officials have discriminated against the movement on the basis of religious belief.[3]

While ISKCON's Indian supporters have in recent years proven a valuable resource, during the movement's early days ISKCON often eschewed formal ties with other Hindu groups in America. In part this resulted from its rejecton of certain social and theological elements of orthodox Hinduism (for example, the caste system, the narrowly defined role of women, and the belief that Krishna was the supreme God rather than one of many Gods). Perhaps of equal importance, however, was Prabhupada's desire to avoid being seen as rigidly sectarian. Prabhupada felt that many Americans held negative attitudes toward Hinduism, and he sought to avoid the Hindu label. He wanted Krishna Consciousness to be viewed as universal in nature and not culturally and religiously bound to India.

Only as the level of tension between the movement and the larger society grew did ISKCON attempt to accentuate its Hindu roots. In the face of strong public opinion against it, ISKCON began actively to seek formal ties with the larger Hindu tradition. As one ISKCON leader explains:

> In fact it was even stated in the 1980 North American GBC meeting that the goal of the decade is to have our public image be that of a denomination. In other words, we are no longer a cult but a denomination of the Hindu church.

---

[3]In 1980 the Indian community in Los Angeles came to ISKCON's support when the city tried to stop the movement from staging its annual Rath Yathra festival in the beachside community of Venice. When charges of religious discrimination against the Hindu tradition were made, the city quickly backed off and allowed the festival to take place.

And, of course, it is a tactical strategy to have the Hindu community come forward and say what they really think about ISKCON. "We are Hindus. We are part of the Hindu culture and therefore deserve the same kind of first amendment rights as any religion." I admit that this is strategy. But this is also their feeling as well. I mean, when ISKCON is persecuted they feel that they are being persecuted too.

By aligning itself with the larger Hindu faith, the movement hopes to establish its legitimacy as a religion in the eyes of the public and shed its image as a deviant and threatening movement. In sum, ISKCON hopes that the public will recognize its Hindu roots and extend to it the rights and privileges of any other faith in America.

SOCIAL WELFARE ACTIVITIES

In the most general sense, ISKCON has always been in the business of providing programs for the benefit of the larger society. The movement's weekly Sunday feast, while expressly concerned with recruitment and spreading Krishna Consciousness, has nevertheless fed thousands of needy youth and other down-and-out people throughout America and around the world. Now, however, ISKCON has developed a food program specifically targeted at the needs of the poor. The "Hare Krishna Food for Life" program was quietly inaugurated in 1982, making use of food donated by the federal government to non-profit organizations. While there are certainly altruistic and missionary motives involved, the program was begun primarily to promote ISKCON's public image. As an ISKCON member explains:

> One program that we are undertaking now is what we are calling the *Hare Krishna Food for Life Program*. But it isn't a PR hype. Food distribution is a form of preaching also. A practical part of any religion is social welfare work. . . . Now, in America, with the recessionary economy and the unemployment like it is and with social security being slashed, we saw an opportunity to really gain some improved public image by distributing food. . . . It will show people that we are a group with a concern for society. . . . It's a fact that the way to a man's heart is through his stomach. So hopefully they will have a little more appreciation, be open to those things which they see as odd about us. You get phrases (from the people being fed) like: "I don't care what other people say about you but you're alright in my book." "You may look a little strange but you really helped me out. . . . " I think this program will help people realize that we are a movement that is genuinely trying to help people.

Since ISKCON has a tradition of food distribution, it is likely that the movement will continue such programs in the future. Whether these programs will actually alter ISKCON's public definition is less clear. Rather than appreciating the movement's efforts, for example, some may instead become outraged over the use of public foodstuffs indirectly to support the efforts of the Krishna movement in America. It is just such a possibility that has led ISKCON to keep this program under wraps until it is well established. The movement hopes that its efforts will be brought to the public's attention through the appreciative words of local politicians.

CULTURAL-RELIGIOUS ATTRACTIONS

Following the lead of other religions throughout history, ISKCON is now attempting to educate the public about its beliefs and way of life by building temples and other cultural attractions in an effort to acquaint large numbers of people with its communities. This strategy is meant to nurture a more positive public definition, since preaching is low-key and recruitment is of little importance. As the devotee in charge of ISKCON's public affairs department commented in 1983, the movement is moving into its "cultural phase" (Suplee, 1983).

The beginning of ISKCON's cultural phase started with the vision of Prabhupada's first disciple, and current ISKCON guru, who vowed in the mid-1970s to build a palace of gold in honor of ISKCON's founder. On his two-thousand-acre farm in the hills of West Virginia, Kirtanananda Swami Bhaktipada and his followers have built a beautiful palace, a restaurant, and lodging for visitors, including guest houses and camp sites. The community is presently in the midst of building the first of several temples that will be situated on top of the many hills surrounding Prabhupada's palace.

Initially, the efforts of Bhaktipada were met with mixed support throughout the movement: several ISKCON leaders, and a substantial number of devotees as well, openly criticized the project since it diverted monies that might have otherwise gone to help support the financially troubled Bhaktivedanta Book Trust in the late 1970s. Despite the criticism, Bhaktipada continued to raise money for the project, and he and his followers completed Prabhupada's palace in 1980. Now, without question, it is recognized as ISKCON's greatest preaching and public relations success. As one ISKCON leader explains, Prabhupada's palace has had a major impact on the public's image of the movement in America:

> The palace is like a hook. The people come because it is such a far out thing, and yet when they are there they are actually undergoing a spiritual experience. . . . People often go away saying: "You know I always thought you guys were weird. Now I see that you actually are alright." Before, these people's experience of the movement was limited to some goofy devotee on the street who tried to take them out of a couple of bucks. But now they can see this huge cultural, historical, heritage is there. They see this work of art. . . . Prabhupada's palace. Without doubt that palace has done more towards

changing the public opinion toward us than anything else. Many Americans when they think of Hare Krishna now, they think of the palace as well as these other things.

Since its opening, Prabhupada's palace has become the second largest tourist attraction in West Virginia. In the summer of 1982 more than 300 bus loads of tourists reportedly visited the community. Literally thousands of people have traveled there to see the palace and hear about Krishna Consciousness. The palace and the efforts of the devotees residing at the New Vrindaban community have been hailed by state and local politicians, as well as by members of the local community as their presence has brought considerable tourist money into the state.[4]

Following in the footsteps of the public relations success generated by Prabhupada's palace, ISKCON completed another major cultural attraction in Detroit in the summer of 1983. The opening of the Bhaktivedanta Cultural Center drew national press coverage since the project was financially supported by the grandson of Henry Ford and the daughter of the late Walter Reuther, president of the United Auto Workers. In an old mansion built by Lawrence Fisher, founder of Cadillac Motors, ISKCON built what has been described as a "Disney-like multi-media diorama exhibition" explaining the spiritual tradition of Krishna Consciousness. In the same complex is a vegetarian restaurant and temple room. Like Prabhupada's palace, the Bhaktivedanta Cultural Center is expected to attract numerous tourists. Recognizing this possibility, the state senate of Michigan passed a resolution calling the center an occasion for "glad rejoicing." The resolution was presented by senate representatives at the center's grand opening (Suplee, 1983).

In a somewhat different fashion, ISKCON has also attempted to influence its public image by staging and taking part in a number of major parades throughout America and around the world. Each year the movement stages its Rath Yathra festival in major cities around the globe. These festivals attract many thousands of people who view the parade, eat vegetarian food, and are introduced to the Krishna philosophy and life-style. Since 1980 the movement has also participated in a variety of other festivals and parades, including the 1984 Cotton Bowl Parade in Dallas, Texas. ISKCON built a float reflecting the movement's spiritual tradition for the event which was viewed by a crowd of tens of

---

[4]This reaction contrasts with that received by the movement when it first located in West Virginia in the late 1960s. Devotees tell stories of how local people were very much against the movement's settling in their community. On several occasions local people are reported to have attacked the devotees and their temple, in one instance firing guns into the temple.

thousands as well as a national television audience. ISKCON has also participated in other parades as well. Hare Krishna floats won awards in Hawaii at the 1981 Aloha Week Floral Parade and in Australia at the 1983 Moomba Parade (Back To Godhead, 1984).

CONCLUSION

As ISKCON approaches the twenty-first century, the movement will be faced with increasing pressures to accommodate its values and life-style to the larger American culture. The strategies of accommodation outlined in this paper appear to be only the beginning of ISKCON's adaptation efforts. Despite these efforts, however, the American public continues to view the Krishna movement with suspicion. As a result, the movement will likely be forced to develop still other strategies aimed at managing its level of tension with the dominant society. Given the likely expansion of these strategies of accommodation, the question arises whether ISKCON will be able to resist secularizaton. I believe the answer is yes. Let me briefly suggest why.

ISKCON's apparent accommodation to its environment reflects what Snow (1979) refers to as dramatic ingratiation. This is a process involving a social movement's strategic and instrumental adaptation to the surrounding society for purposes of facilitating its goal-attainment efforts. Dramatic ingratiation reflects accommodation that is dramaturgical in character. The movement seeks to further its objectives by fostering the impression that it is trying to adhere to the values and normative standards of the society. What appears from the vantage point of the outside observer to be accommodation to the demands of the environment is no more than impression management as viewed from within. By fostering the impression that the movement is more or less in agreement with society's values and expectations, the group is better able to manage its tension level with the surrounding environment, and thereby gain a measure of control in the interest of accomplishing group objectives. Secularization can take place only when a religious movement's strategies of accommodation lose their dramaturgical quality, that is, when what was strategy becomes no more than standard operating procedure. In Goffman's (1959, 1963) terms, secularization can occur only when a religious group's front-stage work, performed for the benefit of interested outside parties, merges with the essential reality of members' distinctive worldview, or backstage work. Given the dramaturgical quality of ISKCON's pattern of accommodation, then, the present changes do not necessarily reflect secularization; ISKCON's accommodative strategies reflect more a commitment to its sectarian goals and life-style than commitment to the values and norms of the larger society.

REFERENCES

Back to Godhead
1984 "Lotus-flower Float Dazzles Cotton Bowl Crowd." 19(4):19.

Bainbridge, William Sims and Daniel H. Jackson
1981 "The Rise and Decline of Transcendental Meditation." In *The Social Impact of New Religious Movements*, edited by Bryan Wilson, 135-58. New York: The Rose of Sharon Press.

Bainbridge, William and Rodney Stark
1980 "Sectarian Tension." *Review of Religious Research* 22 (December).

Gelberg, Steven J.
1983 *Hare Krishna, Hare Krishna.* New York: Grove Press.

Goffman, Erving
1959 *The Presentation of Self in Everyday Life.* New York: Doubleday Anchor Books.

1963 *Stigma: Notes on the Management of Spoiled Identity.* Englewood Cliffs NJ: Prentice-Hall.

Johnson, Benton
1963 "On Church and Sect." *American Sociological Review* 28:539-49.

Johnson, Hank
1980 "The Marketed Social Movement: A Case Study of the Rapid Growth of TM." *Pacific Sociological Review* 23(3):333-54.

Rochford, E. Burke, Jr.
1982 "Recruitment Strategies, Ideology, and Organization in the Hare Krishna Movement." *Social Problems* 29 (4): 399-410.

1984 "Movement and Public in Conflict: Values, Finances, and the Decline of Hare Krishna." Paper presented at the meetings of the Southern Sociological Society, Knoxville, Tennessee.

Forthcoming a *Hare Krishna!* New Brunswick NJ: Rutgers University Press.

Forthcoming b "Hare Krishna: From Peculiar to Threatening Movement." In Ralph Turner and Lewis Killian, *Collective Behavior.* 3rd ed. Englewood Cliffs NJ: Prentice-Hall.

Wallis, Roy
1975 "Societal Reaction to Scientology: A Study in the Sociology of Deviant Religion." In *Sectarianism,* edited by Roy Wallis, 86-115. London: Peter Owen.

1983 "Hostages to Fortune: Thoughts on the Future of Scientology and the Children of God." Paper presented at the Fourth International Conference on the New Religious Movement, Berkeley, California.

Snow, David A.
1979 "A Dramaturgical Analysis of Movement Accommodation: Building

Idiosyncrasy Credit as a Movement Mobilization Strategy.'' *Symbolic Interaction* 2(2):23-44.

Suplee, Curt
1983   ''The Temple of Tomorrowland: Heirs of Detroit's Assembly Line Investing in Hare Krishna.'' *Washington Post* 27 May 1983, p. E-1.

Turner, Ralph and Lewis Killian
1972   *Collective Behavior.* Englewood Cliffs NJ: Prentice Hall.

Wilson, Bryan
1959   ''An Analysis of Sect Development.'' *American Sociological Review* 2(2):3-15.

Zald, Mayer and Roberta Ash
1966   ''Social Movement Organizations: Growth, Decay and Change.'' *Social Forces* 44:327-41.

· CHAPTER NINE ·

The Future of an Old Man's Vision: ISKCON in the Twenty-First Century

Larry D. Shinn

To talk about the future stability and durability of the International Society for Krishna Consciousness (ISKCON) as a religious institution is to assume that ISKCON is a single organism. Such is not the case. Consequently, before discussing some internal and external factors that will determine the fate of ISKCON and its mission, I would like to point to the nature of its diversity as a way of qualifying the ISKCON of which I shall speak in this essay.

THE COMPLEXITY OF ISKCON

First of all, ISKCON is an international organization in which various cultural locations have played a major role in determining institutional forms and practices. ISKCON began as a Hindu missionary movement in North America (United States and Canada) by guru Prabhupada and was headquartered in Los Angeles for much of the first decade of its existence. The primary English publications for ISKCON still come from the Bhaktivedanta Book Trust located in Los Angeles, though various regions now also have their own presses and local publications. Furthermore, and on the one hand, ISKCON in America has ceased to grow numerically (dropouts each year approximately equal new converts), has fallen on hard times economically in some centers, and has encountered significant social and legal opposition. ISKCON in India, on the other hand, now thrives institutionally with increasing popular acceptance and lay Indian support. Hence, ISKCON's fate in America will not necessarily be the same as that of its Indian temples and projects. The remainder of ISKCON's international outposts (temples, centers, and farms) are nearly as diverse in setting, support, and likely success as their numbers and locations. Consequently, to limit my discussion to ISKCON in America is to recognize that what I say must be qualified before being applied to ISKCON as a whole international umbrella organization.

A second obvious element of ISKCON's complexity is the autonomous nature of its various farms and temples and the distinctiveness this factor has bred. Los Angeles is famous (infamous?) for its large "fringe" community, loose adherence to the prescribed religious discipline, and for stressing book distribution above all other means for economic sustenance (though practice has not always lived up to this ideal). New Vrindavan in West Virginia, on the other hand, is a close-knit community, has a strong sense of common purpose (that is, provides an appealing architectural and cultural attraction to introduce outsiders to ISKCON), and relies upon tourist trade and mobile fundraising teams, not book distribution, for its primary income. In a similar fashion, the distinctiveness of Gita Nagari's rural location and agricultural emphasis contrasts markedly with the Chicago or Denver temples' city atmospheres and missions. Furthermore, due to ISKCON's confederation type of affiliation, each zone and each temple have a certain degree of legal and economic autonomy that has led to heterogeneity, not conformity. When one adds the impact and authority of the various gurus over certain temples and zones, the complexity is even further increased.

What both of the above characteristics—geographic and institutional diversity—point to is a healthy dissimilarity of ideological emphasis, community, and expression of mission among ISKCON communities that often get lumped together as though there were a single entity called ISKCON. To be sure, the common adherence to certain beliefs and practices does support such a generalization. Likewise, the influence of the Governing Body Commission (GBC) has had a stabilizing and cohesive effect. Yet for any deliberations on the factors that will determine ISKCON's longevity and success, it is important to recognize that whatever factors are discussed, *they must be weighed differently according to the location, type, and history of each ISKCON community.* And this qualification is as true for the Indian and other international communities as it is for the American ones about which I shall speak.

INTERNAL FACTORS OF SUCCESS OR FAILURE

A critical juncture in a charismatic community's history is the death of its founder. In the case of the Indian utopia named Auroville that I studied in the mid-1970s, no successor was appointed to replace the founder, The Mother, although two men fought for control over the whole community.[1] The result

---

[1]For a description of the theological (that is, ideological) source of Auroville's founding and the author's analysis of the factors that have led to this community's failure, see Larry D. Shinn, "Auroville: Visionary Images and Social Consequences in a South Indian Utopian Community," *Religious Studies* (Cambridge, forthcoming).

was organizational and economic chaos and the current slow demise of The Mother's dream. By comparison, and unlike the expectations of ISKCON watchers, Prabhupada appointed eleven successors, not one. His own spiritual master, Bhaktisiddhanta, had also refused to name a single successor. However, the internal bickering and power plays between the appointed leaders of Bhaktisiddhanta's sixty-four missionary centers, called the Gaudiya Maths, led to institutional fragmentation and the disintegration of a coordinated Krishna-conscious mission in India.

Prabhupada learned from his own master's experience that there must be some overarching governance system in order for a multiple-successor arrangement to work. His own master had tried to establish such a governing commission before his death. Prabhupada, however, was successful in creating a Governing Body Commission (GBC) for ISKCON partly because he provided this political structure early in ISKCON's history in America. In fact, it was in July of 1970, when Prabhupada's impending travels to ISKCON's international centers and his lengthy stays in India would require his absence from his fledgling American centers, that the GBC was established as a "nuts and bolts" governance structure.

Made up of twelve (and gradually expanded to twenty-four) of the most advanced devotees who also held positions of authority in ISKCON (for example, temple presidents and book editors), the GBC was viewed by Prabhupada as his "direct representative."[2] Subsequently, the GBC began to meet annually in Mayapur, India to decide ISKCON-wide policy issues. At these annual meetings, problems were discussed, policies set, and institutional strategies confirmed. Governance, personnel, economic, and even theological issues formed the agendas for these meetings. Prabhupada's word was final, but much of the decision-making process rested in the hands of the GBC members. Hence, when Prabhupada died in the fall of 1977, the GBC already had experience in exercising a leadership role for all of ISKCON. Furthermore, most of the eleven new gurus ("initiating *āchāryas*") were already members of the GBC, making a natural link between the spiritual role of the guru and the institutional role of the GBC.

The twofold level of transmission of authority from founder to disciples in the form of the GBC *and* eleven new gurus was not without its inherent problems. The basic unresolved tension was between the authority of the initiating gurus appointed by Prabhupada and the GBC. The ideology/theology of ISKCON asserts that every devotee is dependent upon his or her guru to

---

[2]Satsvarūpa dāsa Goswami, *In Every Town and Village: Around the World, 1968-1971* (Los Angeles: Bhaktivedanta Book Trust, 1982), *Śrīla Prabhupāda-līlāmṛta*, 4:104.

complete the devotional circuit to God (Krishna). The guru is the intermediary between Krishna and his devotees as he exemplifies and transmits Krishna's teachings and delivers to Krishna the devotees' love. The only way this connection can be continued from one generation to the next is through the succession of gurus, *parampará*. Consequently, the life of faith in ISKCON is dependent upon an acceptance of one's guru as standing in an authentic line of disciples.

Given the above reasoning, when one's own guru dies and appoints eleven successors who are also one's godbrothers (that is, men initiated by the same guru as oneself), to whom does one turn for spiritual guidance and institutional governance? This was the plight of hundreds of Prabhupada's disciples when he died in 1977, and hundreds of them left ISKCON after his death. Though the reasons were many and complex, one persistent cause was the tension that arose between godbrothers. Some of Prabhupada's disciples were now spiritual leaders and initiators of new devotees; others were without a guru physically present for guidance and yet did not feel comfortable accepting the leadership of their peers.

The basic guru/GBC issue that evolved in ISKCON can be stated in the question, "Who *is* the ultimate authority for ISKCON?"[3] The tension reflected in alternative answers to this question surfaced in a dramatic way in the spring of 1980 when Hansadutta, the guru for the Northwestern United States zone was accused by police of stockpiling guns in the Berkeley Temple and nearby farm community. Though Hansadutta was already in hot water with his godbrothers on the GBC for a variety of charges against his unorthodox fund-raising, administrative style, and recruiting tactics, the gun ep-

---

[3]Since Prabhupada's death, there has been contention among some of his disciples over the authenticity of the new gurus' appointment. It seems that during the summer of 1977 (several months before Prabhupada died) the ill founder mentioned six or seven successors in one taped discussion with disciples and additional successors in a second taped discussion. Eleven successors ("initiating acharyas") were mentioned in all. But the informal way the old guru mentioned the eleven new gurus and his simultaneous charge that *all* of his disciples should make themselves worthy and capable of such a lofty responsibility opened the door for some devotees to question his intentions regarding succession. Did he really intend that *only* eleven young men were to assume his mantle upon his death? Did he not leave open the possibility that more than eleven gurus could initiate new disciples (a possibility realized the spring of 1982 when the GBC named three additional gurus)? Some of his disciples also questioned the spiritual maturity of the eleven young gurus who were their social and religious peers. Nonetheless, upon the death of Prabhupada the fall of 1977, the GBC and most devotees in ISKCON accepted the eleven men named by the founder as legitimate heirs to his authority.

isode was the final blow to his credibility. After much heated discussion, the GBC decided to ''relieve'' Hansadutta from his post in Berkeley and sent him off to India for ''rehabilitation.'' This was done, and another guru, Hriday-ananda, was sent to Berkeley to try to put that temple back on good footing.

This action of the GBC, however, raised to the fore the question of ultimate leadership over ISKCON that had been simmering only slightly below the sur-face since Prabhupada's death. The debate essentially asked the question whether the GBC, which was an institutional governing body, had the authority to step between a guru and his disciples, a spiritual relationship. The young leaders of the GBC sought the advice of an elder godbrother of Prabhupada, an Indian sage named Sridara Maharaja. He cautioned these young devotees not to interfere with the guru-disciple relationship because such a spiritual bonding is the primary goal of the Krishna faith. The devotees who opposed this view warned of the frag-menting effect of accepting eleven autonomous leaders for ISKCON, but the devotees who agreed with Sridara's advice prevailed. Hansadutta was reinstated to his post in Berkeley although his responsibilities and zone were curtailed.

When Hansadutta returned to his initiating and governing responsibilities after an absence of approximately one year, the debate within ISKCON over ultimate authority had not disappeared. The actions of Jayatirtha, a guru who was located in London and had Western Europe for his zone, occasioned yet another GBC/guru tussle. Accused of taking drugs and engaging in inter-course with some of his female devotees, Jayatirtha was the topic of serious conversations among GBC members who were concerned with these breaches of his asecetic vows. Furthermore, Jayatirtha appeared to be shifting his loy-alty away from ISKCON's leadership to Sridara Maharaja, a godbrother of ISKCON's founder who lived in Bengal. At the spring 1982 GBC meeting in Mayapur, Jayatirtha was told that if he did not immediately alter his behav-ior, that is, cease seeing Sridara and abide by his vows of celibacy and ab-stinence from intoxicants, he would be removed from his post. Jayatirtha immediately sought refuge with Sridara Maharaja and accepted a new initi-ation at his hands. Some of Jayatirtha's disciples in London fled to India to join him and created briefly the first formal schismatic offshoot from ISK-CON (though still related through Prabhupada's godbrother Sridara).[4] The GBC acted to stabilize Jayatirtha's zone by installing new leadership.

When in the spring and early summer of 1983 persistent rumors and charges of illegal and immoral behavior were leveled against Hansadutta

---

[4]This brief and minor schism was short-lived because Jayatirtha essentially had no economic or political base to sustain a separate institution from ISKCON once he fled his London temple and his disciples returned to the ISKCON fold or left ISK-CON altogether. Latest reports in ISKCON claim that Jayatirtha is now wandering about Nepal alone seeking chemical highs to boost his spiritual ones.

again, the debate over the ultimate authority for ISKCON was settled—at least on the institutional level. Hansadutta was excommunicated from ISKCON, and a public announcement was made to that effect. The news release said in part, "The GBC is ISKCON's highest ecclesiastical body and maintains the Hare Krishna religion's spiritual standards, guarding against teachings and practices contrary to those of the religion as determined by its scripture and Founder-*Acharya*."[5] The GBC had clearly asserted its authority not only over the institutional governance of ISKCON but over its spiritual and theological mission as well. When it appointed three new gurus at its Mayapur meeting the spring of 1983, it was clear that ISKCON was a stronger institution than its Indian predecessor had been. The reason was that the charismatic and spiritual role and power of of the guru had been transmitted without permitting any one guru to determine policy or behavior outside certain theological and institutional limits. To use Max Weber's categories, the charisma of the founder had been institutionalized.[6]

With the exception of the two gurus who were finally forced out of ISKCON, the "new" gurus have evidenced an ability to act as independent authorities as well as co-workers on ISKCON's behalf. Their independence is noticeable in their different styles of religious leadership, fiscal management, community building, and sense of their unique contribution to ISKCON's mission. For example, Hridayananda is famous for his acerbic wit and sermonizing and has taken it upon himself to oversee the completion of Prabhupada's translation of the *Śrīmad Bhāgavatam*. Satsvarupa Goswami is nearing completion of the authorized multivolume biography of Prabhupada and is known throughout the movement as one of the most spiritually advanced of the new gurus.

Kirtananda Swami is located in New Vrindavan (West Virginia) and has taken the development of that community as a combination spiritual center and tourist attraction his lifelong project. The assumption underlying this palace and temple-building program is that beautiful and authentic Indian religious architecture set in the context of a living devotional community will bring to it tourists and others who will provide financial support and obviate the necessity of book distribution or proselytizing in public places. In contrast, Rameswar Swami, the guru based in Los Angeles, is noted for his emphasis on book publication and distribution and his adherence to centralized institution-building (centered on the

---

[5]"ISKCON News Release," Miami FL, 9 July 1983.

[6]For a full description of Max Weber's understanding of charisma, see his *The Theory of Social and Economic Organization,* trans. A. M. Henderson and Talcott Parsons (Glencoe IL: The Free Press, 1947) 358-86.

GBC). As evidence of his commitment to book distribution as the primary form of ISKCON evangelism, the temples in his zone have begun an ambitious every-door canvass of homes in major cities (for example, San Diego and Denver) in which a packet of ISKCON paperback books is left on the doorknob of every home in the city free of charge.

Much could be said about the other new gurus who are noted for their distinctive emphases on certain theological or institutional issues. However, now that the dust has settled to reveal a strong, centralizing force in the GBC, it is clear that cooperation between such nearly autonomous leaders is possible without stripping them of their distinctive roles as spiritual guides or as institutional leaders. Consequently, I would suggest that Prabhupada's charisma *has* effectively been transferred *and* institutionalized.[7]

Even though the legacy of Prabhupada still endures with immediacy and authority in the devotees of ISKCON who remember and follow the dictates (written and spoken) of this founding guru, he encouraged his disciples to adhere to the age-old Indian reliance on the threefold test of guru, *sadhu,* and *śāstra.* That is, the new gurus are free to interpret and apply their founder's teachings to new situations *as long as* these applications agree with traditional readings (by the previous gurus or *sadhus*) of the sacred texts (the *śāstras*). Consequently, daily institutional challenges (economic, legal and so forth) can be met in various zones in various ways without incurring the constant paralyzing effects of infighting and acrimony over minor issues and decisions that have spelled the doom of many religious utopias (for example,

---

[7]It is here that I would disagree with the very title of E. Burke Rochford's dissertation chapter, ''The End of Charisma,'' in *A Study of Recruitment and Transformation Processes in the Hare Krishna Movement* (Department of Sociology, University of California, Los Angeles, 1982). In that chapter, Rochford overemphasizes the ''guru controversies'' by treating them all as equally threatening to the institution of ISKCON and to *all* disciples. Many if not most of the persons I interviewed from 1980 to 1983 were simply not interested in challenging the new gurus' legitimacy. They accepted the eleven as Prabhupada's successors. Those who did raise the issue or who pirated the Sridara Maharaja's taped conversation to me secretly felt obliged to remain anonymous unless they were already among the few who publicly questioned the line of succession. Once I moved from the temples on the coasts (East and West), the issue simply did not dominate the thought of devotees young or old as Rochford's chapter suggests. It is true that among fringe devotees in Los Angeles and New York the issue was a hot one. However, compared to succession debates and conflicts in comparable Indian communities (for example, Ramakrishna Mission or the Brahmo Samaj), ISKCON's transmission of authority at Prabhupada's death was remarkably smooth and successful given the individualist and autocratic structure of the guru/disciple relationship.

Auroville) after the death of their founders, not to mention ISKCON's own predecessor in India.

As recently as 1981, a widely distributed *Los Angeles Times* article entitled ''Krishnas—Kingdom in Disarray'' warned that the guru/GBC debates, internal ISKCON arguments over different sankirtan (that is, preaching and fund-raising) ''styles,'' and the struggle for supremacy among three American gurus for the ''top-guruship'' position threatened the very future of ISKCON. That article surmised, ''But it is unclear whether the disputes within the earthly kingdom of Krishna will produce a mystical college of cardinals or a wildly disparate junta of individualistic holy men.''[8] Given the events of the past two years, it seems safe to say that neither of those alternative scenarios is likely. Rather, it would appear that ISKCON has weathered the initial storm caused by the founder's death and the transmission of his authority by allowing a great deal of autonomy and diversity to persist among the gurus while at the same time expanding the GBC's powers to include a *limiting* role over theological and spiritual matters. While the administrative problems occasioned by this kind of leadership arrangement have not disappeared entirely in the wake of recent centralist decisions, they now serve more to produce creative tension and limits than to encourage fragmentation and schisms.[9]

The recent private agreement by the ousted guru Hansadutta to turn over quietly his disciples and temple holdings to other ISKCON gurus is one example of the stabilizing effect of the GBC's setting of limits for *all* of ISKCON's devotees—guru or not. This current centralist tendency bodes well for the longevity of ISKCON as an institution without undercutting the supremacy of the guru-disciple relationship religiously. In sum, it would appear that ISKCON has begun to develop an ''effective mobilization'' (in Rodney Stark's terms) of institutional resources while retaining a high level of intensity of commitment through the guru/disciple relationship. Even though ISKCON in America will never be a large movement, it has both the seriousness of individuals' conviction and the institutional orderliness that are required of organizations that must face a hostile environment.

---

[8] ''Krishnas—Kingdom in Disarray,'' *Los Angeles Times*, 15 February 1981, p. 10.

[9] As of this writing, there are a few sectarian offshoots from ISKCON that have been started by disenchanted ISKCON devotees. For example, a former Los Angeles temple president (then named Kheera Krishna) was reinitiated in 1983 by Sridara Maharaja in India and returned to America as Bhakti Sudhir Goswami and founded the Chaitanya Saraswat Mandal in San Jose, California. On the East coast, the Sri Nitai Gaura Association is a Sridara Maharaja-backed center. Nonetheless, these schismatic groups are small and without significant funds or outside (for example, Indian) support. They certainly pose no present threat to ISKCON and its activities.

The second internal factor that will affect ISKCON's ability to survive in its new American home is its economic stability. From ISKCON's inception its founder linked its economic well-being and survival to its evangelistic missionary activities. In commenting on the primary mission of ISKCON, Prabhupada grounded his preaching emphasis in that of the fifteenth-century Indian reformer Caitanya: "Spreading Krishna consciousness is Sri Caitanya Mahaprabhu's mission; therefore his sincere devotees must carry out his desire."[10] Preaching has been viewed by ISKCON throughout its history as the "best service to the Lord" and the fulfillment of one's whole devotional life.[11]

On the one hand then, ISKCON exists to "spread Krishna Consciousness." This evangelism has usually taken the form of "book distribution." From the early days of Prabhupada's preaching in India (two decades *before* coming to America), he saw his special task as being to bring the Krishna faith to the English-speaking world primarily through the printed word. While Caitanya used drums and cymbals as he danced and sang the praises of Krishna sankirtan) throughout the streets of Bengal and India, Prabhupada's guru called the printing press the "big *mrduṅga*" or "big drum" that could reach the whole world with its sound. Thus Prabhupada stressed book publication and distribution as the best contemporary form of sanskīrtan or preaching from the time he made his first disciples.

On the other hand, to support his ambitious expensive book ministry, Prabhupada urged his disciples to seek donations for the literature that was distributed (again emulating his own pattern of preaching and solicitation in India). His interpretation of the sacred Krishna texts supported this wedding of evangelism with economic survival. His comment on one Caitanya text says, "When such possessions [that is, the money or possessions of a nondevotee] are given to *brāhmaṇas* and Vaisnavas who can engage them in the service of the Lord because of their advancement in spiritual life, this indirectly helps the person who gives the charity, for he is thus relieved of sinful reactions [that is, the "bad" karma or fruits of his sinful life].''[12] In other words, even

---

[10]*Śrī Caitanya Caritāmṛta*, Madhya 16.64, translation and commentary by A. C. Bhaktivedanta Swami Prabhupāda (Los Angeles: Bhaktivedanta Book Trust, 1975) Madhya-līlā: 6:188.

[11]*Śrīmad Bhāgavatam*, 7.6.24, translation and commentary by A. C. Bhaktivedanta Prabhupāda (Los Angeles: Bhaktivedanta Book Trust, 1976) 8:2:32.

[12]*Śrī Caitanya Caritāmṛta*, Antya 3.139, translation and commentary by A. C. Bhaktivedanta Prabhupāda (Los Angeles: Bhaktivedanta Book Trust, 1975) Antya-līlā: 1:280.

if the person giving a donation for a Krishna book is not a devotee nor desires to be one, there is some spiritual benefit that "naturally" accrues to that individual because of his material or monetary contribution.

Put in different terms, the spiritual transaction of preaching to other persons benefits them even when they remain nondevotees *if* they have given money that will benefit the spread of Krishna consciousness. This view is not new to Prabhupada but is as old as the Indian institutions of monasticism and mendicancy themselves. Traditionally, both Hindus and Buddhists have asserted such a symbiotic relationship between the renounced monk and the worldly layperson. The layperson gives tangible gifts to the ascetic in return for spiritual benefits (usually good karma for the next life). Prabhupada states this view bluntly, "Money given in charity to a suitable person is guaranteed bank balance in the next life."[13] And Prabhupada viewed his world-renounced disciples as such "suitable persons."

Passages such as those above have led to conflicting interpretations in ISKCON over the years on what "sankirtan" can and should mean and include. Some devotees have argued that the stress on book distribution as the best form of preaching *and* financing that ministry means that *no* other fund-raising activities are needed to support ISKCON. Others have argued that selling paintings or other "secular paraphernalia" (for example, records, posters, and personalized buttons) can also be considered "sankirtan" *if* the money collected is used for the central preaching mission of ISKCON. Consequently, battles have raged over the years in ISKCON on what constitutes the limits of legitimate economic enterprises (not to mention the questionable selling techniques associated with such economic ventures).

Here is not the place to discuss the history of these debates nor their likely resolutions in the future. Rather, my point in raising this issue is to note the negative implications for economic stability in ISKCON arising out of the ideology of ISKCON, which makes a restricting connection between book distribution as an evangelical or preaching activity and an economic activity. The effect of this linkage has been to discourage creative economic problem solving by eliminating many traditional funding possibilities.

Furthermore, the tension between sankirtan as the primary spiritual obligation and preaching activity of ISKCON *and,* at the same time, its central economic activity has been exacerbated in recent years. When book distribution was at its peak in the mid-1970s in America, the money that flowed from this activity supported hefty monthly budgets in many American temples. However, in the aftermath of Prabhupada's death in 1977 and the resulting institutional uncertainty, and also as a result of the effectiveness of

---

[13]*Śrīmad Bhāgavatam,* 2.3.17, translation and commentary by A. C. Bhaktivedanta Prabhupāda (Los Angeles: Bhaktivedanta Book Trust, 1972) 2:1:149.

antagonists to ISKCON in arousing public suspicion, book "sales" fell off in the late 1970s, leaving some temples in desperate financial straits. Many ISKCON centers were simply forced to abandon book distribution as their primary funding means.

In spite of increased economic support from the Indian community for some city temples in America and the emergence of new "businesses" like the selling of artworks some temples have developed, many American temples are still struggling economically. Most importantly, book distribution seems not to be the long-term answer economically even though that is what the ideology encourages. The economic support for temples and communities in America is as diverse as they are. Some rely almost entirely on book distribution funds. Others support themselves with separately incorporated businesses that sell Asian art reproductions. Still other communities exist to a great extent on what can be raised on and sold from their farms. Yet nearly all call their money-making activities sankirtan (and their money "lasksmi" after the Krishna goddess of wealth) whether those activities are connected to preaching or not. One could compare this Krishna view with some Catholic monastaries' understanding of their vineyards and wineries.

As their antagonists have become more successful at causing public skepticism of their book distribution activities in public places (for example, airports) and even limiting such activities (for example, the Minnesota State Fair decision), many ISKCON centers have relied less on such activities for raising funds and have stressed the need to separate the spiritual and economic sides of this activity. They argue that sankirtan as book distribution must go on as the primary missionary activity of ISKCON *regardless* of its economic utility—or even liability.[14] But what such a decision has meant in practical terms is that stop-gap businesses (like selling art work) only postpone ISKCON's facing its built-in and underlying economic problem, namely, an expensive book ministry with unstable funding in an increasingly hostile cultural context.

The continuing threat of economic instability to ISKCON's future in America is well known in the inner circles of its leadership. One temple president recently said to me, "We know our painting businesses are not a permanent source of income. It is only a matter of time until that source dries up. But Krishna will show us the way when we come to that bridge to cross." Complicating the economic problem is ISKCON's need to make itself a more

---

[14]A case in point is the current practice in the Western Zone of the guru Rameswar to distribute ISKCON paperback books free to every home in some major cities while raising portions of the money for this "preaching" activity through a variety of means—some not at all related to book distribution.

visible and accepted alternative religious community in America (that is, show what Stark calls "cultural continuity"). But that costs money. For example, in the summer of 1983 the Denver Temple held its first Ratha Yatra festival (made famous in Puri, India) but could not afford the traditional carts to carry the Krishna deities and held a truncated version in a local park. One primary goal of such ventures is public awareness and acceptance of ISKCON and its mission. The major impediment in Denver and elsewhere to this task is lack of financial resources.

An additional facet of ISKCON's monetary problems is that the selling techniques used in their book-sankirtan and temple businesses have raised protests from many quarters. Besides the well-known "change-up" and other forms of "transcendental trickery" that have been employed in the past in book distribution, many temples have ignored or been ignorant of the law in the conduct of their painting businesses. For instance, one traveling sankirtan party in Maine was found guilty of fraud in their sales of art reproductions, and one devotee I interviewed had left ISKCON on several occasions because of his discomfort with the tactics he was asked to use to *sell* paintings.

Anticult antagonists have warned that the Krishnas have "gone underground" as they have donned wigs and secular clothes to do their book selling and other businesses. Even though there is nothing illegal, immoral, or subversive about their abandonment of clerical clothes (compare the move toward secular dress among Catholic nuns in America), heightened suspicion of their intentions has resulted from this practice. In short, both deservedly and undeservedly, the Krishnas are finding it more and more difficult to do business when their identity is known. This fact only worsens the picture of their economic future.

A third internal factor that will determine ISKCON's institutional health in the years to come is the devotees' ability to recruit new members. I have already hinted at several dimensions of this problem in my article "Conflicting Networks: Guru and Friend in ISKCON."[15] First of all, throughout ISKCON's history in America it has been dependent on attracting what Stark and Bainbridge call "social isolates."[16] ISKCON grew rapidly during the days of the counterculture in the late 1960s and early 1970s but has had difficulty finding sufficient numbers of such socially isolated and alienated youth to sustain numerical growth in the postcounterculture era. ISKCON in America

[15]*Religious Movements: Genesis, Exodus, and Numbers,* ed. Rodney Stark (forthcoming).

[16]Rodney Stark and William Sims Bainbridge, "Networks of Faith: Interpersonal Bonds and Recruitment to Cults and Sects," *American Journal of Sociology* 8 (1980): 1381-82.

is barely able to maintain its fulltime temple/farm membership in the vicinity of 2,500 adult members.

In the second place, throughout most of its history in America, the primary model for membership in ISKCON has been its monastic temple membership. Though householders have existed and have often held high managerial positions from ISKCON's beginning, the highest leadership (both spiritual and institutional) of the movement has been made up almost entirely of those who have renounced the world (that is, *sannyāsins*) for Krishna and thus who set the standard for ISKCON membership. This extreme level of total commitment and surrender to ISKCON's life and mission necessarily excludes many people who might otherwise be willing to agree to some less inclusive or demanding affiliation.

Some American ISKCON communities have revised their recruiting strategies to emphasize a "lay" Krishna community that would be made up of persons who consented to adherence to the Krishna beliefs and ritual while living and working in the "karmi" or outside world.[17] However, it is not at all clear how such a plan is to be realized or how recruitment will change to meet this new challenge. The every-door canvassing with ISKCON books is too new to be evaluated in this regard; but history indicates that such tactics are likely to produce few new recruits.

In his article "Recruitment Strategies, Ideology, and Organization in the Hare Krishna Movement," E. Burke Rochford, Jr. argues that "neither the movement's religious beliefs and practices, nor its lifestyle, determined its recruitment strategies as it spread through the United States in the 1970s."[18] He then generalizes to say that this disjunction between ideology and struc-

---

[17]One should distinguish several levels of ISKCON membership that are now discussed as alternatives to the clerical or monastic roles of the *brhmachārī/īnī*. There is first of all the level of the householders *(gṛhastha)* who are married couples living within or without the temple complexes. The commitment level and institutional roles of these persons often are indistinguishable from the monks, except that the householders are married. Then there is the "lay" membership represented by the Indian families who provide economic support for ISKCON centers and are active in ISKCON's ritual life. Some city centers are now talking about trying to extend such lay membership to a wider American clientele. And then there are those who have been called "fringies" in the past who seem to fit the designation of "part-time" devotees described by E. Burke Rochford in his essay "Recruitment Strategies, Ideology, and Organization in the Hare Krishna Movement," *Social Problems* 29:4 (April 1982): 407. It is important to distinguish between the "lay" and the "part-time" categories since the first implies a more congregational focus and the second simply a less faithful adherence to the Krishna faith and life-style.

[18]Ibid., 408.

ture on the one hand, and recruitment strategies on the other may well be a common feature of such social movements. Leaving the generalization aside, Rochford's conclusions regarding ISKCON must be modified. It is precisely the textual (that is, ideological) and institutional traditions and history of ISKCON that assert the primacy of one-to-one preaching that has determined the *way* Prabhupada and his disciples have sought new followers.

Because one's surrender to a guru is not debatable in Gaudiya Vaisnavism, and because belief in and devotion to Krishna require the adoption of a worldview at odds with that of most converts, from the very earliest days of ISKCON in America certain recruitment strategies have been determined and others excluded by its ideology. For example, the earliest recruitment techniques used by Prabhupada (for example, *kīrtana* and preaching from the *Śrīmad Bhāgavatam* or *Gītā*) were venerated Indian practices *required* by the ideology arising from Caitanya's movement in India. To be sure, what was expected of a new recruit regarding the understanding of the ideology changed as Prabhupada slowly Indianized his disciples' dress, rituals, and so forth. ISKCON's fundamental techniques of proselytizing have always been variations on the same themes (whether at Sunday Feasts or rock concerts).

I would suggest that one of the liabilities of ISKCON's recruiting has been precisely its ideological insistence on book distribution (that is, preaching from the scriptures in printed form) as the primary proselytizing strategy. Following this ideology and practice has precluded creative thinking in ISKCON on effective ways to preach a truly "foreign" religion to an American public wider than those isolated or alienated from accepted cultural norms and values. To be sure, there are the cooking courses at colleges and universities, the festivals like Ratha Yatra in major cities, and even the anomaly of New Vrindavan's novel "tourist-attraction" approach as alternative recruiting strategies. But throughout ISKCON in America and even worldwide, it is the individual-to-individual preaching of the Krishna scriptures that has marked ISKCON's recruitment strategy from its inception. And this strategy is based on the spiritual linkage of guru and disciple, and disciple and text, that is centuries old in India.

Just as the transmission of authority from Prabhupada to his successors and the GBC was codified by venerable Indian Vaisnava scriptures and traditions, it would appear that ISKCON's economic stability and recruitment strategies have been hindered by them. What the future holds for ISKCON, as presently constituted, will be determined to a great extent by the success of its bright and energetic leadership in finding alternative funding and recruiting strategies that are at once effective (that is, stabilizing) and acceptable to the received scriptural tradition (that is, ideology). Given the liberty Prabhupada took in his interpretation of the classic scriptures, the scriptural leeway is certainly there.

EXTERNAL FACTORS OF SUCCESS OR FAILURE

Perhaps the most immediate and obvious external factor that appears to threaten the future of ISKCON (and other alternative religious groups in America) is the success of the anticult lobbies in arousing hostility against "the cults" in the legal and psychiatric communities. The continued attempt to use conservatorship laws to legislate against "the cults" is one example of these tactics. The efforts of John Clark, Margaret Singer, and other psychologists to mobilize the psychiatric community against the cults' "mind-control" techniques is another example. Little needs to be added to what has already been written about these and other morally questionable anticult strategies in the legal and psychological arenas.[19]

It would seem to this author, however, that the real threat to the survival of ISKCON and other such alternative religious groups in America is not new laws or professional groups that attempt direct attacks on their civil liberties (though this menace is real enough). Rather, the insidious peril to ISKCON's future in America (and elsewhere where similar tactics are successful) is the attempt by anticult groups and literature to engender a pervasive fear in the general public by lumping *all* "cults" together so that whatever has happened in *any* cult (for example, People's Temple, Manson's Family, the House of Judah, or Synanon) is believed to be potential in *every* cult. No one who has studied the anticult groups or literature needs to be told of their attempts to generalize across all cults regardless of vast ideological, life-style, and historical differences. And the groups most often considered in the "destructive cult" category include the Unification Church, the Way International, Scientology, *and* the Hare Krishnas.

The success of the anticult's fear-mongering campaign has been apparent for some time in the media's unwitting parroting of guilty-by-association stories that lump all cults together without making important distinctions regarding their tendencies toward violence, intensity of proselytizing techniques, abuse of children, and so forth. And the practical effects of this "cult" la-

---

[19]These anticult tactics are discussed in all or part of the following recent publications: Thomas Brandon, *New Religions, Conversions, and Deprogramming: New Frontiers of Religious Liberty* (Oak Park IL: Center for Law and Religious Liberty, 1982); David G. Bromley and Anson D. Shupe, Jr., *Strange Gods: The Great American Cult Scare* (Boston: Beacon Press, 1981) and *The New Vigilantes: Deprogrammers, Anti-Cultists, and the New Religions* (Beverly Hills CA: Sage Publications, 1980); J. Gordon Melton and Robert L. Moore, *The Cult Experience: Responding to the New Religious Pluralism* (New York: The Pilgrim Press, 1982); and Herbert Richardson, ed., *New Religions & Mental Health: Understanding the Issues* (New York: The Edwin Mellen Press, 1980).

beling are just now beginning to appear in legal decisions that truly threaten First Amendment rights for the new religious movements. While ISKCON, the Unification Church, and other such groups have won many legal battles related to their status as religious groups (for example, the 1977 Ed Shapiro case), the jury trials in cases involving parental rights over their legal-aged children (for example, Rebecca Foster, 1980) or trials that attempt to punish all cults by excessive judgments against one (for example, Robin George, 1983) evidence an undermining of our trial-by-jury system by a pervasive fear of all the cults.

For example, the jury foreman in the Rebecca Foster case said that one could not trust the "wooden" testimony of the supposed victim, Rebecca Foster. The foreman of the Robin George jury said that the 32.5 million dollar judgment against ISKCON (only nine million had been asked by the plaintiffs) was intended as a warning to all of the cults to leave American children alone. And perhaps the best instance of the horrific effects of pervasive cult fears on our jury system is the Stephanie Riethmiller case in Cincinnati, Ohio in April of 1982. In this case, where charges of kidnapping, false imprisonment, and rape of Stephanie Riethmiller were brought against Ted Patrick and his associates, the foreman of the jury declared that rape and kidnapping were not really the primary issues, "mind control was."[20]

Of all the social and institutional threats against ISKCON and other alternative religions in America, none are so effective in short-circuiting their cultural accommodation as the uncritical and pervasive fear of the cults that has steadily increased since the Jonestown massacre. When one thinks about the future of ISKCON in America, one assumes that some level of accommodation with the dominant cultural norms, values, and institutions (that is, perceived "cultural continuity" in Stark's categories) will have to come about eventually. It is clear ISKCON has moved in the direction of such accommodations (for example, respecting parent/child relationships and communication or abiding by U.S. laws when conducting its fund-raising activities) in recent years. It is also obvious that much of the American public views ISKCON as a cult to be feared and eliminated. But to put this external threat in perspective, nineteenth-century groups like the Mormons have achieved accommodation with and acceptance by an American culture that was extremely hostile to their beginnings. Time is on the side of ISKCON if it maintains or increases its institutional stability in the economic and recruitment spheres.

A second external factor that will affect ISKCON in America over the next few decades is its strong Indian support base. This positive support cannot be

---

[20]*Cleveland Plain Dealer*, 26 April 1982.

underestimated since it involves Indian communities in America and in India. Indian "Life Member" programs now provide economic support for various ISKCON programs and activities, as well as pave the way for acceptance of ISKCON in political and other arenas. In return, ISKCON has provided a home away from home for many Indians who are married in ISKCON temples, send their children there for religious education, or just enjoy the fellowship of the Sunday Feasts. ISKCON obviously will continue to benefit from this support by local Indian communities.

Many commentators on ISKCON have also underestimated the supportive and codifying effect on ISKCON and its ideology that its Indian heritage provides. By 1970 Prabhupada had "Indianized" ISKCON in America by requiring standard Indian dress, names, and other such religious customs; by instituting a regularized ritual calendar and standardized performance of major rituals based on traditional Bengali ritual manuals; and by returning to India to confirm ISKCON's roots in physical locations important to Vaisnava religious history (for example, Mayapur and Vrindavan). All of these actions by the founding guru cemented the American movement to its Indian predecessors and gave it an authenticity and legitimacy that have been recognized by scholars of Hinduism throughout the world and the Vaisnava religious community in India as well.

The day-to-day effect of this bonding of the American movement with its Indian roots is to locate the sacred center of ISKCON in venerable Indian texts, biographies, and holy sites. The Indian focus of ISKCON gives its devotees a broader perspective of their religious life and ideology than its American forms and history alone could do. Hence, the effects of both external opposition and internal difficulties are mitigated by an awareness of this larger historical and cultural context. The recent success of ISKCON centers in Europe (especially in Italy where a "favorable ecology" exists) is additional confirmation of the larger context into which American Krishna devotees put their successes and failures. When I have pointed out to American leaders that ISKCON is barely holding its own in replacing defectors with new recruits in America, I have been informed immediately of the successes of the European or Indian centers and their programs. This is a positive external factor for the self-image of American Krishnas that is hard to exaggerate. Ironically, however, it is also this very same "foreign" nature of ISKCON's ideology and life-style that poses a barrier to widespread recruitment and acceptance in America.

As the GBC has asserted its centralizing authority, it is more difficult to discuss the fate of the American centers separate from that of the International movement as a whole. Yet one must recognize the confederation structure of ISKCON that has divided centers into separate corporate groups. Some ISKCON corporations can succeed economically as others fail. And as the recent Robin George case against the Los Angeles temple and other ISKCON corporations shows, other ISKCON centers will not necessarily rush to one center's economic defense. This feature of ISKCON's legal and corporate structure actually may be its hedge against increasingly unfavorable legal judgments. Only time will tell.

ISKCON'S DIVERSE FUTURE

ISKCON's future is its own to determine. The transmission of authority (both spiritual and institutional) has been surprisingly smooth, given the built-in ideological conflicts about the priority of the essentially hierarchical and individualistic guru/disciple relationship over against the democratic and collective GBC structure. While tensions will arise from time to time as individual leaders' ambitions and programs are thwarted by collective decision making, there appears to be a developing sense of the need for a central governance structure and institution-wide cooperation. Furthermore, as more and more gurus are appointed by the GBC, there should be even more loyalty among gurus shown to this body as the ultimate authority in ISKCON. Also, it is apparent that the current gurus are maturing in both the spiritual and institutional levels of their roles. In short, charisma has been transferred, not ended.

In the end, I believe that finding an institution-wide funding base that is viable and durable and developing a recruiting strategy that is freed from its previous ideological constraints are the most significant challenges that ISKCON must meet in the near future. While the strength of the missionary zeal that marked the early movement has now given way to a more sober mindset in maturing Krishna communities, ISKCON in America will continue to be a diverse Hindu missionary institution that is grounded in its Indian homeland. One should not underestimate the durability of such a dedicated minority religious community (compare the Christians in India). The question that only time will answer is whether ISKCON will remain simply an alternative religious path for ''social isolates'' in America or will be able to fulfill its stated goal of engendering Krishna devotion ''in every town and village.''

• CHAPTER TEN •

Quo Vadis?
The Unification Church

EILEEN BARKER

Of course, the only thing we know for certain about the future is that we do not, cannot, know what it will hold for us. Mankind may not survive to see the twenty-first century. If it does, economic crisis, conventional warfare, natural disasters, the successors of the silicon chip, or even a new messiah could so change balances of power, economic structures, everyday experiences, expectations and perceptions of reality, that almost anything about which we might today wish to speculate concerning religious beliefs and practices in twenty years' time would be, in the light (or darkness) of our present knowledge, utterly irrelevant.

That said, however, there are several generalizations that can be and have been made about the way in which new religions change over time. Insofar as the movements are successful, there is the commonly described trajectory of the sect moving (perhaps by way of, or after, a period as a cult) to become a denomination. The routinization of charisma, the institutionalization of enthusiasm, the creation of schismatic splinter groups, and, indeed, the collapse and disappearance of a millennial hope or the religion itself are all well-documented phenomena.

New religions do not remain as new religions; one way or another—often traveling along well-trodden paths that comprise a motley assortment of progressions, regressions and transgressions—they react, interact, adapt, accommodate, withdraw, grow, shrink, or whatever. In other words, they change.

In this paper, although I shall be drawing on some knowledge of what has happened to other movements, I shall not be attempting to produce generalizations about trends. I shall, rather, confine myself to enumerating some problems, that while not specific to the Unification Church, are evident in the changes it will have to face within the next two decades. I shall, furthermore, confine myself to changes that are inherent in the very nature of the beliefs of the movement, its present state of organization, and the current composition of its membership. This is in no way to deny the possibility (even the probability) that forces external to the movement will have an even greater effect on its future, but merely to concentrate on the tensions likely to arise out of the passage of time insofar as this will, inevitably, result in (a) demographic shifts in the composition of the membership, (b) changes in the leadership and, consequently, the structure of the movement, and (c) some reinterpretation of, and adjustment to, the messianic and millennial hopes of the theology.

But first, in order to understand some of the challenges the movement will face during the next decade or so, it is necessary to understand something of the Unification theology as it is presented in the *Divine Principle* (Moon, 1973)—a book that (and Stark's model suggests that this could be of some significance) contains a special interpretation of the Old and New Testaments as well as further revelations that, it is claimed, have been received by Moon.

According to Unification theology, Adam and Eve were meant to grow to a stage of perfection. They would then be blessed by God in Holy Matrimony and establish what is referred to as the Four Position Foundation of the Ideal Family in which they would have a loving ''give-and-take'' relationship with God, with each other, and, as True Parents, with their children. Unfortunately, however, this did not come about because the archangel Lucifer, to whom God had entrusted the task of helping Adam and Eve progress through the necessary stages of growth, became jealous of God's love for Adam and had a (spiritual) sexual relationship with Eve. Eve then persuaded Adam to have a (physical) sexual relationship with her, and thus it was that the Fall occurred through the misuse of the most powerful of all forces: love. Instead of being a God-centered marriage, Adam and Eve's relationship was both premature and selfish (Lucifer-centered), and their children and their children's children were born with original sin.

The whole of history has, according to the *Divine Principle,* been an attempt by God and certain key persons to restore the world to the state originally planned by God. To do this, the wrongs that have been done in the past need to be, as it were, ''worked backwards'' in order that bad acts are canceled out by good acts. These acts of ''indemnity'' are carried out as a preparation for the only ultimate solution to man's sin: the advent of a Messiah who will fulfill the role that Adam should have filled by not only living a perfect, sinless life, but also by establishing the True (God-centered) Family that Adam failed to establish. Jesus came in the role of the Messiah, and he lived a perfect, sinless life. He had hoped to bring the Kingdom of Heaven on earth at both a spiritual and a physical level, but because his people rejected him he was killed before he could establish the True Family. The *Divine Principle* teaches that Jesus' death was not planned by God, but that through the sacrifice of his crucifixion Jesus was able to offer spiritual salvation to mankind.

A careful reading of history since the time of Jesus, according to the *Divine Principle*, indicates that the Lord of the second coming would have been born in Korea between 1917 and 1930. While the *Divine Principle* itself ends with this conclusion, the members undoubtedly believe that Moon is the perfect man who is performing the role of the Messiah. They also believe that, as a result of his marriage to his present wife in 1960, Moon has succeeded in establishing the Ideal Four Position (God-centered) True Family. It is, moreover, believed that couples who are married by Moon have, through the Holy Wine ceremony that precedes the Blessing ritual, been purified and cleansed of original sin and that, as a consequence, their children are born without original sin.

The Reverend Moon was born in 1920. His threescore years and ten expire in 1990, and one of the central issues that will affect the future of the Unification Church is the question of what will happen when its founder dies. At present, it is Moon who is at the apex of the organization. His is the ultimate word on all questions, religious and secular. Although many decisions are taken at lower levels, Moon is the final arbiter on what the membership is or is not expected to believe and on what the movement does or does not do. The closer a member is to Moon, the more authority he can claim over other members. It is Moon who holds the movement together and forms the focal point not only for members but for outsiders as well.

There has been considerable speculation as to who will take over Moon's position on his death. In one sense, of course, no one will. His is a unique position in Unification theology. Even if a Lord of the Third Advent were necessary, such a person would not be expected to make his appearance for hundreds, if not thousands, of years (there would, presumably, be some parallels in the time-scale between Jesus and Moon as between Adam and Jesus); but were Moon's mission seen to fail as Jesus' did, it is not clear from the *Divine Principle* exactly what would happen next. In fact this is not really seen as a problem for the membership as it is now claimed that Moon has already fulfilled *his* role, and, indeed, 23 February 1977 has been declared as Day One, Year One of the Kingdom of Heaven. Nonetheless, without a clearly recognizable achievement in material or physical terms (Jesus was, after all, able to offer spiritual salvation to the world), it is difficult to see how the millennial hope could continue, in anything like its present form, after Moon's death.

This is not to say that the movement has not already succeeded in some remarkable achievements. On the purely material side, it has, for example, amassed a great deal of property and owns a large number of businesses. But perhaps the most impressive effects the Unification Church has had upon the societies in which it operates are the result of Moon's amazing talent for communicating his existence and some of his ideas to literally millions of people at many different levels. The very fact that most people in the West know about Moonies is in itself quite an achievement, even if *what* the general public "knows" from what they see in the media is not exactly what Moon might wish them to know. But the movement has also had a more direct contact with thousands of people of potential influence in the worlds of religion, journalism, business, academia, and politics through organizations such as The Global Congress of the World's Religions, The Professors' World Peace Academy, the International Conference on the Unity of the Sciences, the World Media Conferences, the Collegiate Association for the Research of Principles (CARP), CAUSA, and Victory Over Communism. It also owns a number of daily newspapers and other publications throughout the world, sponsors a variety of entertainments (such as the Little Angels, the Korean Folk Ballet, and the Go World Brass Band), and has held numerous rallies at which Moon has addressed audiences in the tens of thousands.

All this, and more, the members point to with understandable pride, but such achievements, impressive as they are, would still seem to leave the world a long way to go before it is restored to a Garden of Eden. It is not yet clear just how the Third World War, which the members believe is being waged against communism, is to be won. If Moon were able to die before complete victory over communism (and the ungodly aspects of the free world) is achieved, there could be considerable confusion about exactly how the mission is to be accomplished. Futhermore, the enthusiasm of the members might be expected to lose some of its impetus once there was no longer the excitement and urgency of the Messiah's actually being a physical presence in this world. The millennial expectation will doubtless continue, but it is likely to take a different form and result in different kinds of actions. I shall return to this subject at a later point.

Sociologists tend to eschew "Big Man" explanations of social phenomena. But when, as is the case of the Unification Church, there already exists an authoritarian structure of communication and command (especially one in which there have been, from an external point of view at least, comparatively arbitrary—or at least idiosyncratic—decisions emanating from the top), the personality of the new leader will be of more importance than in a structure that is more democratic or in which the office of leader has already been routinized.

There have been suggestions that Mrs. Moon (who was only 17 when she married the 40-year-old Moon in 1960) might take her place at the head of the movement on Moon's death. Another speculation is that the eldest son will inherit; a further possibility is that it will be Moon's eldest child—his daughter Ye Jin—who was the first "True Child" to be blessed in marriage and who, in so doing, heralded the start of "the Children's Course." Others have said that Moon's children will have to decide among themselves which of them will carry the burden of the future on his (or her) shoulders. Another possibility is that the actual power will go to the early Korean disciples who were among those first married by Moon. Some people think that there will be a distinction between a "monarchy," which is hereditary and passes through the Moon lineage, and a "parliament" consisting of a "Prime Minister" and others who will be responsible for the actual running of the movement.

Which, if any, of these possibilities is taken up will be a crucial factor in determining the future direction of the movement. If the power is divided between spiritual and mundane authority, there is, *ceteris paribus,* greater opportunity for conflict and schism within the movement. As the balance of power shifts, the altered shape of the structure can have various diverse consequences for the movement as a whole. I have, futhermore, been told by one of the early disciples that the question of succession is not all that crucial as Father (Moon) will continue to lead the movement from the spirit world after his death. To the nonmember, however, such a possibility is likely to suggest not so much that there will continue to be a single voice in authority, but that this could lead to a situation in which rival interpretations of Moon's instructions as revealed to different persons could, in turn, result in further schisms.

Let us, however, turn our attention away from contemplating changes in direction that could result from a changing leadership, to changes that are all but certain to emerge as a result of a changing composition of the membership as a whole. Although a fairly high turnover rate has meant that the average age of members of the Unification Church does not increase by a full year for every calendar year that passes, Moonies do get older, and the movement now has a sizable proportion of members who are in their early thirties. These people will have reached their fifties by the year 2000, and, if they are still members, this will mean that the age composition of the movement will be considerably altered by that date.

Already some of the problems to be faced merely because of aging have become apparent. At an obvious, but nonetheless important, level it can be recognized that the tenor of the movement in the West has been one of youthful enthusiasm and a devoted, sacrificial way of life. Young people can endure, even enjoy, spending a few hours in a sleeping bag on the floor, getting up at the crack of dawn for a long day that involves considerable physical activity; they can be happy living out of a suitcase (or knapsack) with the minimum of personal possessions and no settled home. But this kind of life has far less attraction for middle-aged, let alone elderly, people. I have talked to several of the older members who complained that the youthful leaders have not understood about their arthritis or how they need to get a good night's sleep. Although there is more awareness of the problems, and an attempt is usually made to give older members less exhausting work, several have left because they felt they could not stand the pace. As the Moonie population ages, more arrangements will have to be made to allow for the limitations— and potentialities—of a more mature membership. Another related demographic change that will have its effect on the movement is the number of dependents with which it will have to cope. Not only will there be more elderly people; there are, and will continue to be, an increasing number of children who will need to be looked after—and socialized.

Moonies joining in their early twenties have not only been physically fit; they have also tended to join at an age when they are particularly idealistic and when they have little in the way of responsibilities towards others. They are prepared to sacrifice themselves for the ideal of improving the world for others. But this idealistic sense of responsibility for the world can develop into a practical sense of responsibility for dependents once these exist. To sacrifice merely for an ideal may be a primary duty when one does not have other responsibilities, but to sacrifice one's children or one's marriage (and one of the attractions the Unification Church offers is the establishment of the Ideal Family unit) is something different—something that is counter to the initial appeal. Several members (including many who continue to believe in the basic Unification theology) have left the movement (often with the partner with whom Moon had blessed them) when they have been expected to split up, or when they have become anxious about financial security for their children's future.

Futhurmore, Moonies tend to be "doers," active *achievers* who want to see the results of their labor, to see themselves as contributing and being of value in society (Barker, 1984). The Unification Church does in fact offer young members a means of achieving *visible, calculable goals,* (fundraising, recruiting new members), but during three or more years on an MFT (Mobile Fundraising Team) the day-to-day achievement is *not cumulative.* Although the young Moonie may deny any interest in a conventional career in the rat-race of modern society, he is, nonetheless, likely to be the sort of person who (unlike, say, Premies—members of the Divine Light Mission) works to "get somewhere." Within the Unification Church there are, in fact, some exceptional challenges for the members to face and overcome. Young Moonies are given remarkable responsibilities, and many of them do succeed in a Unification career, achieving things they could never have hoped to do in the "outside" society. But the tight pyramidal structure blocks continued promotion even more forcefully than it does in the larger, more amorphous society, and the absence of bureaucratic rules for promotion or following a career pattern means that those who had managed to achieve a certain position can suddenly lose it without apparent rhyme or reason (perhaps he will be told he is not sufficiently ''spiritual''). There comes a time when curtailed opportunity, in an authority structure for which years of service and perhaps Korean nationality are necessary but not sufficient for success, begins to frustrate the ambitious Western Moonie. There is no obvious way ahead; there is no structure that can accommodate his talents—many of which he may, paradoxically, have developed during his early days in the movement.

There has, in recent years, been a development of Unification-based or affiliated businesses in the West (something that has been established in Korea and Japan for some time), and it is likely that members pursuing careers in these businesses will be less subject to (apparently) arbitrary changes than has been the case in the past, but so long as they are full-time ''core'' members of the Unification Church, they will be unlikely to enjoy any security of tenure in any particular ''mission.'' There is, however, always the option of their becoming ''Home Church'' members who, while still associated with the movement, retain responsibility for where they live and what occupations they pursue. This opting out of the Unification organization while continuing to accept the goals and belief system of the movement is, indeed, what an increasing number of members are doing. Such shifts in the kind and degree of membership, should they substantially increase, would contribute to the movement's exhibiting more denominational (as opposed to sectarian) characteristics over the next decade or so.

On the other side of the coin, while the movement gives no security of tenure in a particular mission, only rarely does it actually get rid of members altogether, and often members are frustrated at having to work with people who are ill-suited for the job. This, of course, is not peculiar to the Unification Church, but to work with incompetent leaders—or subordinates—can be a cause of particular frustration if one knows that one has practically no control over the situation. For a child of the modern age, brought up in an achievement-oriented society, ascription and diffuse relationships can have their attractions, but they can also be a cause of extreme irritation. One ex-member told me among the things he particularly appreciated now that he was working in an ''outside'' organization were (1) he knew he would not have someone incompetent put in a position of authority over him just because he was an American and the other person a Korean, (2) he could now sack subordinates who were not suitable for the job, and (3) he was free to do whatever he wanted (with his family) after 5:30 P.M. each day and throughout his weekends.

Once again, one can already observe changes that indicate an increasing accommodation to such practical contingencies in order to achieve business success. For example, the Unification-sponsored newspaper, the *Washington Times,* is run by a non-Unification editor who has been quite ruthless in not allowing Moonies into jobs for which nonmembers were more suited. One has to go down to the fifth level of management before one can find a Moonie working in the editorial departments of that organization; and the *Washington Times* appears to be considerably more successful than the *New York Tribune* (successor of *Newsworld*) which, although it employs outsiders, has always used far more Moonies in positions of authority. It is, indeed, claimed that the *Washington Times* is one of the four newspapers most favored by the President of the United States.

My point is that, (1) in order to meet the growing demands of a maturing membership that comes mainly from an achieving, middle-class background, and (2) in order to achieve economic and political success in a competitive world (the Unification Church's stated aim is, let us remember, to bring about the physical restoration of the Kingdom of Heaven), there are already signs that the movement is having to shift from feudal family values in which loyalty, ascription, and diffuse relationships are of primary importance, to more of an emphasis on individual achievement and a competitive outlook. Of course, this *need* not occur. There are plenty of examples of how a feudal, family orientation in an organization can function remarkably well, especially in Japan. But the Unification Church in the West is *in* the West; its membership has been brought up with Western values, and it has to operate within Western society.

This leads us to a further potential dynamic within the movement. Although Unificationism affirms that all the races will be united and work together in harmony (the mixed marriages are seen as an important step toward this unity), certain nations are definitely seen as more important than others, South Korea being the most important. Korea is in the "Adam position" to Japan's "Eve's position" (and Britain is meant to unite from the Eve position with Germany in the Adam position). These "positions" are meant to be reflected in individual relationships. Although there are many Western Moonies who will testify how wonderful it is to work with Korean and (to a lesser extent) Japanese members, and how much can be learned from their nature, there are also many signs of resentment or downright dislike, not just of individuals but of the preferences given to Eastern members and of some of the values that the Westerners find difficulty in adopting. The complaint I have heard most often is that for the Orientals honor and loyalty have a higher priority than truth or "common sense" (Western style, presumably). In other words, there are as many signs of cultural differences producing disunity within the movement as there are of their producing unification, and this could well contribute to both defections and schisms during the next few decades, especially after Moon's death.

Let us finally return to some of the ways in which the passage of time is likely to affect the millennial message of Unification theology and, consequently, the future of the movement. Already one can see the development of complicated numerological reckonings on stages of the restoration of the Kingdom of Heaven. The sense of urgency is still present, but there is far less expectation that a miraculous change will occur within the very near future than there was when I first met the movement in 1974—and the expectations for 1967 held by the group that Lofland (1977) studied in the early 1960s have no parallels by the mid-1980s. Although it is at present believed that something important has got to happen between 1985 and 1988, the year 2000 also crops up fairly frequently. Indeed, some Moonies are resigned to the possibility that they cannot hope to see the Kingdom on Earth fully established during their own lifetime (despite the fact that Day One has been announced), and there is already talk of "perhaps our children's children will be the first generation."

In fact, it is possible that the children will present one of the greatest challenges to the movement during the next twenty years. There will, of course, be the usual difficulties, to which Stark refers, of socializing a second generation into a new movement. Unificationists are, however, facing an additional challenge to their theology and, indeed, their *raison d' être,* as they watch their offspring pass through the stages of growth that should lead to their perfection. It will be remembered that, according to the *Divine Principle,* the Fall was the result of Adam and Eve's sexual relationship before they had reached a stage of sufficient maturity to be blessed in marriage by God, and Moonies believe that children born to the couples blessed by Moon are free of the original sin that has tainted mankind ever since the Fall. There is, however, no reason why these children, like Adam and Eve who were also free of original sin, could not themselves fall before reaching the stage of perfection. This possibility has been accepted by some Moonies, who argue that even if the occasional blessed child does fall, it will be less difficult to correct because they will not be the *only* parents (as Adam and Eve were when the original Fall occurred), there will be plenty of others who will not fall, and there can be a better environment to help pull them up.

There is, however, a Catch-22 situation that twentieth-century Moonies are having to face. They are meant to be creating Ideal, God-centered Families who provide the perfect example for how to have a loving, horizontal relationship between a couple, and a loving, vertical relationship between a couple and God and a couple and their children (the Four Position Foundation). Such a family is meant to be the basic unit of the Kingdom of Heaven on earth. But so long as the Moonies have to operate in the Fallen world, they are in difficulties. It is not enough for them to withdraw from the rest of society and build their own private Kingdom: their task is to change *all* of society. To do *that* it appears necessary for many not only to split away from their own family of origin, but also to separate from their spouses and even to leave their children to be brought up by others while the mothers go fundraising or witnessing, sometimes hundreds (or even thousands) of miles away. Moon himself, who is meant to provide the perfect example of a family man, has divorced at least one wife and, we are told, has not been able to see as much of his present wife or his children as the Ideal Father would do, were conditions perfect (Barker 1983). In other words, the pursuit of the goal of the Ideal Family seems to require methods that militate against actually enjoying such an institution in practice.

How threatening these sorts of difficulties will be to the theology over the coming years remains to be seen, but there is, I think, a high probability that the beliefs will be watered down or at least not accepted with the sort of literal fervor that has given the movement much of its impetus in the past. In other words, accommodation to a Fallen environment could become more necessary over time on theological as well as on purely practical grounds. This is especially likely since Unification theology has gained some (although by no means all) of its credibility because Moonies believe that they actually see that it "works." In other words, many members have been persuaded to join and stay in the movement because they believe they they can see the *Divine Principle* in operation—that, for instance, Ideal Family units are being created, children are being born without original sin, and a God-centered Kingdom of Heaven has been, or is being, established on earth through the leadership and example of the Messiah and the dedication and sacrifice of the members.

But this kind of confirmatory support can be a two-edged sword. There is a growing number of ex-members who have left the movement because they no longer believe that the *Principle* was working or because they did not agree that the right means were being used to achieve God's goal. Furthermore, the fact that there have been so many defectors brings into question the belief that if only people could be persuaded to hear the *Divine Principle,* they would be eager to follow Moon and play their part in the work of restoration.

There are, of course, always "escape clauses" for those who find themselves facing what might to others seem disconfirmatory evidence (Festinger et al., 1956). One can hear Moonies explain that apparent difficulties are due to the success the movement is having because Satan is getting worried; or that setbacks occur not because the *Principle* is wrong, but rather, members (and/or nonmembers) are not doing their part; or that important changes *are* occurring, but these are mainly at a spiritual level and have not yet been fully translated into physical restoration. At the same time, there is an increasing number of those whose concept of restoration has already undergone drastic changes with the passing of the years. They say that they no longer believe the Kingdom is attainable in the way they had originally imagined but still feel that the movement can offer a *better* way of life, *higher* standards, and *more* hope any other alternative. One member who had been in the movement for more than ten years told me: ''When I first joined I thought that if I stuck around long enough I would be there among the chosen when God waved his magic wand. Now I realize that if anyone is going to build the Kingdom of Heaven on earth, it's got to be people like me.'' ''Magic-wanders'' will, of course, continue to exist—and to enjoy ''proofs'' and to suffer disillusionment—but all the evidence points in the direction of an increasing proportion of members adopting what can, depending on one's perspective, be seen as either a diluted or a more realistic interpretation of the *Divine Principle*. Such shifts in emphasis are, moreover, likely to affect recruitment—not necessarily so that it is greater or less than before, but in that, as the Unification message changes, it will appeal to a different type of person and/or lose its appeal to the sort of person who would have previously been attracted.

In this paper I have not attempted to predict what the Unification Church will look like in the year 2000. As I said in my opening paragraph, we cannot know what the future will bring. Since this paper was first drafted, there have been two important occurrences that will undoubtedly affect the furture of the movement. First, Moon has lost an appeal to be heard by the Supreme Court and has served a prison sentence for tax evasion. Second, one of his children, Heung Jin Nim, died as the result of an automobile accident. This tragic loss has been interpreted as a sacrifice of immense significance and importance for the movement and, indeed, for both the spirit and physical worlds (*Today's World*, April 1984); and messages received from Heung Jin Nim (who has, since his death, been married to the [still living] daughter of one of Moon's closest disciples) are already affecting the lives of several of the members.

What I have attemped is to sketch some of the theological and demographic challenges inherent in the dynamic relationships between the present state of the movement and the inevitable passage of time. The death of the leader and the consequent changes due to the succession, the aging of the present membership and the presence of second-generation members, and the testing of the millennial promise are all factors that will alter the internal power structures, the cohesiveness of the group, the success it has in achieving its goals and its relationship with the rest of society (including its ability to attract new first-generation members). Some of these changes can be seen as pressures towards an increasing accommodation to Western values through a ''denominationalizing'' process with a greater emphasis on Home Church or associate members supporting a small core of a fully committed ''priesthood.'' But at the same time, the same factors could result in both fundamentalist and liberal factions developing under different leaders. Whether such schisms would result in disruption, renewal, or both—or neither—only time can tell. But, despite the still small membership in terms of absolute numbers (I suggest that there are well under ten thousand full-time members in the whole of the West), I would be extremely surprised if the Unification Church did not continue in some form into the twenty-first century. In Unification language, the movement has, during the last thirty years, laid a foundation and fulfilled conditions for ''something''—even if it is not restoring the Kingdom of Heaven on earth.

REFERENCES

Barker, Eileen
   1983   ''Doing Love: Tensions in the Ideal Family.''In *The Family and the Unification Church,* edited by Gene G. James. Barrytown NY: Unification Theological Seminary.

   1984   *The Making of a Moonie: Choice or Brainwashing?* Oxford: Blackwell.
Festinger, Leon, Henry Riecken, and Stanley Schachter
   1956   *When Prophecy Fails: A Social and Psychological Study of a Modern Group That Predicted the Destruction of the World.* Minneapolis: University of Minnesota Press.

Lofland, John
   1977   *Doomsday Cult: A Study of Conversion, Proselytization, and Maintenance of Faith* (enlarged edition). Irvington Publishers, New York (original edition, 1966).

Moon, Sun Myung
   1973   *Divine Principle.* Washington DC: Holy Spirit Association for the Unification of World Christianity.

· CHAPTER ELEVEN ·

Organization, Ideology, and Mobilization: The Case of Nichiren Shoshu of America

David A. Snow

In his theory of how new religions succeed, Stark proposes that success is partly contingent on how effectively a religious movement mobilizes individuals to act on behalf of its collective interests. Few, if any, students of social movements would take exception to this proposition. Indeed, it constitutes one of the central assumptions of the currently fashionable and influential resource mobilization approach to social movements (Gamson, 1975; Jenkins, 1983; McCarthy and Zald, 1977; Oberschall, 1973; Tilly, 1978). The focal question, from this perspective, is not whether effective mobilization is a requisite for movement success but concerns, instead, the factors and conditions that account for effective mobilization.

Insofar as the target of mobilization is a movement organization's constituency or membership, which appears to be Stark's concern, mobilization entails the process of increasing their readiness to act collectively. The analytic task thus becomes one of specifying the factors that produce and sustain "a change from a low generalized readiness to act to a high generalized readiness to act collectively" (Gamson, 1975:15). The creation of such commitment is generally explained in terms of organizational and ideological factors that produce instrumental, solidary, and purposive or moral incentives to act (Etzioni, 1961; Kanter, 1972; Wilson, 1973). Stark alludes to both organization and ideology but is rather vague about the dimensions of each that facilitate mobilization. The primary objective of this study is to extend Stark's observations by examining how components of the organizational structure and ideology of Nichiren Shoshu of America produce and maintain among a sizable portion of its membership a high generalized readiness to act. Since the analysis is informed by literature pertaining to the broader study of social movements, a secondary aim is to further our general understanding of how movement organizational structure and ideology affect constituent mobilization.

Before pursuing these objectives, it is necessary to provide an overview of Nichiren Shoshu's historical development, goals, and basic rituals, especially since the movement has gained neither the visibility nor notoriety of some of the other ''new'' religious movements. Additionally, the overview will provide a context and some of the material for the subsequent analysis.

The materials on which the overview and analysis are based were derived largely from my observations and experiences as a participant-observer in the movement for a year and a half and from an examination of 240 randomly selected editions of the movement's newspaper, the *World Tribune,* covering a ten-year period from 1966 through 1975. The information obtained from the newspaper provided a more thoroughgoing understanding of the movement's historical development and operation, allowed for more systematic examination of certain questions and propositions, and functioned as a validity check for my own observations and experiences. The ethnographic phase of the research began in February 1974, when I assumed the role of a naive, curious, and moderately willing but skeptical rank-and-file member, and extended into the summer months of 1975. During this period seldom did a day or evening pass when I was not in contact with a movement member or engaged in some movement activity. My involvement was thus participatory, consistent, and intense. Since that time the movement has been observed through periodic visits to Los Angeles, published materials, media coverage, and information provided by a network of current and former members

OVERVIEW OF NSA'S HISTORICAL DEVELOPMENT, GOALS, AND RITUALS

Nichiren Shoshu of America—which is also known as Nichiren Shoshu Academy or by the acronym NSA—is a noncommunal, proselytizing Buddhist movement that seeks to change the world by changing individuals in accordance with its own version of Buddhism, regarded by core members as ''orthodox'' or ''true Buddhism.''

The origins of NSA's basic rituals and much of its doctrine date back to thirteenth-century Japan and the person of Nichiren Daishonin, who, in the pre-dawn hours of 28 April 1253, uttered a chant that allegedly had never been heard before. It was *Nam-Myoho-Renge-Kyo,* what he considered to be the essence of the Buddha's teachings. Fueled with the belief that he had found the key to happiness and enlightenment, Nichiren embarked on a mission to save the world.

Despite a prophetic zeal and fanaticism unique among Japanese religious figures (he suggested Japan would collapse if it did not repent and convert), neither Nichiren nor his revelations commanded a sizable following during his lifetime (Anesaki, 1916). Today, however, some 700 years later and in corners of the world even the peripatetic and reportedly omniscient Nichiren could not have envisioned, *Nam-Myoho-Renge-Kyo* is being chanted and promoted with the same determination that characterized Nichiren.

The modern-day resurrection of Nichiren's revelations began shortly after World War II, when there occurred in Japan a phenomenal flowering of a diversity of religious cults and sects. The defeat of the Imperial regime, the resultant discrediting of state Shintoism, and the guarantee of religious freedom as one of the constitutional principles of postwar reconstruction had combined to create, in the language of Stark's scheme, a "favorable ecology" characterized by an unregulated religious economy. Thus, "the way was open for innumerable captive and incipient religious movements to become independent sects and for new 'prophets' to let their voices be heard" (McFarland, 1967:4). It was during this period of religious proliferation, aptly characterized as "the rush hour of the Gods" (McFarland, 1967), that Nichiren's revelations and teachings were given new life in the form of an active proselytizing movement known as the Sokagakkai (Dator, 1969; Murata, 1968; White, 1970).

With a militaristically organized and highly spirited corps of youthful devotees spearheading its propagation efforts, the Sokagakkai began to gain ascendancy over its competitors. By 1970 it had become a significant religious and political force in Japan, with an estimated membership of more than ten million and its own political party (The Komeito or Clean Government Party). It also claimed an international following of roughly one million, with the largest and most active branch in the United States.

The movement was formally introduced in this country in 1960, when its leader and president, Daisaku Ideda, commissioned one of his devoted followers (now known as George M. Williams) to begin propagating the faith abroad.[1] At that time it claimed no more than 500 adherents, nearly all of whom were Japanese brides of American servicemen . By the mid-1970s the movement claimed more than 200,000 variously committed followers, most

---

[1]Williams immigrated to the U.S. from Japan as Masayasu Sadanaga (his birth name) in 1959. In 1972, a year prior to his becoming an American citizen, he had his name changed from M. Sadanaga to George M. Williams, apparently to strengthen the American identity of both himself and NSA. He received his first name, George, from Ikeda. Wanting a common American name, he selected Williams as his surname because it was one of the most frequently listed names in the Los Angeles phone directory.

of whom were Occidental and had joined since 1966, the year the movement began to make a concerted effort to broaden its constituency and become something more than a Sokagakkai outpost and spiritual aid station for Japanese females and their families.[2]

In contrast to other culturally imported movements born in the East, such as ISKCON and Zen, NSA appears to be remarkably materialistic and worldly. Rather than promising transcendence of the material world, it promises the attainment of personal regeneration and happiness in the immediate present through the realization of an endless stream of material, physical, and spiritual "benefits." Yet, as Nichiren is said to have preached, no person's happiness is complete until the happiness of all humankind is assured. Accordingly, NSA insists that its ultimate objective is to create a peaceful and happy world by changing individuals. The "one way" or path to the realization of these objectives is believed to reside in the practice of chanting *Nam-Myoho-Renge-Kyo* to the *Gohonzon* (a small sacred scroll inscribed in Japanese and regarded as the most powerful object in the world) and in the practice of *Shakubuku,* the act of bringing others into contact with the *Gohonzon* and the key to unlocking its power: *Nam-Myoho-Renge-Kyo.*[3]

NSA'S ORGANIZATIONAL STRUCTURE AND MOBILIZATION

Students of social movements are not of one mind regarding the relationship between organizational structure and movement mobilization and success. At one extreme is the resource mobilization contention that centralized, bureaucratic structures tend to maximize mobilization and the likelihood of success (Gamson, 1975; McCarthy and Zald, 1977). At the other extreme is the grass-roots argument that formal organization is incompatible with constituent mobilization because it stifles enthusiasm and rechannels energy from

---

[2]Consistent with this shift in course and character was the 1966 decision to change the movement's name from Sokagakkai of America to Nichiren Shoshu of America. Although an official reason was not given for this action, my reading of events at the time suggests that it was prompted by two interrelated considerations: to provide the American movement with an identity separate from the Sokagakkai in Japan, which had suffered a barrage of public criticism for several years (Brannen, 1968; Fujiwara, 1970); and to strengthen the movement's American identity by giving it a name with more of an American ring to it, which is clearly the case with NSA in comparision to Sokagakkai. For further discussion of this name change and the movement's broadening of its appeal and constituency, see Snow (1976: 124-37).

[3]*Nam-Myoho-Renge-Kyo* is variously translated as "Adoration to the scripture of the Lotus of the perfect truth," "I devote myself to the inexpressibly profound and wonderful truth embodied in the *Lotus Sutra*," or, as NSA members prefer, "Devotion to the mystical, universal law of cause and effect through sound."

collective action to organization building (Piven and Cloward, 1977). In between these two extremes is Gerlach and Hine's (1970) contention that informal structures are more conducive to effective mobilization. Based on their field studies of the Pentecostal and Black Power movements, Gerlach and Hine propose that a movement is more likely to be successful when its leadership and decision making are decentralized and when its component parts are loosely coupled in a segmented fashion but still linked together in a reticulate or netlike manner. These contrasting propositions are not necessarily inconsistent, however. Nor are formal and informal structures mutually exclusive (Jenkins, 1983; Zurcher and Snow, 1981). To the contrary, mixed or intermediary forms of social movement organizations are probably more common. NSA provides an interesting case in point.

Organizationally NSA is composed of numerous loosely coupled units and cells linked together vertically by a charismatically infused leadership hierachy and horizontally by crosscutting associations incorporating members of the various units and cells. The movement's organizational structure can thus be described as centralized, segmented, and reticulated. Several features of this mixed structure combine to mobilize members to act on behalf of the movement.

Generating Solidary Incentives

The segmented yet reticulated structure of the movement enmeshes members in a set of overlapping and interlocking relationships that produce strong, reciprocal, interpersonal bonds that function to generate fairly powerful solidary incentives to act collectively. When individuals join or are recruited into NSA, much of their initial association with the movement is with and through the members who recruited them and several other members who are linked together by successive instances of recruitment or *Shakubuku*. This handful of members comprises what is referred to as a Junior Group, which is linked vertically to a larger cell known as the Group or *Han*. Two or more Groups constitute a District, which usually has 50 to 100 members and functions as the movement's basic campaign unit. As indicated in Figure 1, which sketches the cellular and segmented nature of NSA's "vertical line," there are a number of organizational components above the District. But it is primarily at the district level that mobilization for recruitment and promotion occurs. And what makes the District particularly effective as a mobilizing unit (it also functions as the basic conversion and socialization unit) is that it constitutes a kind of extended family involving numerous primary relationships, particularly among Junior Group and Group members. Thus, when NSA members act collectively, they do so in part because of solidary bonds and incentives developed at the Group and District levels of the organization.

Figure 1
DIAGRAM OF NSA's VERTICAL
ORGANIZATIONAL STRUCTURE

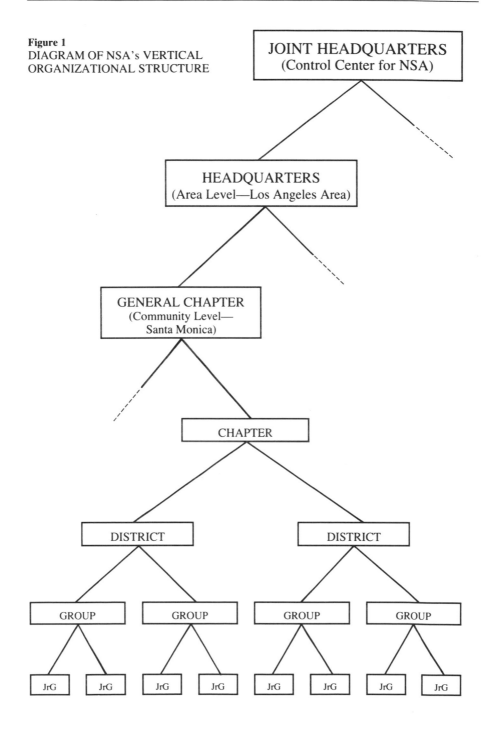

JOINT HEADQUARTERS
(Control Center for NSA)

HEADQUARTERS
(Area Level—Los Angeles Area)

GENERAL CHAPTER
(Community Level—
Santa Monica)

CHAPTER

DISTRICT

DISTRICT

GROUP

GROUP

GROUP

GROUP

JrG   JrG   JrG   JrG   JrG   JrG   JrG   JrG

In order to neutralize the potential for factionalism and sectarianism that inheres in its segmented, vertical structure, NSA, like the Sokagakkai, has developed a "horizontal line" that cuts across the vertical structure and incorporates members into a number of age- and-sex-based peer groups. There are four such groupings: the Men's Division, the Women's Division, and the Youth Division, which is divided into the Young Men's and the Young Women's Divisions. These peer groups are broken into smaller units and involve members in various activities ranging from traffic control, first aid, and child care to learning how to play musical instruments and marching in drill teams and bands (Brass Band, Bagpipe Band, Fife and Drum Corps) that perform at both public and NSA-sponsored parades and celebrations.[4] Through participation in these activities, along with other peer group campaigns and functions, members' commitment to the movement and their readiness to act on its behalf are strengthened. The incentives are both solidary and personal or instrumental. The solidary incentives result from peer relationships and pressures; the instrumental flow from the time and energy invested and the opportunity to learn various skills. Additionally, participation in many of the peer group activities is, as members hasten to say, "a lot of fun."

This horizontal structure of peer groups thus links together in a reticulated manner the movement's members and the various segmented units that comprise its vertical structure. The result is twofold: a more cohesive and highly integrated movement, and a more highly committed and mobilizable constituency.

Generating and Maintaining Enthusiasm and Anticipation

Organizational integration and membership cohesion are obviously necessary for enduring success, but it can also be argued that movements can be excessively organized and integrated. As noted earlier, Piven and Cloward (1977) have raised a number of serious questions about the assumed positive relationship between movement organization and success. Along similar but less extreme lines, Gerlach and Hine (1970) contend that more informal structures maximize mobilization and the probability of success. The problem, however, is not organization per se, but organizations that fail to develop and maintain a sense of enthusiasm and anticipation among their respective constituents. "Participants who no longer harbor a sense of expectancy about what tomorrow will bring, participants who no longer feel strongly or passionate about the cause, are participants who can no longer be counted on for action" (Zurcher and Snow,

---

[4]For elaboration of the nature and functions of these and other NSA information dissemination and promotion activities in public places, see Snow (1976: 162-77).

1981:478). Zablocki (1971:149-92) clearly recognized this when he wrote in *The Joyful Community* that "the secret of the Bruderhof" is its ability to create and sustain a sense of "collective behavior" or enthusiasm and anticipation among communal members.

My research suggests that NSA's success to date is due in part to its ability to generate and maintain among its members a sense of enthusiasm and expectancy. It has done this organizationally and strategically by establishing various proximate and attainable goals and by simultaneously promoting competition and cooperation among Chapters, Districts, and Groups on the vertical line and among the various peer groups on the horizontal line. The secondary goals range from higher monthly *Shakubuku* and *World Tribune* promotion targets to bigger and better annual conventions. The enthusiasm generated by these proximate goals and the intergroup competition to attain them is reflected in such comments as the following:

> Getting ready for the convention is really exciting. Working late at night on floats at the warehouse gives me something to look forward to each day. There's always something in the air. It kind of reminds me of the 1960s, you know, that sense of excitement that was in the air.
>
> What really makes the *Shakubuku* campaigns fun and exciting is all of us working together to do better than the other districts in the Chapter, and then the districts pulling together to beat the other chapters.
>
> One of the things I like best about NSA is that there is always something happening. There's never a dull moment. There's always something to look forward to—*World Tribune* promotion, another *Shakubuku* campaign, our annual convention. It's really exciting.

The incentives to work collectively to achieve these secondary goals are both solidaristic and personal. Working to attain campaign goals and to outdo competing units not only benefits vertical and peer group members, but it also brings recognition to oneself for being part of a winning team. By establishing new campaign goals and promoting intergroup competition, NSA is thus able to generate the enthusiasm and anticipation necessary for maintaining among many of its members a high generalized readiness to act in pursuit of its interests.

Generating Moral Incentives

A third feature of NSA's organizational structure that facilitates constituent mobilization is its centralized, extensive, and charismatically infused leadership hierarchy. The centralization of the leadership and its decision-making activities is clearly indicated by the existence of well-defined leadership roles that are linked together in a pyramidal fashion, much like a military chain of command. That the hierachy is also extensive is indicated by the fact that it reaches into all formalized groupings within the movement, including the Junior Group—the most elemental organizational unit, and thus incorporates a sizable portion of the membership. The last and most interesting aspect of the leadership hierarchy in relation to mobilization is that it is charismatically infused in the sense that charisma is diffused throughout the ranks. The nature of this diffusion process and its mobilizing power are elaborated below.

Drawing on the work of Dorothy Emmet (1958), Gerlach and Hine (1970) distinguish between (a) charismatic leaders who inspire devoted obedience because of the almost hypnotic powers attributed to them and (b) leaders who strengthen their followers, heightening their enthusiasm for the cause and inspiring them to devote more time and energy to its attainment. The first type of charisma is the stereotypic variety; the latter represents "a kind of secondary or communicable charisma" (Gerlach and Hine, 1970:39).

Both types are clearly evident and almost constantly operative in NSA. The first type is lodged in NSA's two previously mentioned principal leaders: Daisaku Ikeda, the President of Sokagakkai, and George M. Williams, the organizational head of NSA. Ikeda is referred to as "the Master," is regarded as a kind of wisdom-giving Pope, and is seen by core converts as an historically unique figure. His mere presence elicits among followers a rush "to get close to him," thunderous applause, yelling, tears, and the like. Some members even personalize his waves and glances in public places, assuming that his gestures are earmarked just for them. The relationship between Williams and his American followers is similarly charismatic. Core members frequently speak of him in honorific and inspirational terms, such as "the greatest living American" and "our guiding light." He is said to have special insights into the life situation of all members. And he too stimulates a rush "to get close to him" when in the presence of other members.

One of the problems with this stereotypic charisma is that the individuals with whom it is associated are not always directly accessible to their followers, especially those who are geographically or structurally distant. Consequently, it is often difficult for rank-and-file constituents to get close enough to their charismatic leader to receive the full benefit of his or her inspirational guidance and thereby have their faith and enthusiasm reinvigorated. Movements based in part on charismatic authority thus run the risk of diluting that very authority and its mobilizing power as they expand both numerically and geographically.

One solution to this problem of access is to set in motion a secondary or communicable charisma of the kind alluded to earlier. NSA has done that by diffusing throughout its leadership ranks the charisma associated with Ikeda and Williams. The result is that all incumbents of leadership roles are empowered with a degree of moral authority that they would not have otherwise and that is not usually associated with centralized leadership hierarchies. Since NSA's hierarchy is quite extensive, as previously noted, a rather large number of members are so empowered. But not all leaders are equally empowered. As one moves up the hierarchy and gets closer in rank to Ikeda and Williams, one becomes more "special" and his or her "guidance" becomes more compelling. As a senior leader explained one evening while making a surprise appearance at a district discussion meeting:

> The best way to get close to Mr. Williams and President Ikeda is to follow your district chief and be his right hand. His main function is to get you and keep you connected to Mr. Williams and President Ikeda.

Such instructions were also reiterated, almost continually, in the *World Tribune,* as indicated by the following directive:

> You should try to be with your leaders anytime, anywhere. If you find your leader talking to others in an informal situation, join in and listen. . . . The person who we in NSA aspire toward most is, of course, President Ikeda. The easiest way to get close to him is to communicate sincerely with your immediate senior leaders (*World Tribune,* 20 Nov. 1974).

Thus, not only is charisma diffused throughout the leadership hierarchy, but adhering to leaders is defined as a moral imperative of sorts.

NSA'S IDEOLOGY AND MOBILIZATION

Movements that promise individuals the realization of personal benefit or gain in their everyday lives if only they engage in some seemingly magical ritual, such as chanting *Nam-Myoho-Renge-Kyo* to a small scroll inscribed in Japanese, run the risk of creating a pool of "free-riders" within their ranks. After all, why help the movement attain some larger goal, such as world peace, when that goal constitutes what Mancur Olson (1965) calls a "public good" (that is, indivisible, nonexcludable benefit) and when recitation of some mantra within the confines of one's home is sufficient to yield a continuous stream of physical, material, and spiritual benefits? Movements such as NSA are thus confronted with the task of convincing members of both the need for collective action and the utility of their participation in that action. The solution, according to Olson (1965) and the resource mobilization perspective, resides in the attachment of "selective benefits" (that is, divisible and excludable benefits) to the collective action.

NSA has done precisely that by offering benefits for contributing to its campaigns that cannot be attained by merely chanting. We have seen how several features of the movement's organizational structure generate solidary and moral incentives, as well as some additional personal ones, for acting on behalf of the movement. We now turn to an examination of how NSA's ideology also functions to facilitate mobilization by providing additional, and perhaps even more powerful, incentives for acting in pursuit of its goals and interests.

Movement ideology is broadly conceptualized as a set of interconnected beliefs, values, attributions, and expectations that support and justify movement objectives and practices. For analytical purposes, however, it is useful to decompose movement ideology into at least three component elements: (a) a diagnosis of some aspect of social life as problematic and in need of alteration; (b) a solution to the diagnosed problem and a blueprint for happier days or a better world; and (c) a call to arms or rationale for acting collectively on behalf of the movement (Wilson, 1973:95-130). Since the last ideological component bears directly on the issue of mobilization, our concern here is with that element of NSA's ideology.[5]

Examination of NSA's literature, its leaders' directives, and the talk of rank-and-file members indicates five distinct rationales or ideological inducements for becoming and remaining active in the cause.

A Divinely Ordained Mission

The first major rationale is NSA's contention that its mission is not only preordained, but was divinely given. As one rank-and-file member explained:

> There is a whole history and theory going back 3000 years that point to Nichiren Shoshu as the orthodox practice of Buddhism and the correct philosophy and practice for this time period [referring to the present].

This prophecy, according to another core member,

> was predicted by the Sakyamuni Buddha. He said that during the time of Mappo, which is the third period after his death and which would last for thousands of years, his teachings would lose all their power. And when this time came, he said a Buddha greater than he would appear to propagate the *Lotus Sutra*. The *Lotus Sutra* is *Nam-Myoho-Renge-Kyo*, you know. He also predicted that anyone who practiced other forms of Buddhism in Mappo would not become happy or get any benefits. This is why so many people in much of Asia, and all over the world for that matter, have so much suffering—they practice the wrong philosophy. As Sakyamuni prophesied, the only correct teaching for this time period is *Nam-Myoho-Renge-Kyo*.

It is NSA's firm contention, as these statements suggest, that not only was the prophecy fulfilled, but that it was Nichiren himself who was the "new

---

[5]Aspects of the diagnostic and prognostic components of NSA's ideology were presented in the earlier overview. For detailed discussion of these two ideological components, see Snow (1976: 42-89).

Buddha'' prophesied to appear for the purpose of saving humankind. As Nichiren's heirs apparent, members are continually reminded of their responsibility to carry out and complete this divine mission. Such mobilizing guidance is reflected in part by the frequency with which the leadership refers to members as *the* ''Bodhisattvas of the Earth,'' who are mentioned repeatedly in both the *Lotus Sutra* and Nichiren's writings.[6] As Ikeda stated in a 1975 edition of the *World Tribune*:

> We were born into this world as Bodhisattvas of the Earth whose greatest wish is to propagate true Buddhism throughout the world. If we forget this wish, we will find no true meaning in our existence. Therefore, I hope you will advance with me to fulfill our noble goal.

Thus, one of the rationales for acting on behalf of the movement is that in doing so one is not participating in some fly-by-night fad or cult but is contributing, instead, to the realization of a kind of cosmic plan that was divinely prophesied years ago.

The Only "Proven" Religion

A second ideological inducement for becoming active in the cause resides in the movement's claim that it is the only ''proven'' religion. This claim is grounded in the contention that when all religions are assessed and compared in terms of Nichiren's ''three proofs'' (literal, theoretical, and actual), only Nichiren Shoshu satisfies all three. Literal proof refers to written documentation, such as the *Lotus Sutra* and Nichiren's writings; theoretical proof addresses the question of whether a religion is logical; and actual proof refers to the results that come from practing a particular religion. Since literal and theoretical proof are regarded as ''imperfect without actual proof,'' the ultimate criterion for assessing the quality of a religion is simply to observe the extent to which its theories and promises are borne out by reality (*World Tribune,* 7 April 1971). When this is done, other religious practices are said to pale beside Nichiren Shoshu. As a district leader

---

[6]The *Lotus Sutra* (Kern, 1963) is the sacred source of Nichiren's theology and, in turn, of part of Nichiren Shoshu/Sokagakkai's philosophy and practice. Just as other sacred religious texts, such as the Old and New Testaments of the Judeo-Christian tradition, are ridden with countless phrases and parables that can and have been interpreted in different ways, such is also the case with the *Lotus Sutra*. And just as numerous cults and sects within the Christian tradition have drawn on various biblical passages and parables as a source of inspiration and rationalization for their existence, so Nichiren drew upon certain passages in the *Lotus Sutra* not only as a source of prophetic inspiration, but also as pointing to him as the ''true Buddha'' in the age of Mappo. For discussion of Nichiren's unique reading of the *Lotus Sutra,* see Anesaki (1916).

explained in response to a question concerning the difference between chanting *Nam-Myoho-Renge-Kyo* and Transcendental Meditation:

> The real difference is in what's going to happen to you once you start chanting. But you have to try it in order to compare the two. . . . When you do chant, its effect is going to really astonish you. It's really shocking. They may seem similar, but if you chant you will see the difference. I'm not denying that other practices might have effects on you, but how great is that effect and how far does it go? As you will discover when you chant, the effect is far greater and far more positive than the effect produced by any other practice.

Few members are so bold as to denounce other religious practices as being false or pointless. The normative response, as suggested in the above statement, is to acknowledge the claims of other religions while emphasizing that the results they produce do not quite measure up to the consequences of the NSA practice of chanting. To do so is not to vitiate the mobilizing power of NSA's claims. Rather, it is a wise accommodative practice consistent with Stark's contention that new religions must exercise caution so as not to disavow fully the prevailing religious paractices and traditions of the communities in which they are attempting to gain a following. As NSA members go about the business of promotion, then, they are cautioned to temper their public appeals and enthusiasm, but not at the expense of surrendering the belief that theirs is the only religious practice that is consistently valid and effective. And for good reason: possession of what is thought to be an historically unique practice can provide, according to some members, a powerful incentive to do *Shakubuku*.

Carrying On the Pioneer Spirit and Tradition

A third ideological call to arms is the contention that NSA is the reincarnation of America's early pioneer spirit and traditions, and that members are therefore the new pioneers carrying out the unfinished work of America's forefathers. Although this value linkage is articulated most frequently in the *World Tribune* and in the speeches of Mr. Williams, it is also expressed occasionally among rank-and-file members and during district discussion meetings, as illustrated by the following remarks of a district leader during a meeting on 5 July 1974:

> As you know, many of the members from this district and chapter are in Estes Park at Ft. Pioneer tonight. Along with 1500 other members and Mr. Williams, they are sharing the experience of life in the wilds. . . . They're not just having a vacation or playing cowboys and Indians, though. Mr. Williams is giving continuous guidance and encouraging members to develop a pioneer spirit—the spirit which charcterized our forefathers and made possible their accomplishments. . . . What Mr. Williams is stressing is that the early pi-

oneer spirit is seemingly lost in the U.S. today, but that the philosophy of Nichiren is exactly in the same spirit of the founders of our country—the spirit to develop ourselves and make something great out of our society. This is the philosophy of true Buddhism. And Mr. Williams stresses that the mission of NSA today is to keep alive that pioneer spirit and awaken many, many people to the values of such a high philosophy.

Not surprisingly, this alleged congruence between NSA and America's heritage became more pronounced as America's Bicentennial approached. It is important to note, however, that this value linkage had been used as a mobilizing prod for a number of years. A November 1967 *World Tribune* editorial, titled "Pioneers of Happiness Observe Thanksgiving," refers to the original pilgrims, for example, and suggests that the members of NSA are the new pilgrims who are reviving the true spirit of Thanksgiving. And a July 1971 editorial succinctly summarizes this articulation with its title: "America's Heritage: Our Mission for Peace and Happiness."

By linking its mission with the values and ideals of America's founding fathers and early pioneers, NSA provides an additional rationale for becoming active in the cause, and one that is especially powerful for those who accept the linkage and who are ardently patriotic as well.[7]

Greater Tangible Benefits

The fourth lever to action contained within NSA's ideology is the widely articulated belief that those who act on behalf of the movement will receive greater benefit than those who sit on the sidelines and chant. This mobilizing belief is grounded in the earlier observation that NSA revolves around two basic practices: chanting and *Shakubuku*. Since the latter is considered the only way to attain world peace and happiness, it is regarded as the greatest cause one can make for the sake of humankind. But it is also a source of individual benefit. According to NSA's interpretation of the karmic law of cause and effect, *Shakubuku* reinforces and adds to the positive life-force one has

---

[7]This value linkage is also illustrative of NSA's accommodative flexibility and its efforts to render itself respectable and legitimate in the public eye. This and other accommodative tactics, along with the previously mentioned name-changes (see nn. 1 and 2), have been interpreted elsewhere as indicative of a strategic attempt by the movement to gain "idiosyncrasy credit" (Snow, 1979). As a stock of "positively-disposed impressions residing in the perceptions of relevant others" (Hollander, 1958: 120-21), idiosyncrasy credit buys license for movements to operate with a measure of impunity. This interpretation bears directly on Stark's first two propositions by suggesting conceptually how a new religious movement might establish and retain cultural continuity with the host society without diluting, at the same time, the "uniqueness" of its claims and practices.

begun to accumulate through chanting. "By doing *Shakubuku,*" in the words of one member, "you do something great for others and get benefits at the same time."

Activity on behalf of NSA is equated primarily with the practice of *Shakubuku,* with reaching out and acting on the ambient society so as to promote the movement's interests and extend its span of influence. To be active in the cause is, in short, to do *Shakubuku.* As we have seen, it is rationalized not only in terms of the movement's mission, but also on the grounds that it is a source of greater personal benefit and fortune in one's daily life. And therein lies what is perhaps NSA's most compelling answer to the potential problem of "free-riders" within its ranks: in order to receive the greatest possible benefit, one must not only chant but also do *Shakubuku.* In NSA, then, there are really no free-riders but only members who receive greater or fewer benefits.

Status Enhancement

The final mobilizing strand of NSA's ideology addresses the question of what it means in terms of personal status and identity to be in the vanguard of a movement "upon whose shoulders," in the words of Williams, "rest the dreams, wishes and all the hopes of the world" and that "will certainly," according to Ikeda, "develop into a movement of mankind, the greatest in its history." The answer is implicit in these claims as well as in the previously mentioned rationales for climbing aboard: to become active in this "unprecedented" venture is to become, among other things, part of an elect group that provides one with the basis for forging a unique and special status and identity in both the present and the future. As Ikeda noted before 5000 members on the occasion of the ground-breaking ceremony for the first Nichiren Shoshu temple in the United States:

> The day will come when each of you will appreciate Nichiren Shoshu. . . .
> In the coming 10, 20, 30 and 50 years, you will see proof of this and each of you will come to realize that you have been very fortunate.

In a similar vein, Williams, in a speech before 700 members of the Santa Monica Youth Division, links participation and future status consequences, but he is more specific as to what that linkage might mean for individual members:

> We have a mission to propagate the Gohonzon all over the world. That is why we were born at this time. . . . Very soon the responsibility of the country may fall on your shoulders. Some of you may become governors, presidents of large corporations, educators, doctors, and so forth. . . . It is immeasurably fortunate to have faith in Nichiren Shoshu at this time.

While such statements reflect the manner in which NSA's leaders draw upon the ideas of election and special status in their attempts to urge members on to greater action, the following illustrate the way in which some core members have internalized these ideas, thereby hinting at the efficacy of this mobilizing prod.

> The people who laugh at us now will be asking for our advice and help before too long.
>
> Within the next 15 to 20 years people will be wanting to know more and more about NSA.
>
> You should feel lucky to be in NSA. It is those who feel such fortune and who work for world peace who will get the greatest benefit now and in the days to come.
>
> I hope you will see me in twenty years. I'll be an important leader in this country.

SUMMARY AND PROJECTION

This chapter has sought to extend our understanding of the factors that account for effective mobilization among new religious movements and thereby contribute to their relative success. Drawing on data derived from field research on the Nichiren Shoshu Buddhist movement in America, the study has focused on several components of the movement's organizational structure and ideology that function in part as mobilizing prods or levers to action. We have seen how its charismatically infused leadership hierarchy and its segmented yet reticulated organizational structure have functioned to generate fairly powerful solidary and moral incentives to act on behalf of the movement. Several strands of NSA's ideology have been identified that also facilitate mobilization by providing additional inducements to support the cause. These ideological strands include the assertions that NSA is the manifestation of a long-standing Buddhist prophecy, that its religion is the most valid and effective one, that its mission is in keeping with the values and ideals on which this country was founded, that those who act on its behalf receive greater benefit than those who just chant, and that participants in its cause comprise an elect group that will occupy a special niche in the future. Taken together, these ideological claims provide the basis for a sense of mission, enthusiasm, and expectancy that are not only necessary for sustained collective action, but that make it well-nigh impossible for those who believe them to stand on the sidelines and watch. And if some members do choose just to watch, most will not do it for long, given the solidary bonds they are likely to have developed and the force of NSA's leadership.

These observations suggest that insofar as effective mobilization is a requisite for success, then NSA has clearly satisfied one of the necessary conditions. Yet the analysis is incomplete. There are other organizational dimensions that might also relate importantly to mobilization. Movement organizations can vary considerably in terms of whether their membership requirements are "inclusive" or "exclusive" (Curtis and Zurcher, 1974; Zald and Ash, 1966). They can also differ as to whether they are communal or noncommunal. Because communal movement organizations tend to be more "greedy" (Coser, 1974), Stark intimates the noncommunal ones are likely to be more successful. Whether this is in fact the case, however, remains an empirical question. Noncommunal movements tend to diffuse more widely and rapidly because they constitute open networks (Snow et al., 1980). Yet communal movement organizations probably tend to have a greater proportion of highly committed members because they are generally more demanding and constitute a dense network of social relations. It would thus appear that there is a trade-off between communal and noncommunal movement organizations. If so, then it would seem to follow that "mixed types" of religious movement organizations might be the more successful ones. Indeed, Stark suggests as much when he proposes that "successful movements consist of dense, but open social networks." Interestingly, both characteristics apply to NSA. That NSA constitutes an open social network has been documented and discussed elsewhere (Snow et al., 1980), and we have seen here how its segmented and reticulated structure produces strong solidary bonds that give rise to what Stark calls "a dense network of internal attachments." There are, then, a range of organizational variables that can affect movement mobilization and success and that therefore warrant further empirical examination.

The same can also be said about ideology. However, in recent years ideology has received scant attention in comparison to organizational and macrostructural variables. Much of the work associated with the resource mobilization perspective assumes that relevant beliefs and ideas are ubiquitous and therefore relatively unimportant determinants of movement emergence, mobilization, and success (McCarthy and Zald, 1977; Oberschall, 1973; Tilly, 1978). Stark similarly glosses over ideology. He suggests that perhaps some attention might be given to variation in its content and plausibility, but it does not figure prominently in his model. This tendency to ignore or sidestep the relevance of ideology to mobilization success is misguided in several respects. First, it fails to consider the possibility that just as the effectiveness of constituent mobilization can be influenced by various components of movement organization, so different components of movement ideology can have a similar effect. Drawing on Wilson's (1973) decomposition of ideology into three structural components, we have seen how the mobilizing component of NSA's ideology includes a varied assortment of richly elaborated claims. There is no reason to assume, however, that the mobilizing components of all movement ideologies are equally variegated and elaborated. Similarly, there is no reason to assume that the diagnostic and prognostic components of ideology are equally developed and persuasive across movements. Accordingly, it seems reasonable to hypothesize that variation in the development and richness of the different components of movement ideology, both within and across movements, accounts in part for variation in movement mobilization efforts and success.

Movement ideologies can also vary according to the vulnerability of their claims to disconfirmation. Some movement ideologies contain within them various validation logics and other self-confirming elements that provide immunity from seemingly disconfirming evidence. Machalek and I have shown this to be the case with NSA's ideology, for example, and have suggested that it may help explain the viability of a number of other religious movements as well (Snow and Machalek, 1982). This suggests, then, that a movement's mobilization efforts and relative success may also hinge on the resiliency of its ideology, such that movements whose ideological claims do not lend themselves to falsification may be more adaptive and successful.

In summary, this chapter has identified several features of NSA's organizational structure and ideology that have contributed to its success to date by producing and sustaining among a portion of its membership a high generalized readiness to act collectively. A number of other organizational and ideological dimensions have also been identified as hypothetically affecting movement mobilization and success. A more thoroughgoing understanding of new religious movements and their differential success requires further empirical consideration of these and related propositions pertaining to mobilization.

REFERENCES

Anesaki, Masaharu
    1916   *Nichiren: The Buddhist Prophet*. Cambridge: Harvard University Press.
    1963   *History of Japanese Religion*. Rutland VT: Charles Tuttle Co.
Brannen, Noah S.
    1968   *Soka Gakkai: Japan's Militant Buddhists*. Richmond: John Knox Press.
Coser, Lewis
    1974   *Greedy Institutions*. New York: Free Press.
Curtis, Russell L., and Louis A. Zurcher
    1974   ''Social Movements: An Analytical Exploration of Organizational Forms.'' *Social Problems* 21:356-70.
Dator, James
    1969   *Soka Gakkai: Builders of the Third Civilization*. Seattle: University of Washington Press.

Emmet, Dorothy
1958   *Function, Purpose, and Powers*. London: Macmillan.

Etzioni, Amitai
1961   *A Comparative Analysis of Complex Organizations*. New York: The Free Press.

Fujiwara, Hirotatsu
1970   *I Denounce Soka Gakkai*. Tokyo: Nisshin Hodo Company.

Gamson, William A.
1975   *The Strategy of Social Protest*. Homewood IL: Dorsey Press.

Gerlach, Luther P., and Virginia H. Hine
1970   *People, Power, Change: Movements of Social Transformation*. Indianapolis: Bobbs-Merrill.

Hollander, E. P.
1958   "Conformity, Status, and Idiosyncrasy Credit." *Psychological Review* 65:117-27.

Kanter, Rosabeth M.
1972   *Commitment and Community: Communes and Utopias in Sociological Perspective*. Cambridge: Harvard University Press.

Kern, H.
1963   *Lotus Sutra: Saddharma-Pundarika or The Lotus of the True Law*. New York: Dover Publications.

Jenkins, J. Craig
1983   "Resource Mobilization Theory and the Study of Social Movements." *Annual Review of Sociology* 9:527-53.

McCarthy, John, and Mayer Zald
1977   "Resource Mobilizaton and Social Movements: A Partial Theory." *American Journal of Sociology* 82:1212-41.

McFarland, H. Neill
1967   *The Rush Hour of the Gods: A Study of New Religious Movements in Japan*. New York: Harper and Row.

Murata, Kiyoaki
1969   *Japan's New Buddhism: An Objective Account of Soka Gakkai*. New York: John Weatherhill.

Oberschall, Anthony
1973   *Social Conflict and Social Movements*. Englewood Cliffs NJ: Prentice-Hall.

Olson, Mancur
1965   *The Logic of Collective Action: Public Goods and the Theory of Groups*. Cambridge: Harvard University Press.

Piven, Francis F., and Richard A. Cloward
1977   *Poor People's Movements*. New York: Pantheon.

Snow, David A.
  1976   *The Nichiren Shoshu Buddhist Movement in America: A Sociological Examination of Its Value Orientation, Recruitment Efforts, and Spread.* Ann Arbor MI: University Microfilms.
  1979   ''A Dramaturgical Analysis of Movement Accommodation: Building Idiosyncrasy Credit as a Movement Mobilization Strategy.'' *Symbolic Interaction* 2:23-44.
Snow, David A., and Richard Machalek
  1982   ''On the Presumed Fragility of Unconventional Beliefs.'' *Journal for the Scientific Study of Religion* 21: 15-26.
Snow, David A., Louis A. Zurcher, and Sheldon Ekland-Olson
  1980   ''Social Networks and Social Movements: A Microstructural Approach to Differential Recruitment.'' *American Sociological Review* 45: 787-801.
Tilly, Charles
  1978   *From Mobilization to Revolution.* Reading MA: Addison-Wesley Publishing.
White, James W.
  1970   *The Sokagakkai and Mass Society.* Stanford CA: Stanford University Press.
Wilson, John
  1973   *Introduction to Social Movements.* New York: Basic Books.
Zablocki, Benjamin
  1971   *The Joyful Community.* Baltimore: Penguin Books.
Zald, Mayer, and Roberta Ash
  1966   ''Social Movement Organizations: Growth, Decay and Change.'' *Social Forces* 44: 327-41.
Zurcher, Louis A., and David A. Snow
  1981   ''Collective Behavior: Social Movements,'' 447-82. In *Social Psychology: Psychological Perspectives.* Ed. M. Rosenburg and R. Turner. New York: Basic Books.

VIEWS
IN THE MIRROR

CHAPTER TWELVE

Future Prospects
of the Unification Church

Michael L. Mickler

INTRODUCTION

Discussion about the future of new religious movements (NRMs), particularly those with strong millennialist bents such as the Unification Church, typically focuses on the impact of such inexorable factors as the death of charismatic founders, the aging of the first generation (converted) membership, the emergence of a "birthed" (unconverted) second generation, the seductions of upward mobility and higher education, failed prophecies, and shifts in macrocultural, political, or demographic patterns over which a new movement has limited, if any, control. The usual conclusion follows that the future of NRMs, if they are to have a future, will be in a form unrecognizable to their original adherents: they will have become churches. When expressed within a "sect-to-church" framework, this view presupposes a basic discontinuity between the first and subsequent generations of religious traditions that survive. This "sect-to-church" formulation, while influential, has drawn mixed reviews from within the sociology of religion. Rather than review those discussions here, however, this treatment will focus on some of the deficiencies of the "sect-to-church" model from the standpoint of participation in a first-generation religious movement. Then it will introduce an alternative approach for examining the future prospects of the Unification Church.

Briefly, the deficiencies of the "sect-to-church" model to be considered here are three: the assumption of passivity on the part of a new movement with regard to its future; the assumption that change implies deviation from an originally pristine and unitary faith; and the assumption that first-generation religious movements, at least those that survive, become churches.

The assumption of passivity on the part of a new religious movement toward its future is the most obvious defect of the "sect-to-church" formulation, at least from an insider-participant perspective. Change, according to this view, is something that *happens* to a movement and only secondarily something that is initiated from within. This scenario, however, misses the more essential dynamic of movement development. That is, although environmental factors and organizational processes exert significant influence, the more crucial question is how external events and internal processes are understood and assimilated; and here there is ample room for subjectivity and choice. Put another way, any movement will face numerous crisis situations, but what is devastating for one movement—social repression, for example—may be a boon for another, at least in its subsequent interpretation. Any notion that movements are a "neutral medium through which social forces operate" does not take into account differential responses to similar stimuli.

A second deficiency of the "sect-to-church" formulation is the "golden age of faith" assumption that change implies deviation from an originally pristine and unitary faith. While this assumption may be alluring for some converts to first-generation religious movements, it is primarily a mythic construct and has little basis in fact. The reality is that new religious movements are in constant flux, if not downright turmoil. They tend to emit mixed signals about belief, carry pervasive cultural biases, and reflect high levels of disaffection and turnover. In fact, it could be argued that NRMs are more complex, more worldly, and less unified than more settled and established expressions of faith that have worked out the "bugs" of ideology, purged their more destructive chauvinisms, and socialized several generations in the faith. This is not to push a mythic golden age forward but to note that change need not mean defeat; positive values not apparent at the beginning may appear after traditions have had a chance to develop.

A final deficiency of the "sect-to-church" formulation is the assumption that first-generation religious movements, at least those that survive, become churches. This is simply not the case, especially within the pluralist American context. Some NRMs persist as "sects"; and others develop both "churchly" and "sectarian" tendencies and persist as "denominations"; still others merge into the environment and persist as diffuse cultural impulses. On the other hand, some NRMs, with marginal beginnings as "sects" or "cults," develop rapidly as "churches." Others prosper as "sects" but lose all appeal and collapse as "churches." In short, success or failure cannot be correlated with any single line of development. Put differently, NRMs don't *have* to become anything but can survive or perish in a variety of forms—of which the "sect-to-church" formulation is a poor predicter.

AN ALTERNATIVE APPROACH

Given the above-described deficiencies of the "sect-to-church" model, this treatment will utilize what has been familiar in the field of collective behavior as the "life-cycle" approach to analyze the future of the Unification Church. Although much less utilized within the sociology of religion than its "sect-to-church" counterpart, it offers several potential advantages including a more active role for movements in their own development, an emphasis on process rather than static dichotomies, and an "organization of knowledge about movements so as to permit prediction of future events." A "typical life cycle" to be adapted here contains four stages of development.

The first, or *preliminary stage of social unrest,* is characterized by unfocused restlessness, increasing disorder, cultural drift, and susceptibility of alienated and marginal masses to appeals of agitators.

In the second, or *popular stage,* unrest is transformed into collective excitement during which individuals participating in the mass behavior of the previous stage become aware of each other. Resultant *esprit de corps* and utopianism are conducive to the talents of the prophet who speaks with an air of authority, revealing a new message and a new philosophy of life, though always in general terms. The prophet popularizes unrest but provokes intensified resistence to an emerging movement.

Transition to the third, or *formal stage,* is a "crucial point" in development as a movement faces disintegration if it cannot buttress group morale and ideology on essential desires of people. Further, hope for enduring social change demands formulation of issues and formalization of procedures. Finally, as during this stage issues emerge over which there are differences of opinion, leadership passes from the prophet to statesmen who are able to formulate policies in accordance with prevailing social forces and convictions of membership constituencies.

In the final, or *institutional stage,* a movement loses its stigmatized status and becomes an organic part of society. Frequently, due to psychological exhaustion, moral letdown, or economic distress, a compromise is effected between the values of the decadent old order and the emergent new society. When this occurs, institutionalization is "incomplete," and a movement comes to rest at a point short of its expressed purposes. Still, it acquires "organization and form, a body of customs and traditions, established leadership and enduring division of labor, social rules and social values; in short, a culture, a social organization, a new scheme of life." It now requires the services of the administrator-executive as "policies formulated by statesmen—to satisfy demands for action voiced by the prophet in consequence of unrest generated by agitators—must be administered."[1]

Given this "typical life cycle," the Unification Church may be depicted as having entered the "crucial point" of transition between popular and formal stages of its development. This is evident primarily in that *opinion within the church as to its present options and future development has begun to coalesce into four major ideological subgroupings*. These subgroupings may be identified as liberal, prophetic, theocratic, and cultic. Each of them, in balancing millennialist prospects against current realities, poses a distinctive answer to the church's fundamental eschatological and methodological question, "How shall the Kingdom of God on earth be established?" For the liberal, the answer is "through the embodiment and synthesis of what is best in culture." For the prophetic witness, the answer is "through identification with the oppressed." For the theocrats, the answer is "through establishment of God's own nation." And from the cultic perspective, the answer is "through loyalty to church leadership and traditions." Based on these answers, various spokespersons have begun formulating issues and formalizing procedures. This process is consistent with the church's transition from popular to formal stages of development and will be described in sections on each of the four major subgroupings. Having outlined their ideological underpinnings, emergence, and respective agendas, we will find it possible to evaluate more adequately the church's future prospects.

Liberal

The liberal orientation is animated, most fundamentally, by the idea that "God is immanent in human cultural development and revealed through it." In practical terms, this means three things. First, it means the conscious, intended adaptation of religious ideas to modern culture and, in particular, to the insights of science and philosophy. Second, it means understanding the "essence" of a religious message and how it can be applied in different cultural settings. Third, it means initiating programs in accordance with the belief that human society is moving toward realization of the Kingdom of God.[2]

To an extent, adaption, cultural immanentism, and a religiously based progressivism have been integral parts of the Unification Church's program

---

[1]Adapted from Rex Hopper, "The Revolutionary Process: A Frame of Reference for the Study of Revolutionary Movements," *Social Forces* 28 (March 1950): 270-79. See also Ralph H. Turner and Lewis M. Killian, *Collective Behavior*, 2nd ed. (Englewood Cliffs NJ: Prentice-Hall, 1972) 245-68.

[2]See William R. Hutchison, *The Modernist Impulse in American Protestantism* (Cambridge: Harvard University Press, 1976) 2.

in the United States for some time. The problem, however, is that the church has been perceived as holding to a less "liberal" and more authoritarian set of standards in its internal life. Widespread recognition of this discrepancy has not only undermined its cultural outreach but has introduced a new element into the internal dynamic of the church, that of the self-conscious liberal. Demanding consistency of approach, the emergent liberal has begun to call for theological openness, cultural affirmations, and resource expenditures not only *vis-à-vis* society but also *vis-à-vis* the church. Given the critical nature of this stance, most early proponents of the liberal point of view are no longer with the church. Recently, however, the liberal position has coalesced into a more affirmative posture, and its adherents are remaining affiliated. In general, their emerging agenda takes either a more reformist or a more radical form.

In its reformist form, the liberal agenda advocates policy and life-style changes while leaving the church's basic belief structure intact. Characteristic of emerging bureaucratic and business class constituencies, the idea has been that if the church is to gain a hearing and accomplish its objectives, *it must become more reputable*. Rhetorically, this has meant "contrition" from PR representatives for past mistakes and expressed willingness to work within the American denominational framework. Substantially, it has meant the emergence of "careerism" both within and outside of the church. The rationale here is that for church membership to have any appeal in the eighties, at least among the "baby-boom generation," it needs to take on a "young urban professional" or yuppie profile. Also to be included within this general grouping are an increasing number of immigrating Korean nationals, most of whom appear primarily intent on achieving rapid upward mobility.

In its more radical form, advocacy of policy and life-style changes is augmented by a rethinking of basic beliefs from a liberal perspective. Characteristic of academic sectors within the church, the trend has been toward a fairly thoroughgoing "demythologizing" process that has subjected church doctrine to the rigors of higher criticism. In general, this has involved efforts to distinguish the essential "kerygma" or message of the Reverend Moon, to detach it from a precritical, theologically fundamentalist formulation at the hands of early Korean disciples, and to reinterpret or translate it into contemporary thought-forms. At the same time, usage of the historical-critical method has facilitated retreat into the subjective domain of self-awareness and self-fulfillment. In this sense, the liberal orientation, taken to its logical extreme, has led to a "privatization of faith."

Prophetic

The prophetic orientation, as distinct from that of the liberal, is animated less by the bourgeois "God of culture" and more by "a liberating God," a God "who intervenes in history in order to break down the structures of injustice and who raises up prophets in order to point out the way of justice and mercy.'' Not surprisingly, the practical implications of this view are at variance with the agenda just presented. Rather than adapt religious ideas to the modern intellectus, the prophetic orientation would ground them in ''praxis'' or experience, particularly the experience of the oppressed. Rather than tailor its message to cultural norms, the prophetic point of view would judge those norms. And for the liberal doctrine of progress, the prophetic perspective would substitute a conceptualization emphasizing the redemptive quality of voluntary suffering and sacrifice.

To an extent, in its humble post-Korean War origins, in its communitarian-collectivist organization, and in its generally stringent, sacrificial lifestyles, the church has lived out some of the themes described above. However, just as a perceived discrepancy within the church gave the liberal impulse a ''life of its own,'' what has detached the prophetic orientation from its previous moorings is a growing consciousness of discrepancies in American culture. This emerging consciousness is due to the coming together of two separate but interrelated developments. The first stems from the church's treatment by American society, which—while asserting pluralism, toleration of religious minorities, and open, democratic procedures—was pursuing a different, more repressive line with regard to the UC. Painful recognition of this discrepancy as well as of its own outcast status is the primary reason for the coalescing of the prophetic impulse within the church. A second key development has been the church's increased interaction with other outcasts in American society, the only ones to have anything to do with the UC ecumenically. In particular, these would include socially conscious black clergy and a number of dissident-misfits from a variety of traditions. This interaction has added definition and substance to the church's emerging ''pedagogy of the oppressed,'' which has taken both reformist and radical forms.

In its reformist mode, the prophetic agenda advocates a primarily ameliorist ethic that, while ''naming'' abuses, is willing to work within the system. Characteristic of the church's ex-radical, black, feminist, and European socialist element, the idea is that if the UC is to retain credibility as a world-transforming social movement, it must identify with the dispossessed. Rhetorically, this has meant a fair amount of ''name-calling'' and ''political posturing''; that is, depictions of the United States as racist, sexist, imperialist, and even genocidal, along with articulations of anti-Reaganism and support for Jessie Jackson, detente, nonviolence, mutual disarmament, and full employment. More substantially, it has meant establishment of minority alliances, social-action organizations, the advocacy of life-styles lived in solidarity with the poor, and the setting up of house churches in depressed neighborhoods.

In their more radical form, societal critique and social action are accompanied by a "politicization of belief." Thus, from the prophetic perspective Reverend Moon is not a liberal "Horatio Alger" hero but a suffering servant: a "man of color," a onetime dockworker and draft-resister who has suffered, first, as part of an underground liberation movement against fascist Japan; second, under North Korean totalitarian and South Korean "strong-man" regimes; and now, at the hands of the United States government. Similarly the "third-world" origins of church doctrine are stressed in depicting it as a "theology of liberation." The goal here is *not* the creation of another ecclesiastical institution but the realization of a just social order, usually conceived along the lines of democratic socialism. In this sense, the prophetic viewpoint, taken to its radical extreme, would advocate not the privatization of faith but a "withering away of the church."

Theocratic

The theocratic orientation, as distinct from both bourgeois and proletarian idealisms, is animated by a more "realistic" appraisal of power and power relationships. Theologically, this translates into the notion that "God works through nations" and, in particular, through the leadership of "chosen" nations. This idea has several practical implications. First, it implies a "top-down" rather than the "bottom-up" approach advocated by the prophetic types. Second, it implies the necessity of adapting religious ideas to political as well as to intellectual and ethical realities. Third, it implies the unity of projecting internal ambiguities, especially those within a "chosen" nation, onto an external threat.

Again, as with the subgroupings already described, the theocratic impulse has been an integral part of the Unification Church's program in the United States for some time and is reflected in its all-out support for Richard Nixon, in its frequent interminglings of civic and religious symbolizations, and in its fervent anticommunism. However, whereas increased consciousness of precarious balances between freedom and oppression *both in the church and within American society* helped coalesce the orientations already described, the emergence of a more clearly defined theocratic position has been fostered by a heightened consciousness of the same tension at work on the geopolitical level. This has been due partly to a recent intensification of the "ideological struggle" between the United States and the USSR but more centrally to the serious destabilization of political conditions in Central America. This latter situation, in facilitating UC access to high-ranking officials in several Latin American countries, has fueled significantly an emerging theocratic agenda.

In its more provisional form, the theocratic agenda seeks to point out the "lies and deceptions of communism." Typified by Korean and other "captive nation" constituencies within the church, as well as a vocal cadre of campus activists, the idea here is that the church will not fulfill its mission until communism, the primary obstacle hindering realization of an "ideal" world, is stopped. Rhetorically, this has meant the same kind of "name-calling" and "political posturing" that marks the prophetic agenda but along a different line. Rather than U.S. abuses, Soviet atrocities are enumerated along with staunch support for Reagan administration policies and opposition to peace movements, detente, and disarmament. Substantially, the ideological offensive against communism has meant significant monetary outlays to support international conferences, media outlets, research studies, and even (through proper channels) the "right" political candidates in defense of "human freedom and democracy under God."

In its less provisional and more radical form, anticommunism is augmented by initiatives more explicitly suggestive of theocratic intent. The assumption here is that the church and its message will neither be secure nor empowered to fulfill its calling until it can attain sovereignty within at least a limited geopolitical setting, which then would become not only the standard for other societies but also a base from which to "liberate" those under communist rule. From this perspective, Reverend Moon is viewed less as a suffering servant than as a potential world leader. Similarly, church doctrine is redefined in nonsectarian terms as "Unificationism" or "Godism," a theocentric worldview that could be applied with benefit within any number of political contexts. To this end, the church has begun cultivating contacts and stockpiling investments in several candidate-countries. In this sense, the theocratic orientation, carried to its radical extreme, would advocate not a withering away of the church but its embodiment in a state.

Cultic

The cultic orientation, as distinct from those already described, takes as its organizing principle not intellectual knowledge, social justice, or power but rather purity. Expressed theologically, the notion is that "God works through the pure in heart." This view has several key implications. First, it implies that church doctrine is not to be adapted but *is to be believed*, basically in literal terms. Second, it implies a renunciation of the world, usually reinforced by communal solidarity, a distinctive ritual life, and a rigorous personal ethic. Third, it bases hope for the future not on human achievement but on divine intervention, generally either as a sudden transformation or as a succession of "dispensations."

To an extent, literal belief in church doctrine, separatist communalism, and supernaturalism have been long-standing staples of UC church life in the United States. What led, however, to the coalescing of these elements into a distinct subgrouping was a growing awareness of tension, not as externalized organizational, social, or geopolitical levels but rather in the interior life of church membership. To a certain degree, this awareness has been fostered by high turnover rates and the leveling off of conversions. More significant, however, was the sense that in reaching out to the world—intellectually, socially and politically—individual members have either lost or compartmentalized their faith. In this sense, the cultic agenda can be described most accurately as a reaction to secularizing trends. And, as with the subgroupings already discussed, it has both reformist and radical dimensions.

In its reformist mode, the cultic agenda promotes spiritual enrichment within the context of diverse worldly involvements. Characteristic of less educated, grassroots membership, the idea is that external accomplishments are meaningless if they become attenuated from church authority and traditions. Rhetorically, this has meant sermonic condemnations of individualism, materialism, rebelliousness (especially in women), and immorality, as well as approbations of obedience, self-sacrifice, filial piety, and chastity. More substantially, it has meant the development of a hagiographic tradition, a burgeoning of publications dedicated to internal edification, home-study courses, the development of Sunday school and nurseries for the socialization of children, and, most importantly, the emergence of ritual traditions and church calendar. In short, the cultic agenda has meant the formalization of mechanisms designed to stimulate interior life, bolster group cohesion and distinctiveness, and resist, or at least ameliorate, secularization.

In its more radical form, general spiritual enrichment is augmented by challenges to existing life-styles. Characteristic of Korean elite and mainstream Japanese membership, these challenges are of two types. On the one hand, they include calls for greater loyalty to church leadership, usually within the context of extended millennial timetables and dispensational ''emergency time-periods.'' In this sense, marriage or career are not occasions for withdrawal from church life but rather occasions for even greater sacrifice as frequent separations are called for. On the other hand, calls for more loyalty to church traditions often imply the affirmation of neo-Confucian culture, which has been granted quasi-normative status within the church. Conscientiously applied, this requires significant adjustment of life-styles in a Western context—from relatively minor details of daily etiquette to more basic issues of arranged marriages and strictures that Korean be the spoken language of the church. In this sense, the cultic agenda, taken to its radical extreme, would favor the ''orientalization of culture.''

CONCLUSION

Here, then, are four major subgroupings within the church, and the temptation is to conclude by ''picking a winner.'' This, however, is a hazardous approach given both the unforeseeable character of future social trends and the fact that there need not be a winner at all. The ''life-cycle'' model utilized here does not postulate an inevitable series of stages but, to the contrary, allows that in a variety of ways development may be indefinitely postponed or completely redirected. Put succinctly, there are no guarantees that any movement will achieve lasting institutional form.

From this perspective, the fact that the Unification Church has generated four ideological subgroupings can be seen in either positive or negative terms. On the one hand, differentiation could offer the church more flexibility in coping with future contingencies while, at the same time, sharpening its faculties of critical analysis. On the other hand, it would be a mistake to minimize the risks attendant to the coalescing of variant options. Most obvious are the dangers of factionalization, dissension, and outright schism. Less obvious, though equally debilitating, are the possibilities of exhaustion with the whole procedure, boredom with intramural debate, and a feeling that the sorting out of issues simply is not worth the effort. In short, the emergence of options, while unavoidable if a movement is to develop, can have devastating consequences.

Given the ambiguities of its present situation, the only sure conclusion about the future of the Unification Church is that it remains highly indeterminate. This is so not only because of the emergence of alternative agendas but also because current environmental conditions are subject to change. Nonetheless, a projection of church development is possible based on two alternative scenarios: first, that environmental conditions remain relatively constant, reflecting a continuation of present trends; or second, that geopolitical and religious conditions change radically. Given the first set of circumstances, the church's prospects for organizational continuity are good if it can hold together its emergent sub-groupings. On the other hand, given catastrophic change, the church's survival in all likelihood will depend upon whether one or another of its ideological subgroupings gains dominance, probably in its most radical form. In order to assess the church's future prospects, it is necessary to examine each of these scenarios in more detail.

If present geopolitical and religious conditions remain relatively stable during the next 25-50 years, the church stands a good chance of maintaining organizational continuity and achieving a viable institutional form if it is able to hold together its various tendencies. The way to do this is *by accommodating more moderate demands of intra-organizational subgroupings and channeling more radical impulses into controlled settings.* For example:

The church needs to institute its *liberal culture-affirming agenda* insofar as it promotes cultural continuity and, at the same time, formalize settings in which more radical intellectual reflection can occur with minimal disruption. The church has already done this by establishing a theological seminary and will need to broaden this development by establishing a university within the next 25-50 years.

The church needs to institute its *prophetic social-justice agenda* insofar as it promotes community welfare and, at the same time, formalize settings for more radical societal critiques. The church has already moved in this direction by setting up relief agencies and home-church ministries. It will need to establish more broadly based service networks and further initiatives in "third-world" and socialist world settings in the next 25-50 years.

The church needs to institute its *theocratic political-action agenda* as it facilitates organizational objectives and, at the same time, channel more radical theocratic impulses into the building up of a strong corporate institution. The church has already moved in this direction by legally incorporating, by property and business investments, and by pursuing its interests in the public sphere. It needs to continue this approach in the next 25-50 years by formalizing a clear internal governing polity, a viable means of economic support, and permanent lobbyists.

The Church needs to institute its *cultic spiritual-edification agenda* as it preserves church distinctiveness and resists secularization; at the same time, it needs to formalize settings for more radical devotionalizing. The church has already moved in this direction by encapsulating more radical demands within increasingly well-defined "novitiate" periods and by generating a variety of ceremonial and ritual practices, mostly derived from its Asian roots. In the next 25-50 years, the church needs to continue and begin to standardize these developments.

If the church takes the above-listed steps, its prospects for "success" in a relatively stable environment are good, especially given progress already made. If, however, the geopolitical and religious situation changes drastically in the next 25-50 years, the church's survival will depend on one or another of its ideological subgrouping's achieving dominance, probably in its most radical form. The idea here is that radical change calls for a radical agenda and that the four scenarios of radical change commonly envisaged within the church—that the United States will go secular; that socialism will win; that the political situation in Central America and elsewhere will further destabilize; or that Asia will become the center of global civilization—are roughly congruent with radical expressions of its four ideological subgroupings and, to an extent, embody their secret hopes.

Rather than speculate further on how current church subgroupings correspond to these radical scenarios, a more pertinent way to close this discussion is to note the ambiguity of such congruity. On the one hand, regardless of the specific character of social disruption, it is the case that alterations of the status-quo tend to produce "market opportunities" for new faiths in that

NRMs adapt more swiftly to change. The flip side of this, however, is that once the disruption or crisis has passed, so too have the new faiths. This problematic holds true for the Unification Church and is the reason why, though time and circumstance favor the preeminent emergence of one or another of its fundamental tendencies, other tendencies must be retained and protected as fully legitimate minority perspectives.

CHAPTER THIRTEEN

The Future
of Krishna Consciousness
in the West:
An Insider's Perspective

Steven J. Gelberg (Śubhānanda Dās)

As an "insider," a committed member of one of the "new religious movements" under discussion in this volume, I find myself feeling a bit like a laboratory frog who, in the midst of being dissected, is requested to comment on the proceedings. It is a little difficult to comment dispassionately upon a matter that is of such vital personal significance. Besides that, active participants in new religious movements are rarely asked to respond to scholarly studies done on them, and when so requested usually lack the specialized theoretical training and technical social-scientific language to relate productively to their experimentors. "As a sociologist I have always envied anthropologists the impunity with which they may write about their usual subjects—preliterate groups," says Rodney Stark. "Remote tribes do not publish criticisms of anthropological studies, nor do they retain libel lawyers."[1] The editors of this volume are to be commended, then, for their courageous willingness to face a few restless natives.

In this essay, I will be providing an "insider's view" of the future of the International Society for Krishna Consciousness (ISKCON), better known as the Hare Krishna movement. I am not trained as a social scientist (my own fields of interest, academically speaking, are Hindu studies and comparative spirituality), but as an object of sociological study, I think I've developed some sensitivity to

---

[1]Personal communication.

and even appreciation for social-scientific perspectives on religion. As one yet uninitiated into the arcane mysteries of sociological theory, though, I will not presume to comment at great length on it vis-à-vis new religious movements and questions of their future. Instead I will try to directly assess ISKCON's future prospects in light of Rodney Stark's success/failure model and then suggest some further success/failure criteria (with application to ISKCON) and explore how this issue is viewed within the movement itself.

Before proceeding to discuss ISKCON's future, it might be in order first to ask what ISKCON *is,* at present. It is often referred to as a "new religious movement," but this categorization is a little problematic. In the United States ISKCON might be defined, according to nonpejorative sociological parlance, as a "cult movement"—an unconventional or "deviant" faith, in this case one representing an alien religious tradition. The movement was founded in America in 1966 by A. C. Bhaktivedanta Swami Prabhupada, an elderly Indian holyman, scholar, and saint who led the movement until his passing in 1977. In India, ISKCON is also a new movement (in its institutional form reimported from America in 1970), but there it is an authentic modern expression of a major Hindu denomination, Caitanya Vaishnavism.[2] In India, as well as in America, "Hare Krishna's American-born missionaries appeal to Indians as representatives of a greatly reinvigorated, activist, and innovative movement within the conventional Hindu tradition."[3]

In the West, Krishna Consciousness is no more a new religion than was the Christianity imported into India by European missionaries in the sixteenth century. ISKCON may appear new and strange to those unfamiliar with its parent tradition abroad, and in fact it may *act* like a new religion in its struggle to forge roots in inhospitable cultural territory. But inasmuch as it draws quite heavily on a long-standing religious tradition rich in theology, doctrine, ritual, and distinctive cultural and social forms—and has a large and solid constituency among Indian Hindus in the West—theories concerning the future prospects of new religious movements may at times need to be applied to ISKCON in a slightly modified form.

When confronted with the sheer complexity and variety of ISKCON, it seems quite difficult to paint a distinct picture of the present, much less the future. In many ways, ISKCON differs from one geographical region to another. In spite of a high degree of ideological and life-style uniformity, or-

----

[2]Caitanya Vaishnavism was itself an important sixteenth-century revitalization movement, founded by the saint, mystic, and divine incarnation Sri Caitanya. It is currently "the strongest single religious force in the eastern part of the Indian subcontinent" (Dimock, 1972:ix).

[3]Rodney Stark, personal communication.

ganizational matters vary significantly. Regional ecclesiastic leadership ranges from efficient to haphazard; leaders from brilliant and charismatic to mediocre; administrative regions from economically prosperous to impoverished, democratically governed to semiautocratic. Some centers are recruiting new members heavily while others are barely maintaining their numbers. Within ISKCON there is considerable attitudinal variety as well with a rich plurality of opinion on almost everything save fundamental theological doctrine, and a variety of perspectives on the current and future status of the movement. In view of all this sheer diversity, speculation about the future of ISKCON—a phenomenon so little understood in the present—may seem a questionable; even frivolous academic pastime. What we can do, nevertheless, is try at least to discover those strengths and weaknesses that may have some bearing on the future direction of the movement.

THE STARK MODEL APPLIED TO ISKCON

Cultural Continuity

Stark begins by suggesting that new religious movements are likely to succeed to the extent that they "retain cultural continuity with the conventional faiths of the societies in which they appear or originate" and cites as prime offenders of this principle Hindu and Buddhist groups in the West, which are "wholly discontinuous with the conventional religious culture." On the surface, certainly, ISKCON seems to fit this description neatly. Its sheer exotic strangeness seems to set it light-years apart from conventional Western civilization.

However, Stark modifies his idea further on where he explains that cultural discontinuity will restrict movement growth "at least until a religion has succeeded in at least one society." Hence, ISKCON may be a special case among the "new religions" discussed in this volume due to its deep roots in India. In the West, ISKCON has taken advantage of popular interest in "things Indian"—vegetarianism, yoga, meditation, Mahatma Gandhi, and concepts such as karma and reincarnation—to convey its message. Although popular interest in Indian thought apparently peaked in the late sixties, there is a residual Western fascination with things Indian, with which ISKCON has tried to connect its own message and mission and in that way "build upon the familiar." Recent ISKCON publications have highlighted a long history of support in the West for some of its core Indian values, ideas, and practices: Emerson's and Thoreau's reverence for the *Bhagavad-gita;* the reincarnation beliefs of Plato, Benjamin Franklin, Walt Whitman, and Henry Ford; the vegetarianism of Pythagoras, Leonardo da Vinci, Leo Tolstoy and George Bernard Shaw; and the Hare Krishna chanting of Allen Ginsberg and the Beatles.

Another way ISKCON gains legitimacy from its Indian roots is through the rather substantial support it receives from the immigrant Indian communities in the West. Thousands of Hindu Indians attend weekly services at ISKCON temples, participate in traditional Hindu festivals, provide monetary support, and even send their children for religious instruction at ISK-CON schools and summer camps. Some ISKCON centers are even beginning to resemble ethnic churches. As ISKCON has gradually begun to get the message of its legitimate "ethnicity" across to the American public, it has begun to enjoy some of the polite respect (from government bodies, the courts, and the media) due ethnic minorities.

If we look back to ISKCON's first several years in America, we find yet another line of cultural continuity linking it to American society. ISKCON's early explosive growth occurred within the milieu of the hippie- counterculture, as clearly evidenced by the content and language of some of its early informal publications and by the geographical placement of its early missionary efforts. J. Stillson Judah (1974) has elaborately documented how ISKCON appealed strongly to hippies and others subscribing to countercultural values such as rejection of materialism, nonviolence, and the search for "higher consciousness" and transcendence. As the counterculture fragmented and faded, however, ISKCON lost its most lucrative source of recruits. So closely tied was ISKCON to the counterculture in terms of ideology and recruitment that, much like the early Jewish followers of Jesus who assumed that pagans would first have to convert to Judaism before they could follow Christ, some early ISKCON members were certain that a genuine understanding of Krishna Consciousness required contercultural initiation, and were a little suprised when "straight" youth began to join the movement by the early seventies. The death of the counterculture as a social movement in the early seventies was survived, however, by perennial countercultural values such as disillusionment with materialism and the quest for self-knowledge and mystical experience, and ISKCON has continued to draw many of its members from this residual if fragmented counterculture.

In his writings and lectures, Srila Prabhupada, ISKCON's founder, claimed a commonality with the religions of the West, particularly by pointing out a common monotheistic heritage. He even suggested that by chanting the "non-sectarian names of God" of the Hare Krishna mantra, Christians would become better Christians and Jews better Jews and, further, that if Western religionists found the Hare Krishna mantra a bit too exotic, they could simply chant "Jesus Christ" or "Yahweh." These and other examples of cultural and religious continuity do help to mitigate the "foreignness" of ISKCON and ease the task of setting roots.

Medium Level of Tension

ISKCON is a movement in a fairly high state of tension with Western society. Increasingly, however, one begins to detect accommodative tendencies, and it is the tension within the movement between accommodative and purist attitudes and policies that will increasingly become a major theme in the future.

ISKCON is now experiencing classic tensions between its radical ideological rejection of the "material world" (often expressed in uncompromising antiworldly rhetoric) on the one hand, and its desire to become legally and financially stable, forge alliances, and gain respectability on the other. While the movement might not openly admit to be seeking respectability (which might contradict its missionary rhetoric), there are nevertheless symptoms of an evolving accommodationist tendency such as its willingness, described earlier, to seek active or passive endorsement of its values and teachings from conventional sources, to allow itself to be identified with a respectable émigré Indian community (most of whom are Hindu more in ethnic than activist terms), to cater to popular tastes in music by broadcasting its message through a variety of popular music styles, to seek dialogue with and support from the academic community, and to encourage the development of a less committed lay community (as I'll describe later in more detail). Although ISKCON is hardly on the verge of becoming a tolerant, world-accommodating religious movement, it has begun to take a few steps in that general direction.

Pressure to accommodate may come from various and conflicting sources, such as the desire to evangelize more effectively by lowering tension, and latent worldliness in members themselves. Some of the pressure to accommodate has come, no doubt, from a highly vocal and persistent anticult movement that seeks to stigmatize ISKCON as a major threat to society. Although this anticult lobby has failed, thus far, to effect legislative sanctions against "cults," it has had some success in gaining public acceptance of its message through the media as well as through "preventive education" in schools and churches. Perhaps greater even than the danger of stigmatization and persecution, however, is the danger of accommodation itself, whereby ISKCON might gain public acceptance at too high a price—not only to itself but, as Harvey Cox argued in a *New York Times* editorial (1977), to the greater society:

> Some oriental religious movements bother us because they pose a threat to the values of career success, individual competition, personal ambition and consumption. . . . We forget that Christianity, taken literally, could cause similar disquietude. . . . American culture has an enormous capacity to domesticate its critics. . . . My real fear about the new religious movements is not that harassment will drive them out of existence, but rather that it could

push them into premature accommodation, and we would lose the critical perspective that religion can bring to a culture in need of renewal.

Along with accommodative tendencies, there has also come some pressure within the movement to avoid accommodation, insofar as it is equated with compromise. Some devotees detect in certain accommodative tendencies a pandering to mundane sensibilities and a diluting of the purity and pristine otherworldliness of ISKCON's spiritual message. Such "purists" view the liberal accommodationist at times as being preoccupied with public approval and lacking the spiritual conviction to preserve the radical, transformative message of Krishna Consciousness, no matter what the consequence. Both views are diffuse (albeit the accommodationist is more influential), and no battlelines are drawn, but the issue of accommodation could well heat up in the future. In the meantime, the creative blending of purist and accommodative approaches has effected a healthy variety of styles of public interaction.

Sociologists tend to view stigmatization as a powerful liability to instrumentalist success, but that is so only when we define success in quantitative terms—recruitment of large numbers of followers. Stigma can also serve as an asset. The fact that a movement like ISKCON carries the stigma of social and cultural deviance—that it stands in radical opposition to the status quo—can be a real source of attraction to young people seeking radical alternatives to what they view as an academic-sexual-career rat race. Such social and ideological dissidents, although certainly a small minority of the total population, form the committed inner core of new religious movements and supply much of their strength and vitality. They are not reveling in eccentricity but seeking—often with deep and disarming sincerity—an alternative to a banal existence in a meaningless world. Freedom from stigma and attainment of respectability are often purchased at the price of secularization, whereby the movement "loses the power to provide potent other-worldly religion" (Stark, herein).

Effective Mobilization

ISKCON has been able to generate a very high level of mobilization, that is, to mobilize individuals to "act on behalf of the collective interests" of the movement, largely because of its guru authority system, which inspires high levels of individual commitment. Referring to a study of Larry Shinn (1984), however, Stark suggests that guru authority systems "are inimical to effective organization and are subject to constant fission and schism, since members are committed to a particular guru, not to a large organization." In ISKCON, guru-disciple bonding is theologically integral and so can never be dispensed with as politically inexpedient, but it no doubt could potentially create awkward conflicts of loyalty.

However, this diffusion of loyalties is not as clear-cut as Stark indicates. Although the potential for schism certainly exists (ISKCON has already had a few minor ones), there are certain theological and practical safeguards in ISKCON that would seem to lessen the danger somewhat. In the movement's theology, the guru's authority is not absolute but derives from his adherence to scripture, tradition, and to his own guru, of whom he remains a ''servant'' in perpetuity. Because Prabhupada himself had placed a very high priority on institutional solidarity and many times had implored his leading disciples to work together cooperatively after he was gone, defection by any guru would be viewed, almost on the face of it, as an act of disrespect for Prabhupada, fealty to whom is a fundamental criterion of orthodoxy. Further, the central ecclesiastic authority of ISKCON, the Governing Body Commission, has clearly defined regulatory powers over all its gurus (to appoint, censure, excommunicate, and so forth). An errant guru can find his powers and prestige sharply curtailed by the GBC. In one case of guru defection (resulting from ideological deviation complicated by personal scandal), although the guru in question strongly urged his disciples to exist along with him, most of them were successfully prevailed upon by members of the GBC (and other leaders) to remain within ISKCON, and later were reinitiated by other ISKCON gurus. Of those who did exit with their guru, it appears that most eventually returned to the organization. Moreover, by training, disciples of the various current gurus come to hold Prabhupada in very high esteem as their own guru's spiritual master, the founder and perpetual spiritual force behind the movement, and the greatest of modern saints. This reverential attitude towards the founder of ISKCON acts as a cohesive force that at least partially transcends ''sectarian'' guru-disciple bonds.

My argument here is not that ISKCON has some built-in immunity to schism or that the guru system of authority is not potentially destructive of centralized institutional authority, but that given appropriate organizational and ideological safeguards, commitment to guru and to institution can coexist without ''constant fission and schism.''[4]

There is one other aspect of the issue of individual member commitment that deserves note. In his essay, Stark warns that high levels of mobilization achieved by ''removing converts from the normal secular world . . . results in isolation, in reliance on collective economic activities which often deflect

---

[4]I must weaken my argument by reporting, as this volume goes to press, that there are two ISKCON gurus (in separate cases and divergent situations) who conceivably separate themselves from institutional ISKCON, retaining large, geographically distinct bodies of loyal disciples and major ISKCON properties and buildings. If schism eventuates in either of these cases, it will be ISKCON's first such experience on a major scale.

from religious goals." As organizations, new religious movements must of course concern themselves not only with individual religious discipline and worship but with organizational maintenance and missionary enterprises (fundraising; recruitment; publishing and distributing teachings; forming economic, legal, and bureaucratic policies and practices; and so forth). Yet, as Bryan Wilson (1982:13) explains, "They must carefully avoid the appearance of making efficiency an end in itself, of becoming too preoccupied with purely instrumental issues, occasioning a deflection of goals from the higher purpose of the movement to the intrinsic problems of organization *per se.*" This tension between instrumental concerns and substantive goals has generated some controversy and dissent within ISKCON over the past several years and has had some negative effect upon individual member commitment, an effect that could have serious implications for the future.

In America in particular, financial difficulty has compelled some ISKCON centers to shift manpower from public chanting and the distribution of literature (and other "direct" missionary activities) to various economic pursuits. Some members who would rather contribute to what they view as the movement's "substantive" aims (by distributing religious texts, for example) are induced, out of economic necessity, to perform more "instrumental" functions such as fundraising. Although the theology explicitly sacrilizes the act of collecting funds to be employed in "Krishna's service," some devotees find it difficult at times to experience these "instrumental" activities in their broader theological context and to internalize their theological rationale. Especially when fundraising is performed in a secular, public context without the usual monastic dress ("identity baggage"), the devotee may feel the outside world impinge dangerously upon his own cognitive and sacred universe. In the following passage, Wilson (1982:108) explains the necessity for sacrilizing the instrumental components of a religious movement. Because of the powerful tension—especially in the West—between the sacred and the profane,

> the profane aspects of a religious movement [such as organizational or economic maintenance] need to become sacrilized in order to prevent these essentially secular elements from tainting and secularizing the sacred. If they become sacrilized, they reinforce the adherent's commitment by reducing the tension that otherwise might arise between the instrumental and organizational concerns and the substantive and arbitrary goals of the movement. The secular world is kept at bay by making even expedient matters into matters of religious principle and religious poetry.

If, however, the devotee fails to experience the instrumental activities in their intended social context (due either to spiritual weakness or instrumentalist peer pressure), the devotee might come to view his or her activity as primarily economic *rather than* devotional, and resultant dissatisfaction or disillusionment may undermine institutional commitment. Although such a disillusionment may not be theologically justifiable, it does take place and can potentially develop into a serious problem in the future, unless the movement establishes a more stable economic base (one that does not consume the energies of a large portion of its core membership) or creates a system of vocational specialization more sensitive to individual psychological temperament.

Internal Perception of Success

Professor Stark suggests that for enthusiasm to remain high, new religious movements "need to perceive serious success within the lifetime of the first generation." Most members of ISKCON do perceive the movement as having achieved considerable success in less than a generation. Many scholars have commented on Prabhupada's remarkable early success in attracting thousands of young Westerners to the intensive practice of an authentic Hindu religious tradition (for example, Hopkins and Basham in Gelberg, 1983). Within little more than a decade, devotees were able to perceive substantial progress: centers had been opened in more than one hundred major cities throughout the world; over 100 million books and magazines in numerous languages had been distributed; many farm communities and children's schools had been founded and were thriving; large impressive centers had been constructed in important cities and religious sites of India and a strong indigenous following attracted; there had been significant artistic and intellectual achievements; and "Hare Krishna" had become a household mantra. The imposition of negative stigma by the mid-to-late seventies did little to detract from internal perceptions of institutional success.

Network Ties

For ISKCON, one source of institutional cohesion is its communal life-style with its "dense network of internal attachments" that create bonds between individual members and the organization. In spite of ISKCON's theological emphasis on what Shinn (1985) calls the "vertical communitas" of the guru-disciple relationship, the "horizontal communitas" of disciple-to-disciple social bonding does play a major role in maintaining commitment to the movement, and conversely the lack of it tends to subvert commitment.

However, Stark makes the point that some religious movements with these kinds of strong internal social networks suffer from social exclusivity in that they lack social ties to the outside world. "In the absence of such attachments," he writes, "a movement will be unable to make converts, for it is through attachments that people are recruited to movements." True, core members of ISKCON follow a somewhat cloistered, monastic life-style, maintaining few ongoing social relationships with nondevotees (outside of family), and so the movement has tended to attract mainly "social isolates." This is changing, however. The need for broad social network ties conducive to recruitment is beginning to be fulfilled by a growing lay membership.

In the early years of the movement, most devotees assumed that to practice Krishna Consciousness one necessarily had to cut all ties with the secular world and live a communal, monastic life. This idea derived less, perhaps, from the Hindu scriptures (the *Bhagavad-gita* preaches, in part, an ethic of detached involvement in the world) than from the hippie "dropout" ideology. The recruitment policy engendered by that idea encouraged outsiders to establish intense commitment (as ashram dwellers) as soon as possible rather than allowing commitment to ripen more gradually within familiar social surroundings. This policy tended to abort potential linkage between *emergent* and *potential* recruits and the obvious advantages of recruitment through friend and relative networks.

But as the pool of socially disenfranchised youth began to evaporate, and as the movement increasingly began to attract people unwilling to accept the rigors of asceticism and the demands of ashram life (and also as many core members began to move towards lower stages of institutional commitment[5]), the emphasis on rapid commitment building and the almost exclusive emphasis on the ascetic, world-renouncing model of commitment began to undergo a significant change. Devotees began to acknowledge and then even to encourage the notion of a Krishna Consciousness lay movement. The organic, grass-roots evolution of an informal lay community was in full swing by the late seventies and formalized in some locations with programs such as F.O.L.K. ("Friends of Lord Krishna"). One survey (Gallup, 1978) indicated that one percent of U.S. teenagers (or roughly one-half million) were "involved with the Hare Krishna group," a figure

---

[5]Like all new religious movements before it, ISKCON has suffered to some extent from what James Richardson calls the "domestication effect": long-committed members marry and raise families (sometimes obtaining outside employment) and in the process become somewhat secularized. As concerns for family, economic, and career security increase, the secularizing member becomes less willing to sacrifice on behalf of the movement and, to use ISKCON lingo, "fringes out." It might be said that the early stage of laity formation in ISKCON began not predominantly with outsiders moving upward toward increasing commitment, but with insiders moving downward toward slackened commitment. Although these two types of members may meet in some hypothetical center of the commitment-noncommitment continuum, those moving downward from higher commitment tend to carry a stigma in the eyes of more seriously committed members.

more than one hundred times the actual core membership of the movement in the United States.[6] The publication of that survey (along with the knowledge that most lay members are not teens but older youth) awakened many in ISKCON to the fact that the movement's influence had spread far beyond its own institutional borders. There is every indication that this informal lay movement will continue to expand into the future, with benefits accruing to ISKCON in terms of increasing recruitment (both high and low level) through friend-and-relative social networks.

Along with the development of intentional differential recruitment, the very concept of membership in ISKCON may undergo significant change over time. The movement will need to more clearly and systematically address certain classic issues concerning the appropriate social and bureaucratic interrelationship between clergy and laity, the distinction between the two in terms of possible spiritual attainment, and the ultimate religious role of the movement in the world—whether or not, for example, the movement's traditional minimal rules of moral/spiritual discipline observed by initiates will come to be redefined as a specialist regimen rather than one of potentially universal relevance, and the movement itself as an elite core of ascetics rather than a practical and all-encompassing model for spiritual life. These issues will call for sophisticated theological reflection—and the implementation of pragmatic policies—by ISKCON leaders.

INTERNAL CRITERIA FOR SUCCESS

Most of Stark's essay discusses factors that he feels contribute to the success or failure of new religious movements, but only a few lines are devoted to the question of what success *is,* what it really *means.* He briefly defines success as "the degree to which a religious movement is able to dominate one or more societies,"—his emphasis throughout the rest of the essay being on institutional growth, particularly in terms of "absolute numbers" of members. This approach to the question of success reveals a quantitative bias that underlies the entire conceptualization of his criteria. Growth in "absolute numbers," or in terms of public influence or institutional longevity, may or may not be the same as meeting

---

[6]Obviously, the respondents were not involved as core members residing in ISK-CON centers but as outside practitioners or sympathizers. Even before a movement-wide rule was instituted (around the mid-70s) that people under the age of eighteen could not reside in ISKCON centers without parental permission, relatively few younger teenagers joined the movement. This particular survey was designed to test interest and involvement in new religious trends among teenagers thirteen to eighteen years old. Even if only one in ten of the respondents who indicated involvement in ISKCON actually were involved, the number is still highly significant.

a movement's substantive spiritual aims and expectations. There are Christians who have argued that if strict discipleship to Christ (with all its implications for self-denying commitment) or depth of Christian holiness were taken seriously as criteria, Christianity might be judged a colossal failure. As Professor Wilson asks in his essay, "What shall it profit a religious movement if it 'shall gain the whole world and lose [its] own soul'?"

There certainly are no universally agreed upon criteria for measuring success and failure in new religious movements, as the diversity of opinion in this volume attests. To look to criteria other than quantitative growth and longevity, therefore, is not an exercise in hairsplitting as Stark argues, but an acknowledgement of the fact that some religious movements do emphasize nonquantitative measures of institutional success—not necessarily as strategies for the rationalization of quantitative failure, but as expressions of fundamental theological conviction. One must take seriously a movement's internal perspective of success and failure, at least inasmuch as such internal views do affect institutional decision-making and development. It is my task, now, to bring this issue to light with regard to ISKCON.

To be sure, there have always been Caitanyite Vaishnavas in India who have defined their tradition in broad, expansionist terms. One important Caitanyite saint and reformer of the late nineteenth century, Bhaktivinoda Thakur, wrote longingly of a future in which fair-skinned foreigners would chant in ecstasy, with drums and cymbals, through the streets of Western cities and towns.[7] In Prabhupada's writings also, one finds expression of hope, and occasionally conviction, that the Krishna Consciousness movement will spread throughout the world or at least exert wide influence. Citing Sri Caitanya's declaration, "My name shall be heard in every town and village." Prabhupada exhorts devotees to "spread Lord Caitanya's message all over the world" (Prabhupada, 1975a:188). If the movement can distribute huge quantities of

---

[7]"Lord Caitanya did not advent Himself to liberate only a few men in India. Rather, His main objective was to emancipate all living entities of all countries throughout the entire universe and preach the Eternal Religion. Lord Caitanya says in the *Caitanya-bhagavata:* 'In every town, country, and village, My name will be sung.' There is no doubt that this unquestionable order will come to pass. . . . Very soon the unparalleled path of *hari-nama-sankirtana* will be propagated all over the world. . . . Oh, for that day when the fortunate English, French, Russian, German and American people will take up banners, mrdangas and karatals and raise kirtana through their streets and towns. When will that day come? Oh, for the day when the fair-skinned men from their side will raise up the chanting of *jaya sacinandana, jaya sacinandana ki jaya* [All Glories to Lord Caitanya! All Glories to Lord Caitanya!] and join with the Bengali devotees. When will that day be?" (Swami, 1974:6-7).

its books and magazines throughout the world, "we will have a great effect on the mass population of Europe and America. If we can get the masses in the Western countries like Europe and America to become Krishna conscious, then all the rest of the world will follow" (Goswami, 1982:102). If book distribution is managed properly, and if the devotees are spiritually strong, "the whole world will become Krishna conscious" (Goswami, 1982:105).

In addition to these kinds of statements and claims, there are, however, many others that clearly indicate a more qualitative (and modest) conception of movement success. These more qualitative expressions cannot be easily dismissed as mere rhetoric adopted to de-emphasize growth and conversion—ad hoc strategies to rationalize failure. They were spoken or written not during periods of institutional decline, but throughout all stages of movement development and, moreover, are expressive of primary doctrine.

Before beginning his mission, Prabhupada's hopes were high but his expectations modest. Upon his arrival in the United States from India in 1965, he wrote a poem in Bengali in which he expressed some doubt whether Westerners would even understand the teachings of Krishna Consciousness and whether he himself would be able to convince them of its truth (Goswami, 1980:5-6). Years later, in a 1975 letter to a disciple, he explained that before coming to America he "never imagined that even one person would accept" his strict prohibitions against meat-eating, intoxication, gambling, and illicit sex (Goswami, 1983a:72).

When speaking about the development of his movement, Prabhupada often affirmed that he was more interested in having a few sincere disciples than in achieving mass popularity. While expressing concern that his disciples should develop philosophical and spiritual depth, Prabhupada asked, "What good are many, many disciples if none of them are knowledgeable?"[8] In a 1975 lecture to disciples in Berkeley, Prabhupada expressed a favorite theme: he would have been satisfied with having only one sincere disciple. Criticizing charlatan gurus who accept large followings of nominally committed, undisciplined disciples he said:

If I say that you can do all nonsense, simply take this mantra and give me $125, [people will become attracted]. So I would have collected millions of

---

[8]"It is better to maintain a devotee [in serious commitment] than to try to convince others to become a devotee. Your first job should be to make sure that every one of the devotees in your zone of management is reading regularly our literatures and discussing the subject matter seriously from different angles of vision and see that they're somehow or other absorbing the knowledge of Krishna conscious philosophy. What good are many, many devotees if none of them is knowledgeable?" (Goswami, 1983a:62).

dollars if I would have cheated like that. But I do not want that. I want one student who follows my instructions. I don't want millions. . . . If there is one moon in the sky, that is sufficient for illumination. There is no need of millions of stars. My position is that I want to see that at least one disciple has become a pure devotee. Of course, I have got many sincere and pure devotees. That is my good luck. But I would have been satisfied if I could find out only one. (Goswami, 1983b:94-95)

During a stroll along Commonwealth Pier in Boston in May of 1968, one disciple asked Prabhupada, "What if people don't want to hear our message?" Prabhupada replied:

The people might not understand our message, but Krishna will be pleased. And that is our mission. . . . We must not be disappointed that no one is hearing Krishna Consciousness. We will say it to the moon and stars and all directions. We will cry in the wilderness, because Krishna is everywhere. We want to get [recognition] from Krishna that, "This man has done something for Me." Not popularity. If a pack of asses says you are good, what is that? (Goswami, 1981:64)

Why then the apparently conflicting internal attitudes towards success? ISKCON, like almost any religious institution, declares universal acceptance of its teachings and principles as an institutional goal. But making lofty statements of ultimate aims is one thing, and pragmatic assessment of present reality is quite another. The eschatological formulations of scripture may hold out promises of universal salvation, and movement pioneers, emboldened by initial rapid growth, may articulate ecstatic visions of missionary triumph, but these expectations cannot be pinned down as specific institutional goals in the ordinary sense, and their nonfulfillment does not put vital missionary enterprises out of business.

Since the very beginning of ISKCON in America, Prabhupada and his disciples have defined "spreading Krishna Consciousness" as something which, on one level, happens subtly and very gradually. Success is measured not only in terms of numbers of newly shorn recruits but in terms of effecting a gradual "purification" of the material world. Public chanting (*nama-sankirtana*), for example, has never been viewed as a recruitment tactic *per se* but as a means to expose large numbers of people to the sacred sound of the Hare Krishna mantra, consisting of "holy names of God" that, according to Vaishnava theology, have immense, spiritual purificatory power. So powerful is the name of Krishna, according to Prabhupada, that even a hostile newspaper report on ISKCON benefited readers spiritually because it contained numerous references to the "Hare Kirshnas."

There are other subtle effects as well. Anyone who partakes of ritually sanctified food (*prasadam*) at ISKCON temples or festivals obtains tangible spiritual blessings. Those receiving a copy of one of the sacred texts ISK-CON disseminates benefit simply from *touching* the book, even if they do not actually read it. Anyone even unknowingly donating funds or services to ISKCON—or one who merely has a positive thought of the movement—benefits from such pious acts performed unconsciously or circumstantially (*ajñāta sukrti*). The benefits of such pious acts accumulate life after life and entitle one eventually to come to Krishna Consciousness. The success of ISKCON's spiritual mission is calculated, therefore, in other than tangible, immediate, and quantitative terms.

Quite apart from the impact of internal and external social dynamics on institutional success, a movement's theology can play a key role in attracting new members and deepening commitment. Along these lines Professor Stark suggests in the latter part of his essay (hesitatingly, he admits) that his model may need "greater development in terms of ideological or theological elements." He suggests we need to "confront the possibility that some theologies are inherently more plausible, some are more easily and effectively communicated, some are more able to satisfy deeply felt needs of large numbers of people, indeed, some probably are inherently more interesting, even exciting, than others."

Stark makes an important point here. As an insider, I would argue that part of the appeal that Krishna Consciousness has always had (and will continue to have) is precisely the kind of theological allure Stark refers to. Vaisnava-Hindu theology appeals to many as plausible, for example, in its clear distinction between the spiritual self (*atma*) and the material body, the primacy of consciousness over matter, the personhood of God, its ethic of nonviolence and vegetarianism, and its elaborate critique of life in the material world. As for communicability, in his writings Prabhupada has conveyed Vaisnava thought in simple, direct prose, intuitively deep yet unencumbered by abstruse intellectual nuance. Vaisnava theology is inherently interesting (even "exciting") in that it encompasses and explores in great depth every theological and philosophical category. Its cosmology is teeming with demigods, demons, divine incarnations, heroes, heroines, and saints—inhabiting infinitely variegated worlds. Compared with the "stupendous and cosmogonal philosophy of the *Bhagavad-gita*," exults Thoreau in *Walden*," "the modern world and its literature seem puny and trivial" (Thoreau, 1960:198). Finally, the theology of *bhakti*, theistic devotion, has for centuries given solace and joy to millions of Hindus because it speaks of a personal and loving Deity who is, indeed, vivid and close at hand, who compassionately appears to be faithful in a multitude of divine forms, who asks only for simple, spontaneous devotion (Hopkins in Gelberg 1983:115-16)—a God with a radiant transcendental form with eyes like lotus petals, skin the bluish-gray color of autumn rainclouds, who plays a divine flute beckoning all animate and inanimate beings. There is certainly nothing vague or remote about Lord Krishna, so it is not difficult to understand His attractiveness to seekers bored by an Occidental God made distant by Scientism, this-worldly humanistic piety and theological cerebration.[9]

For an insider, individual or personal success is conceived most fundamentally in explicitly spiritual terms: the progressive and ultimate attainment of "Krishna Consciousness," a state of perpetual, direct, profound loving apprehension of God. This state is attained, gradually, through adherence to the principles and practices of bhakti-yoga, a spiritual path delineated in venerable ancient and medieval Vaisnava scriptures. In one very important sense, then, ISKCON's ultimate strength lies in the possibility of its members conforming to this time-tested spiritual path and contacting a powerful, transforming experience of the sacred. To speak in these terms is not to deny the value of sociological perspectives on conversion and commitment, but to point out that we ignore the role of felt, intuitive experience at our peril.

Some scholars, including Bryan Wilson in this volume, assert that it is difficult to rate religious success or failure because "what religions promise [in experiential or salvific terms] is incapable of empirical verification." Of course, spiritual states of consciousness do not easily lend themselves to social-scientific measurement, but there are "internal" means of assessing spiritual progress. Religious texts have been quite graphic in their description of ultimate spiritual states, as well as various progressive stages along the way. There are medieval Sanskrit texts that report on the varieties of Vaisnava mystical experience with the analytical rigor of a laboratory manual. These kinds of texts provide rather specific criteria by which the adept can monitor his or her progress.

Larry Shinn has pointed out that during his study of Krishna devotees he encountered many instances of what he called "genuine religious searching" as well as "the experience of a relationship with a sacred power" (Shinn, 1983:133-34). If we are to take at all seriously the notion of "genuine religious searching" and the possibility of "a relationship with a sacred power," then we must acknowledge that one factor determining whether ISKCON will be successful in recruiting new members is the degree to which it continues to embody and transmit "sacred power." The entire spiritual tradition sustaining Krishna Consciousness asserts that orthopraxis (correct practice) leads to heightened awareness of divine reality and offers a rather clear set of cri-

---

[9]This may help scholars (like Indologist J. F. Staal [in Prabhupada, 1977b:90-93]) who find it puzzling that people dissatisfied with Western monotheism should turn to an Indian theology that is monotheistic and devotional rather than to one that is impersonalistic.

teria for the "measurement" of that higher state. If orthopraxis is preserved and is evidenced through felt transformation of consciousness, member commitment will remain high, and sincere spiritual seekers will continue to be attracted to the movement.[10] If, however, attention to practice weakens, along with a diminution of religious enthusiasm, if there come to be fewer living models of sanctity within the movement, if instrumentalism andd organizational maintenance come to supersede personal holiness as the predominant internal value of the movement, ISKCON will wither and cease to meet its own basic goals.

If the movement is to prosper, it must have spiritual depth. There is a perennial danger that pragmatic, instrumentalist concerns may detract from the quality of spiritual training (what Catholic writers call "formation") of members. For instance, in spite of the fact that all full-time ISKCON members attend at least one scripture class daily, there remains a lack of structured, systematic religious education, the result being that some members tend to pick up the teachings of Krishna Consciousness in a somewhat haphazard and superficial manner. Prabhupada strongly emphasized the importance of scripture study and theological reflection.[11] Yet, many ISKCON members fail to penetrate the depth of their Vaishnava heritage and to explore and be transformed by the profundity and richness of the scriptural and literary foundation of that tradition. Although they may be dedicated and hardworking members of the community, these devotees fail to become impressive embodiments, much less credible communicators, of their own tradition. This is not an appeal for a dry scholasticism (in *bhakti*, piety is more important than punditry) but rather for the spirituality that flows from a deeper absorp-

---

[10]"Our Krishna Consciousness is meant for this purpose: we want to create pure devotees so that other people will benefit by their association. In this way the number of pure devotees increases. Professional preachers cannot create pure devotees. . . . To make a show of devotional service will not help one. One must be a pure devotee following the pure devotional process; then one can convert others to devotional service. . . . Otherwise his preaching will have no effect." (Prabhupada, 1975b:132-33).

[11]"I am very much stressing . . . that all of my students shall be very much conversant with the philosophy of Krishna Consciousness, and that they should read our books very diligently at least one or two hours daily and try to understand the subject matter from varieties of angles. . . . [We should] discuss the subject matter very minutely and inspect it from all angles of approach and savor the new understandings. . . . [I]f the students get knowledge more and more, they will automatically become convinced and very easily perform their duties for tapasya or renunciation of the material bondage, that will be their successful advancement in Krishna Consciousness." (Goswami, 1983a:61-62).

tion in spiritual practices. There is similar laxity in the manner in which some devotees approach basic spiritual practices, such as individual contemplative chanting. The path of *bhakti* calls for much more than mere attendance in routinized devotional and ritual activity—it demands a patient, deliberate cultivation of interior, and active, devotion.

Lack of sufficient attention to basic spiritual formation has sometimes led to weak and uncommitted—and thus transitory—membership. In spite of some initial show of enthusiasm and commitment, in the long run insufficiently "formed" members fall away, unable to surmount personal (or institutional) crises when they come. The historian of religion Thomas J. Hopkins has explained that one of the principal strengths of the Vaisnava *bhakti* tradition has been its healthy balance between the practical (instrumental), intellectual, and devotional aspects of the religious life, and he warns that religious movements failing to achieve a good balance between these three elements lose their transformative impact and vitality (Hopkins in Gelberg, 1983:138-39).

One other major criterion for institutional success should be noted, and that is the quality and solidarity of administrative and spiritual leadership, especially after the death of a movement's founder. Elsewhere (Gelberg, 1985) I've described the factors that contributed to the relatively smooth transmission of authority in ISKCON from Prabhupada to his successors. For Prabhupada, the continued success of his movement rested on the hope that his leading disciples would cooperate to maintain institutional solidarity after his passing. Having witnessed how the religious institution founded in India by his own spiritual master (the Gaudiya Math) had quickly disintegrated for lack of unitive governance after the master died, Prabhupada had resolved that ISKCON should not suffer the same lamentable fate. Back in 1970, he established the GBC (Governing Body Commission) to oversee the spiritual and institutional development of the movement. By the time of his passing away in 1977, the GBC had been trained as a semiautonomous administrative body, meeting annually to formulate policy under Prabhupada's direction and each member being responsible for supervising ISKCON centers in separate geographical regions throughout the world. Thus, Prabhupada's departure did not create a power vacuum, and authority was transferred to a new generation of leaders. For Prabhupada, the continued success of his movement rested on institutional solidarity based on the intercooperation of his leaders. He was quite firm on this point: "If you love me you will not fight. Stay united. Don't let this become another Gaudiya Math. Maintain the Society in my absence. Do not let it deteriorate" (Goswami, 1982:108).

A major question for the future of ISKCON, then, is whether its current leaders will remain united, inspired by personal loyalty to the memory of their spiritual master and to his vision of a worldwide Krishna Consciousness movement. Another important question still to be answered is whether strong loyalty to Prabhupada will continue to be a unifying factor when the first generation of members—direct disciples of Prabhupada—are no longer present. Should the memory—indeed, the perceived living presence—of Prabhupada not be kept in the forefront of member consciousness, there may be little to save ISKCON from gradually transforming into a tenuous federation of submovements defined by distinct guru-allegiances or worse, from fracturing into separate, schismatic movements.

Prabhupada held his leaders responsible not only for preserving political cohesion, but for maintaining a high standard of spiritual practice in the movement—a standard they were enjoined to diligently follow themselves. He requested his leaders to travel from center to center to see that the basic religious practices he had instituted were being strictly adhered to and, if not, to rectify discrepancies (Goswami, 1983a:xviii-xix). He insisted that the movement would survive and prosper only to the extent that the leaders set a high personal example of spiritual and moral integrity.[12] Especially in a movement like ISKCON where leaders, both spiritual and administrative, are reverenced, the exposing of moral improprieties on the part of leaders (which has happened from time to time) has tended to damage the faith and commitment of rank-and-file members and to generate cynicism. Also Prabhupada felt that effective administration of the movement would derive more from spiritual strength and purity than from bureaucratic professionalism. When presented with the minutes of one early GBC meeting that included elaborate plans for bureaucratic and economic reorganization of ISKCON, Prabhupada became irate and scolded, "Your material formulas will not help. We must become made after Krishna!" (interview with GBC member).

A new kind of challenge to the quality of leadership in ISKCON derives from the inherent dangers that come with the elevation of some leaders to the role of guru. In the Vaisnava system the guru, by the very nature of his role, commands a very high degree of submission and reverence from his disciples. Power and status can certainly corrupt a spiritually immature guru, and what may start out as a healthy and progressive guru-disciple bond can lead to self-aggrandizement, misguidance, and manipulation. The most serious internal problem ISKCON has had to face in the early 1980s is the abuse of authority by, and the moral misconduct of, a number of its gurus (thus far,

---

[12]"The movement will go on increasing more and more, provided the leaders of the movement remain firmly Krishna conscious by following the regulative principles and the primary activities of chanting the Hare Krishna mantra regularly." (Prabhupada, 1977a:146). "The GBC should personally observe strictly all the rules and regulations and it should become the practical example to others. Then everything will be all right. Then there will be no fear of being victimized by maya [illusion]." (Goswami, 1983a:xviii)

five of the eleven named by Prabhupada) with the resultant emotionally painful disillusionment of their many disciples, some of whom have left the movement. The disgrace of formerly highly respected leaders has engendered wide debate and dissent among devotees in the movement, and set into motion a powerful and increasingly influential movement for reform. The continued existence of ISKCON—at least as a unified international organization—will depend in large part on the success of such reformist efforts, and on the emergence of leaders of high moral and spiritual character capable of inspiring faith. Of those among Prabhupada's disciples who have remained in ISKCON through difficulties, many have done so not chiefly out of loyalty to the current ISKCON leadership, but rather out of spiritual loyalty to Prabhupada, whose sacred mission and movement they feel is important enough to redeem and renew. The continued health of the movement will depend to a large extent on the spiritual genuineness of its gurus, and their willingness to exalt Srila Prabhupada as the preceptorial centerpiece of the movement. ISKCON will remain a vital spiritual and social movement to the extent that it is guided by genuinely charismatic (that is, spiritually gifted, ''Krishna-conscious'') leaders. Such leaders strengthen the movement both through the force of their personal piety and by the vision they can bring to the practical management of the movement. Charisma in leadership must not be merely of the ''transferred'' variety—the charisma of designation or of office—but ''personal'' charisma, generated through tangible connection with the sacred. The movement's success will depend on its capacity for producing authentically charismatic persons as well as its capacity for acknowledging them. There is always a danger that the bureaucratization of authority may preclude recognition of genuinely charismatic souls.

In the higher echelons of ISKCON leadership, one does find (besides a few prosaic types) some individuals of uncommon talent: powerful intellects, gifted orators, brilliant administrators, and a few saints. These individuals generally had the opportunity to associate closely with Prabhupada, learn from him at close range, and absorb and internalize his aura of devotion and heroic self-sacrifice. Some are not mere reflections of charisma, however, but people of genuine personal holiness. Without such individuals, it is hard to imagine ISKCON continuing to exist as a vital spiritual enterprise, easy to imagine it dissolving into an effete ecclesiasticism. Devotion cannot be taught in the abstract—*there must be devoted people*. The life of ISKCON, or of any religious movement, is those in whom the movement's cherished principles and message are embodied—those who are living examples of what scripture and tradition preach. Without them, perfection becomes mere doctrine, salvation a metaphor, and ecstasy mere sentimentality.

There are other important issues relevant to the future of ISKCON that I would have liked to explore in this essay but cannot for lack of space. One concerns how the movement might in the future come to deal with internal dissent and redress of grievances (at present the groundwork is being laid for a full-scale judicial system within ISKCON). Another concerns the attempt of academically trained movement intellectuals to bring the Indian Vaisnava tradition—and ISKCON itself—into active encounter and dialogue with the Western intellectual and religious community.[13]

Another issue that needs further exploration is the evolution of ISKCON as a communal, social organization *per se,* apart from its purely religious and missionary functions. In the future, the movement will need to devote more systematic attention to, and develop more well-defined policies concerning, the practical issues of child rearing and education, marriage, the role of women, the care of older members, and so on. One of the challenges facing ISKCON in the future is the task of completing the transplantation of an ancient religious culture—with all its implications for social life—to the contemporary West.

In conclusion, ISKCON will be with us for many years to come. In time, the movement will achieve a certain measure of acceptability as other high-tension religious movements have done throughout history. The question, though, is whether ISKCON will emerge as simply another quaint addition to the luxuriant American religious landscape, or will it be able to contribute to a genuine spiritual reformation in Western society. The future beckons.

REFERENCES

Brahmananda, Swami
    1974   "How the Teachings of Lord Caitanya Came to the Western World" (Part 2). *Back to Godhead,* No. 68.

Cox, Harvey
    1977   "Playing the Devil's Advocate, as It Were." *New York Times,* 16 February 1977.

Deadwyler, William
    1984   "The Devotee and the Deity: Living a Personalistic Theology," in Joanne Waghorne and Norman Cutler, eds., *Gods of Flesh/Gods of Stone: The Embodiment of Divinity in India.* Chambersburg PA: Anima Press.

    1985   "The Scholarly Tradition in Caitanyite Vaishnavism: India and Amer-

---

[13]See, e.g., Gelberg, 1980, 1983, 1986: Deadwyler, 1984, 1985.

Graham Schweig, an ISKCON member now working on a doctoral dissertation at Harvard Divinity School, founded (in 1980) the Institute for Viasnava Studies, which brings together devotees and scholars involved in the study of the Vaisnava traditions of India. The author of this paper edits *ISKCON Review,* an annual, interdisciplinary journal devoted to the academic study of ISKCON, publishing articles both by "insiders" and "outsiders." A third issue is in preparation now.

ica." *ISKCON Review* 1.1(Spring): 15-23.

Dimock, Edward C.
1972   Foreword to *Bhagavad-gita as It Is* (Complete Edition), by A. C. Bhaktivedanta Swami Prabhupada. New York: Macmillan.

Gallup, George
1978   "New Religious Movements Popular," *Los Angeles Times* 13 September 1978.

Gelberg, Steven L.
1980   "Is the Krishna Consciousness Movement 'Hindu'?" Paper presented to the annual meeting of the Australian Association for the Study of Religions, Canberra.

1983   *Hare Krishna, Hare Krishna: Five Distinguished Scholars on the Krishna Movement in the West*. New York: Grove Press.

1985   "ISKCON After Prabhupada: An Update on the Hare Krishna Movement." *ISKCON Review* 1:1 (Spring): 7-14.

1986   "The Catholic Church and the Hare Krishna Movement: An Invitation to Dialogue." *ISKCON Review* 2:1 (Fall).

Goswami, Satsvarupa dasa
1981   *Prabhupāda-līlā: Chapter Four*. Port Royal PA: Gita-nagari Press.

1982   *"Distribute Books, Distribute Books, Distribute Books": A History of Book Distribution in ISKCON 1970-1975*. Port Royal PA: Gita-nagari Press.

1983a   *Vaiṣṇava Behavior*. Port Royal PA: Gita-nagari Press.

1983b   *Śrīla Prabhupāda-līlāmṛta*, Vol. 6. Los Angeles: Bhaktivedanta Book Trust.

Judah, J. Stillson
1974   *Hare Krishna and the Counterculture*. New York: John Wiley & Sons.

Prabhupada, A. C. Bhaktivedanta Swami
1975a   *Śrī Caitanya-caritāmṛta*, Madhya-līlā, Vol. 6. Los Angeles: Bhaktivedanta Book Trust.

1975b   *Śrī Caitanya-caritāmṛta*, Madhya-līlā, Vol. 9. Los Angeles: Bhaktivedanta Book Trust.

1977a   *Śrīmad-Bhāgavatam*, Canto 10, Vol. 1. Los Angeles: Bhaktivedanta Book Trust.

1977b   *The Science of Self-Realization*. Los Angeles: Bhaktivedanta Book Trust.

Shinn, Larry D.
1983   "The Many Faces of Krishna," in Joseph H. Fichter, ed., *Alternatives to American Mainline Churches*. New York: Rose of Sharon Press.

1985   "Conflicting Networks: Guru and Friend in ISKCON," in Rodney Stark, ed., *Religious Movements: Genesis, Exodus and Numbers*. New York: Rose of Sharon Press.

Thoreau, Henry David.
1960   *Walden and Civil Disobedience*. New York: New American Library.

Wilson, Bryan
   1982   *Religion in Sociological Perspective.* Oxford: Oxford University Press.

CHAPTER FOURTEEN

Reflections on the Scholarly Study of New Religious Movements

David G. Bromley
Jeffrey K. Hadden
Phillip E. Hammond

New religious movements (NRMs), often referred to as cults, are, generally speaking, unpopular—not just in the United States, but elsewhere as well. They have thus given rise to anticult activity (see chapter 15 below), including legislative initiatives, criminal charges, and public harrassment. This societal hostility has been directed not only at new religious movements, however, but also at scholarly efforts to study and understand them. The authors represented in this volume know something of what the first pathologists to study diseased corpses must have felt: the firsthand study of condemned objects is itself condemned by some. At the very least, this prompts reflections by the investigators of the investigative process, and we want to share several of these reflections.

Of course, the new religions are not condemned by everyone, least of all their members. But even among the latter, social science investigations may be suspect, especially when they purport to tell (predict?) what these movements are going to do. As one thoughtful member said to us, "We tend to conceive of our movements more in theological than in sociological terms—as creations of Divine Will or important chapters in salvation history." Given this point of view, therefore, how can any social scientific analysis merit respect? "We would be naive not to recognize," continues our informant "that we are not merely in the world, but 'of it' as well. We come into movements wherein horizontal relationships with other devotees impinge on our consciousness with at least equal force with the vertical relationship with God."

Such forthrightness seems to us valuable, an exercise in reflection we ourselves might undertake. After all, here we are claiming to tell the future of NRMs. Knowing that anticultists oppose our efforts, and knowing that cult members themselves are ambivalent about being studied, the scholarly student of new religious movements is made rather self-conscious.

1. A first self-consciousness is to admit that any discussion of success or failure in a religious movement is an act of supererogation. An organization's health can be assessed, perhaps, but whether organizational health constitutes religious success is a different question. This point has been made elsewhere in this volume, especially by Byran Wilson in Chapter Two, but it bears reiteration.

2. A second self-consciousness is to be sensitive to the demonic as well as the angelic in religious movements. The analogy is the limitation on so-called privileged communication as found in medicine, law, and ministry. Surely nobody doubts the right and obligation of professionals in these fields to know intimate details of clients' lives, but just as surely, such knowledge should be accompanied by intervention if life and health are endangered. To say this, however, is to provide very little indeed in the way of counsel. For someone to threaten antisocial action (''You'll pay for this; somehow I'll get even!'') is a common enough occurrence—even in humdrum daily life. If every such revealing encounter led to interventionist tactics, society would come close to shutting down altogether.

Surely, however, scholars with intimate knowledge of the bizarre, the irrational, the borderline crazy should drop their shield of neutrality and sound the alarm. True enough. But this is easier to advise than to execute. Even in the case of the mass suicide of 913 People's Temple members in Guyana, who was in the position to warn society? The public, including scholars, largely ignored the People's Temple until the tragedy took place. Certainly, Jim Jones—an ordained clergyman in a mainstream denomination, accomplishing something desired by many of his counterparts by developing an interacial congregation and getting the ear of politicians—aroused little curiosity until just prior to the migration to Guyana. Many members had ''inside'' knowledge and might have blown the whistle, but, generally, they appear not to have recognized its significance. The People's Temple was not even considered a ''cult'' until after the suicides. Granted, the Jonestown massacre is a limiting case—the carnage was very high while the prognosis was not particularly unusual—but it nonetheless illustrates a more general point, which becomes our third reflection.

3. Science, including social science, is woefully misunderstood if its goal is thought to be prediction. It is true that prediction, derived from theoretical principles, permits the most stringent test of those principles. The prediction is made, time passes, and events then occur that confirm, disconfirm, or sug-

gest revision of the principles. But throughout this process, understanding the theoretical principles is the goal. Not prediction, then, but understanding is what scientific work is all about.

Actually, social science understands a great deal about social life and on that basis is able to predict enormous amounts of behavior with remarkable accuracy. These predictions, however, can be made and are made by just about any socialized human being, with or without an understanding of the theoretical principles they derive from. Thus, we all predict that oncoming traffic will stay on its side of the road; that mail deposited in a post office will get delivered; that the store clerk will return our change along with our purchase; and so forth. But these are all trivial as stated, true as they may be. What we want to know is how to anticipate the drunk driver, the wayward letter, and the dishonest clerk.

However, such specificity of prediction may be impossible or, at least, cost too much in money, time, and human freedom. And when it is not just an individual's actions that concern us but a whole complex of interrelated actions by many persons, then prediction becomes even more unlikely. Often overlooked in this issue, however, is that all scientific predictions are conditional; that is, *if* certain conditions are met, *then* a certain event will occur. In much of the physical world, these conditions can be manipulated or at least known, but in much of the social world, they cannot—because to do so is immoral, illegal, and/or simply beyond human capacity. Thus, ''prediction'' in social science tends to be far less satisfactory—*on those questions people would ask of it*—than ''prediction'' in those sciences dealing with the nonsocial world. To put it another way, social engineering is harder to achieve than physical engineering.

Such an admission does not mean that the social sciences trail in their capacity to ''understand,'' however. As unsatisfying as it may be to those who would intervene if they ''knew'' in advance what would happen, the fact is that social science is quite good at explaining after the fact. Thus, how wars came to be fought, how depressions came to be experienced, or how divorce rates came to increase are all understandable after they have occurred. But it may be totally unrealistic to expect the social scientist to *predict* such things. Someone close to international government, to the money market, or to the family counseling scene may have a greater capacity to predict trends. Oddly enough, such insiders, unless they also understand the underlying theoretical principles, will not know after the fact *why* their predictions were correct. Despite his lesser record as a seer, then, the social scientist will excel at explaining what *did* happen. An analogy can be seen in predicting and explaining the dropping of an apple from the tree. The experienced farmer will have a better *prediction* of when a particular apple *will* drop, but a botanist will have a better *explanation* for why the apple *did* drop.

4. A fourth reflection brought on by the self-consciousness that comes from studying new religious movements has to do with the *effects* of such study. What are the implications for social scientists of getting close to NRMs in the course of conducting their research? One major issue of contention has been that individual social scientists, by attending various functions sponsored by NRMs, have lent visibility and credibility to groups of questionable repute. That controversy has now been superseded, however, as behavioral scientists have expanded their activities. For example, in addition to attending conferences (at which they have comprised an audience and been presenters), individual behavioral scientists have authored articles in books published by movement-controlled presses, served as consultants to movements on various issues, served as expert witnesses in trials involving new religious groups or their members, and acted as lobbyists regarding legislation designed to regulate new religious groups.

Two observations need to be made about the involvement of social scientists in such activities. First, most scholars get close to new religious groups because they regard this contact as imperative if they are to understand them adequately. These groups typically are divided into numerous levels of organization, semiautonomous or even warring factions, and geographic units with distinctive histories and practices. They change rapidly and, public images of monolithic organization notwithstanding, they are characterized by a great deal of turmoil and conflict. Virtually the only way to understand one of these groups is to be quite close to it. Researchers find that, at least during the last decade when growth and change were extremely rapid, being out of touch with a movement for any extended period affected their access to informants and their understanding of organizational developments. Indeed, as our third reflection above suggests, the very sense of where these groups are headed can best be gained intuitively through sustained close contact.

Second, a number of social scientists appear to be closer to new religious groups than they really are. These individuals are monitoring and studying the conflict in which new religious groups are involved. As a result, they gather data from NRMs and their opponents as well. At least some of the research on the mental health of members—as well as on conversion, socialization, and defection—in reality is research on the conflict and probably would not have been conducted at all were it not for allegations about mind control and the deleterious mental health effects of belonging to a ''cult.'' Most of these social scientists have limited interest in particular NRMs and are not very close at all to them.

There is, finally, the question of what posture social scientists should assume as close contact with NRMs reveals their errors and excesses, on the one hand, and the prejudice and mistrust directed toward them, on the other hand. Intensive research on organizations will almost always unearth institutionalized arguments that violate the organization's professed goals and values. Research on new religious groups is no exception; a number of scholars have discovered and reported practices that, it seems clear, they find personally reprehensible. However, in many cases, scholars have concluded that whatever the sins of these groups, the blanket indictments and public fear of "cults" is hardly warranted. In the process of studying these groups, therefore, numerous scholars have ended up challenging anticult accusations. In some cases, this has involved "defending" new religious groups.

Nonetheless, most social scientists have defined for themselves the kinds of personal and professional commitments they have vis-à-vis new religious groups (for example, Barker, 1983; Wilson, 1983). There is, at least for some, a moral issue involved when they disagree with accusations made against new religious groups. As one sociologist put it

> As to becoming "spokespersons," even apologists, for these groups, I doubt if any of us are compelled at all, but I would say this: it is the social scientist's business to say what is so about society. Saying what is so may sometimes conflict with what perfectly virtuous and respectable persons and agencies believe to be so, and may sometimes accord with what persons and agencies who are not generally viewed as virtuous and respectable claim to be so. This does not make them spokespersons or apologists. It makes them responsible social scientists and citizens. Surely Horowitz would not prefer us to hold our peace when religious groups are attacked on what seem to those of us who make it our business to study them in depth—rather then relying upon the . . . newspapers or the hysterical commentary of parents, political or religious opponents and other interested parties for their information—very poor grounds indeed. (Wallis, 1983:218).

Probably at the very least, social scientists have an obligation to offer a fair interpretation of new religious groups to the world. Barker (1983:204) asserts that

> a necessary element in preserving one's integrity as a researcher, who has been granted access to an alternative perspective of reality, is to continue, in the face of negative pressures or "discouragement," to try to make it more understandable to others how it could make sense, for example, for Moonies to belong to the Unification Church, and to believe and act as they do.

5. Lying behind all of the above reflections, however, is a larger issue yet—a major disagreement regarding the proper interpretation of human behavior. We conclude this chapter, therefore, with some comments on what may prove to be an interpretive clash between sociology and psychology.

It would be an unwarranted oversimplification to assert that psychologically oriented behavioral scientists have lined up on one side of the conflict and their socially oriented colleagues on the other, because many representatives in each discipline have recognized the limitations of their own disciplinary perspective. Nevertheless, it is clear that scholars less critical of the new religious groups tend more often to be sociologists; those more critical, psychologists.

There are several reasons for this difference. First, sociologists are more likely to have employed a participant-observation methodology. This approach affords researchers a contextual understanding of behavioral patterns that, if examined out of context, might appear bizarre or irrational. Second, psychologists and psychiatrists have often worked with *former* members who are in the clinical throes of personal dislocation accompanying their major status change, and generalizing to an entire population from such a sample has long been viewed as problematic. It might be observed, however, that while psychologists are prone to exaggerate emotional problems by virtue of studying exceptional cases, sociologists may *underestimate* these problems since current members may be reluctant to discuss them. Third, there is a tendency among psychologists, particularly those who view personality as "fixed," to be very suspicious of sudden shifts in behavioral responses; sociologists, by contrast, are more likely to view such shifts as role changes rather than personality changes, and, thus, quite normal.

Opponents of new religious groups have overwhelmingly opted for the psychological interpretation of these groups, with its focus on the allegedly manipulative recruitment techniques and deleterious mental health consequences of membership. The major pillar on which the anticult movement's position rests is that individuals who are members of "cults" were subjected to some combination of deception and manipulation that reduced their autonomy and ability to make choices of their own "free will." Terms like "mind control" and "brainwashing" frequently are used to describe this process. Correspondingly, the anticult-proposed remedy for brainwashing has been deprogramming, a technique that presumes to strip away the cult-imposed personality and allow the reemergence of the individual's former fixed or "natural" personality. This interpretation involves a number of assumptions about both new religious groups and their members: that individuals are not independently motivated to join them; that there is a one-sided conversion process in which the group imposes a regimen upon members without their full knowledge or approval; that individuals are unable to assess and cope with their situation; and that the effects of membership in these groups is destructive of mental health.

This psychologically based interpretation of cults in many respects represents a frontal assault on the sociological perspective, for it begs the very questions sociologists regard as central to an understanding of new religious groups and their individual members. It ignores such issues as the role of sociocultural forces in the emergence of social movements; the interactional dimensions of affiliation and organizational participation; the role of subordinates in the creation and maintenance of charismatic authority; and the organization problems of social movements. In essence, the brainwashing perspective represents a return to pathology theory, traditionally a perspective portraying social movements as havens for those unable to cope with the rigors of conventional society. The anticult reformulation simply substitutes "manipulated" for "naturally occurring" helplessness. At base, there is a challenge to the more dynamic, interactive conceptions of individual and group structure that dominate current sociological thinking.

There is also, of course, a political component to this clash between the social and psychological sciences. The brainwashing ideology was constructed by partisans seeking to redress their grievances and gain allies to oppose new religious groups. The ideology has been used to neutralize sanctions that otherwise would be brought to bear against those employing extralegal tactics in the conflict. Thus, a sociological perspective obviously presents a distinct threat to the anticult-sponsored ideology, for sociological investigations of "cults" often challenge the strong negative stereotypes surrounding them.

Sociologists, moreover, generally reject "brainwashing" altogether as a scientific concept; even as a metaphor it appears to cloud more than it reveals. Research indicates that converts come into new religious groups by a variety of routes that simply cannot be understood until one jettisons the concept of brainwashing so central to anticult thought. Similarly, sociological investigations have established that there is a great deal of movement out of, as well as into, cults. The notion that cult leaders have hypnotic-like powers that can capture the mind and body does not stand up well to the evidence. Zealous recruiters, high-pressure tactics, and strong resistance to defection do not constitute brainwashing. There is also accumulating evidence that deprogramming produces substantial personal trauma and is hardly constructive mental health therapy.

Beyond these specific issues, sociologists are likely to view current new religious groups as constituting part of a continuing evolution of symbolic systems in response to sociocultural change (with all of its implications for individual biographies). They regard oppositional groups as a predictable response to movements that challenge prevailing values and institutional arrangements; thus, conflicts between religious movements and countermovements are viewed as clashes of interests, not wars with ruthless conspiracies that must be quelled at any price.

Opponents of new religious groups consequently oppose the research findings and the lines of reasoning that sociologists of religion have been presenting about "cults." One result has been the accusations that social scientists misunderstand the problem, lack objectivity, or have "gone native." These allegations obviously place sociologists in a difficult position. At the same time, such charges remind sociologists they are living up to tradition since an enduring element of the sociological tradition has been to critique the cultural mythology regarded by contemporaries as common sense. Indeed, the starting point of much sociological research is debunking prevailing myths.

We regret this tendency to overlook the assault upon the sociological enterprise inherent in the anticult perspective and to focus instead upon the propriety of the relationships of individual scholars to the groups they are studying. In appears that the latter issue pales before the former in terms of the potential impact upon the discipline, for it is precisely in conflicts like this that a sociological interpretation needs to be articulated if the prevailing cultural bias toward psychological reductionism is to be redressed. Similarly, the concern that sociologists may be "lending legitimacy" to social movements is more perplexing in light of the parallel legitimacy lent by the research of many social scientists to such movements as civil rights, women's rights, gay rights, and nuclear disarmament. There has been relatively little public carping in these cases even though their societal impact will probably be greater than in the case of cults. It appears that the real issue, then, is the *religious* base—with the attendant conservatism and authoritarianism—often found in new religious movements. It would be unfortunate indeed, however, if the liberal persuasion of sociologists frightened them off from the study of new religious movements, thus contributing to an entirely one-sided psychological interpretation of this important social phenomenon.

REFERENCES

Barker, Eileen,
    1983   "Supping with the Devil: How Long a Spoon Does the Sociologist Need?" *Sociological Analysis* 44 (3): 197-205.

Wallis, Roy
    1983   "Religion, Reason and Responsibility: A Reply to Professor Horowitz," *Sociological Analysis* 44 (3): 215-20.

Wilson, Bryan
    1983   "Sympathetic Detachment and Disinterested Involvement: A Note on Academic Integrity," *Sociological Analysis* 44 (3):183-87.

The Culture of the Future and the Future of Cults

CHAPTER FIFTEEN

The Future
of the Anticult Movement

David G. Bromley
Anson Shupe

Throughout American history new religious movements have faced hostility and repression. The clash of interests between these movements and the dominant societal institutions typically has triggered oppositional movements that have varied in longevity, intensity, and organizational durability. We would argue that an understanding of the development of countermovements, a topic frequently overlooked in theories of change (Marx, 1979), is crucial to any discussion of the future of new religious movements. New religious groups may solve internal organizational problems and even encounter fairly favorable environmental conditions but be significantly affected by organized opposition. This is as true for contemporary groups such as the Unification Church, Scientology, and Hare Krishna as it once was for the Mormons, the Jehovah's Witnesses and the Roman Catholics.

Most countermovements as well as most of the social movements they oppose experience very limited success by almost any criteria. Indeed, the history of new religious movements is largely a history of groups that either have disappeared or have lapsed into obscurity; the same is true of religious countermovements, as we have shown elsewhere (see Shupe, Bromley, and Oliver, 1984:1-24). Therefore, in examining the development of the contemporary anticult movement (hereafter the ACM), we will be interested in identifying factors bearing on its internal development and external influence.

For heuristic purposes we have divided the development of the modern anticult movement into three stages. The first stage (*formative*) denotes the period of the ACM's initial organization and development. The second stage (*expansionist*) represents the growth of major ACM organizational components and the development of a strategy for exerting external influence. The ACM currently is at this second stage. The third stage (*institutional*) describes the long-term niche that the ACM will occupy vis-à-vis other major societal institutions. The ACM could become a major interest group possessing the capacity to influence in a significant way the definition of "legitimate" and "illegitimate" religion, or it may lapse into relative obscurity as have many countermovements that have opposed earlier waves of new religious groups. In examining the ACM at each of these three stages, we shall briefly consider a number of movement components instrumental to an understanding of the ACM's structure at that particular stage: (1) membership base, (2) financial base, (3) ideology, (4) organizational structure, (5) visibility/legitimacy, (6) coalition formation, (7) strategy and tactics, (8) change in target groups, and (9) organizational impact.

In discussing the institutional stage we recognize that it is risky to wax prophetic and attempt to chart future directions for social movements. However, in this case our analysis and predictions deal with a specific type of social movement—a counterreligious movement—that has been found frequently in American history. The fact that the ACM probably will not become a major regulatory force in the social order does not diminish the importance of examining factors that would facilitate that outcome any more than the fact that most fledgling religious groups do not become major denominations should deter us from attempting to identify the factors that do lead a few to that position. Indeed, it is precisely because there are so few unmitigated successes in this sense that understanding the sources of success (and failure) becomes so important. Furthermore, we maintain that such movements' fortunes have repeatedly depended on tangible, identifiable resources. Thus we can assert, with some confidence, what some of the key determinants of the countermovements' fortunes have been in the past and will be in the future.

FORMATIVE STAGE

The ACM originated from the individual, localized efforts of family members of recruits to new religious movements during the early 1970s. Initially such complaintants concerned themselves with the Children of God (a Jesus-movement offshoot founded in the late 1960s), but soon a network of persons concerned about sons/daughters/siblings recruited into other groups such as the Unification Church, the Hare Krishnas, Scientology, and the Divine Light Mission formed (Shupe and Bromley, 1980). During the *formative* stage, the ACM grew from a collection of individual families with no previous contact to dozens of regional groups, composed of parents and family members, linked in a loosely organized national network. One major factor in the coalescing of these persons was the mass media, which found the families' stories of sudden transformation and alleged "psychological kidnapping" (for example, brainwashing) good sensationalistic press. It was through such press accounts that parents learned of their common plight. However, the countermovement at this point was still difficult to mobilize for any concerted efforts. It was, for example, fragmented in terms of ideology regarding the freedom of will that individuals possessed when they were drawn to such groups (for example, evangelical—which theologically posited an element of free choice— versus secular, which maintained that no reasonable person would voluntarily join a "cult" except through being a victim of a combination of guile, seduction, and brainwashing) as well as by the means appropriate for "rescuing" "cult" members (for example, coercive kidnapping/deprogramming versus noncoercive dialogue). Furthermore, proponents of the secular mind-control theory had yet to delineate precisely how this control was achieved and maintained. There was a motley and often inconsistent set of explanations: sensory deprivation and sensory overload, denial of food and improper dietary mix, physical subversion through drugging and mental subversion through hypnosis.

Organizationally, the ACM's component groups were fragile and small. They were often operated more on the basis of zeal and ideology than from any sound organizational expertise. For example, the membership base was usually limited (*de facto*) to the family members (and a few sympathetic friends) of young adults who had become involved in controversial religious groups, in large measure because the ACM limited the range of issues it addressed and the linkage of those issues to more general public concerns. Since many new religious groups had a fairly high turnover of members, ACM groups likewise faced unstable membership and commitment problems as well as lack of organizational continuity. Further the financial resources of such ACM groups were closely tied to the voluntary donations of members (which were often pitifully inadequate). There were few systematic membership fees or other ways of raising money. A number of groups, including some we researched, never survived this *formative* stage.

These internal features that lent ACM groups organizational precariousness were complicated by several other factors. First, the ACM had persistent difficulties in attaining a viable national coalition. Many small local groups jealously guarded their autonomy. There were frequent disagreements over whether to centralize or federate in setting up any umbrella organization. A number of attempts at unification failed because no consensus (and the accompanying financial support) for such a large group could be reached. Second, ACM leadership was part-time and voluntary, analogous to that found in community service groups. Often, organizational effectiveness was achieved only when some crusading individual assumed personal responsibility for most group functions. Likewise, the questionably legitimate "deprogrammers" who operated in vigilante fashion (and typically had no formal connections to ACM groups) were either amateurs who assumed this role for a limited time or were individuals who tried to carve out a career but eventually experienced serious legal difficulties as a result of their exploits. Third, the ACM had not yet built up a legion of angry ex-"cult" members to testify as to "cult" "atrocities," and the journalistic media had not yet peaked in focusing attention on certain groups. Indeed, as we found in our analysis of early 1970s press coverage of the Unification Church, reporting of the "Moonies" was laudatory and uncritical, Moon being often portrayed as a benign Korean version of Billy Graham (Bromley and Shupe, 1979:149-67). There was a delay of several years between ACM formation and the full-scale negative media coverage of "cults" that eventually ensued.

The ACM's fortunes in mobilizing allies at this early stage were mixed but mostly uphill. Local officials were willing to deal with questionable groups that infrequently appeared, but higher authorities often demurred from following through on ACM complaints. This is in part attributable to the ACM leadership's naivete and ineffective attempts to mobilize the support of political and criminal justice institutions. ACM spokespersons unsuccessfully tried to translate their private problems into public issues, frequently not understanding that their real political presence was that of just another interest group. In sum, other than activists in the ACM, few persons at this time (including scholars of new religions) knew either of the existence of the ACM or of its goals.

The most important single development during the formative stage was the focusing of ACM ideology on one overriding explanation of how otherwise exotic, authoritarian "cults" could attract America's allegedly best and brightest youth. This was the resilent "thought control/brainwashing" explanation resurrected from the Korean War era. Despite the fact that little evidence has been produced that Communist persuasion and coercion resulted in any significant number of defections, there is a substantial scientific literature investigating the phenomenon, as well as a widespread public belief in and fear of brainwashing. Thus, the brainwashing explanation provided families with a superficially plausible model of seemingly "bizarre" behavior that did not place any stigma on either themselves or their errant ("cult") family members, *and* it came embellished with the legitimacy of science. Even more importantly, it created the basis for placing a diverse array of new religious groups under the rubric "cults." Groups referred to as "cults" had as their first and foremost alleged characteristic manipulative recruitment and socialization practices. This combination of "cult" and "brainwashing" as the basis for ACM ideology allowed the coalition of distraught family members to coalesce around what appeared to be a common problem.

EXPANSIONIST STAGE

During the *expansionist* stage, the ACM significantly increased its presence and impact along the lines of enlarged membership, consolidated organizational activities, expanded visibility and credibility, and heightened public levels of fear. The process was frequently discontinuous on different levels and anything but smooth. Nevertheless, this countermovement did more than simply "dig in" to survive and challenge what it perceived to be a "cult" threat. It painfully began to institutionalize.

The changing composition of its membership base was one such sign. Originally, members were almost exclusively parents, siblings, and other relatives of young adult converts to unconventional religions. Gradually, however, there was the creation of a membership corps that included other than directly affected parties: lawyers, clergy, mental health professionals, and social scientists, among others. The professionals in this network were particularly important, for they provided the expertise in drafting anticult legislation, offering expert testimony when former members brought legal suits, and providing exit counseling. While this sympathetic contingent never grew large relative to the majority of family-related ACM constituents (and its members were never representative of the views of their respective professions), it nevertheless was to play a significant part in helping to legitimize and encourage the entire countermovement. Another such sign was the discovery of new and diverse financial bases such as civil suits, corporate and charitable grants, sales of materials, raffles, dues and subscriptions, and workshop fees. The combination of payments to deprogrammers, attorneys' fees for lawyers successful in handling civil suits, proceeds to ACM members from workshops on "destructive cultism," and consulting fees for expert witnesses helped to sustain the network of ACM members in the face of a still inadequate organizational resource base.

The ACM also refined the crude "brainwashing" ideology (for example, in terms of "cult-imposed personality syndromes," "self-inducted personality regression," and "destructive cultism"). The easily disconfirmed allegation of drugs being placed in food and the allegation of spot hypnosis (originated by Ted Patrick, the "father" of deprogramming) gave way to more clinically based conceptions of mind control. These latter conceptions facilitated participation of sympathetic social scientists and mental health practitioners on the ACM's behalf and created the appearance of a strong scientific basis for ACM ideology. In time this brainwashing ideology was widely accepted by many mainstream leaders in both politics and religion (see Boettcher and Freedman, 1980; and Shupe, Bromley, and Oliver, 1984:51-80) as well as by the public at large.

One of the most important developments during the expansionist stage was the aggressive recruitment and cultivation of "apostates" (that is, ex-"cult") members who often had been forcibly abducted from their respective deviant groups, held involuntarily for a time, and eventually convinced to recant their religious memberships and to testify that these previous memberships had never been of their own choosing. Such persons provided the popular media with images of innocent, idealistic youth transformed into fanatical zombies. These ex-members served an invaluable function for the ACM as they were able to provide the firsthand "smoking gun" "evidence" that life within "cults" was indeed as horrible as outsiders (particularly their families) had imagined (Shupe and Bromley, 1981). The simple fact that deprogrammers could physically abduct and confine members of new religious groups and that within a few days (or sometimes a matter of hours) these individuals would renounce the group and testify that they had been brainwashed lent powerful credence to the brainwashing allegations. In this way they added immeasurably to the ACM's credibility and stoked the fires of public concern. Apostates often were brought into deprogrammings to achieve a rapport and common experience base with the deprogrammee that many "professional" deprogrammers could not. These apostates were very effective in recruiting new members for deprogramming teams once they had been convinced of the error of their previous ways. Meanwhile, a series of frustrated attempts to create a national umbrella ACM organization, either centralized or confederated, continued throughout the 1970s (Shupe and Bromley, 1980:87-120). So although the loose confederation of regional groups continued (with each monitoring and opposing the activities of "cults" within its specified territory and on occasion cooperating in unified lobbying and publicity efforts with its allies but not pooling critical financial resources), during this time there was a process of selective survival. The American Family Foundation and the Citizens Freedom Foundation became the dominant organizations within the ACM. New initiatives such as seeking grant funding, establishing a research base, and beginning a dialogue with opponents represented efforts to move the ACM away from its parochial, isolated position. Many of the small regional anticult groups struggled on in relative obscurity or disappeared altogether, never solving the dilemmas of high membership turnover and narrow reliance on memberships and gifts.

At the same time, a number of important alliances portending an indefinite future existence for the modern ACM were forged. Various religious groups (for example, fundamentalist Christians, some representatives of mainline denominations, and many Jewish associations) as well as some sympathetic politicians at state and federal levels supported ACM complaints by offering workshops and conferences, holding public hearings, and even proposing legislation dealing with the "cult" problem. The newer religious groups targeted by the modern ACM also became incorporated into the older conservative Christian category of "cults," linking the new countermovement to a much older sectarian one. Thus it was not unusual by the early 1980s to find anticult books dealing simultaneously with the Unification Church, the Hare Krishna movement, the Church of Scientology, and the defunct People's Temple as well as Christian Science, Mormonism, and Jehovah's Witnesses.

It is ironic that, as the ACM began its period of aggressive expansion during the mid-1970s, many of the highly visible groups it opposed had either leveled off in growth or even entered a state of decline. This is true not only for the more radical millennial groups such as the Children of God, which divorced itself from the more conventional Jesus Movement, but also for visible groups such as the Unification Church, the Hare Krishnas, and the Divine Light Mission (see Bromley and Shupe, 1981:26-46; and Pilarzyk, 1978). Such developments in these religious groups occurred partly for internal reasons but also in large part because of the news media's discrediting reports about their activities. The media disseminated in uncritical fashion ACM claims and apostate accounts to create widespread public acceptance of the "mind-control" and "cult" stereotypes. Although toward the end of the ACM's first decade of operation, there could be seen a gradual trend toward "balanced coverage" (as anticultism alone ceased to be newsworthy), the news media were still dominated by negative images of many religious groups.

The key characteristic of the expansionist stage was a tactical parrying between new religious groups and anticult groups. This parrying occurred on many different levels and in various forums, two of the more notable being the legislative and judicial sparring over deprogramming and anticult legislation. Early in the "cult" conflict, parents began seeking writs of habeus corpus to gain access to sons and daughters who had joined new religious groups. Their assumption was that something deleterious had been done to their offspring and that once they had a chance to meet with their children they would convince them to dissociate themselves from the "cult." Representatives for the latter groups quickly learned that they could simply disavow knowledge of the individuals' whereabouts or any control over them. Parents found that even if the son or daughter appeared in court, there was no assurance that this would lead to disaffiliation since the court would simply release them into their own custody. When this tactic failed, ACM groups began seeking formal custody of their sons and daughters through the use of conservatorship and guardianship laws, which originated in an effort to provide families with a means of appointing legal guardians for mentally incompetent or senile family members. The anticultists sought to expand the use of conservatorship provisions to cover sons and daughters who parents feared had been brainwashed and hence were incapable of conducting their own affairs. For a while parents were able to get conservatorship orders relatively easily, and anticultists developed effective techniques, such as obtaining orders from sympathetic magistrates late on a Friday afternoon so that deprogrammings could be conducted over the weekend when opposing attorneys could not contest the action. As new religious groups protested this unintended use of conservatorship provisions and they became more difficult to obtain, parents and deprogrammers simply moved deprogrammees across jurisdictional lines to thwart law enforcement efforts. In the process, they found that federal agencies regarded abductions and deprogrammings as family matters and hence were reluctant to treat as kidnappings cases in which religious groups alleged that their members had been abducted. Parents and deprogrammers also experimented with the necessity defense, which allowed parents, and deprogrammers as their agents, to resist legal charges brought against them on the basis that their children were in imminent danger and hence abduction and deprogramming constituted the "lesser of evils" from which they had to choose. New religious groups, which were having mixed success in gaining prosecutions against deprogrammers as a result of these various tactics, began turning to civil suits in order to circumvent the problems attending criminal prosecution. Civil litigation could be initiated by the plaintiff (in this case usually an unsuccessfully deprogrammed individual with financing sometimes provided by the religious group), and the preponderance of evidence necessary for conviction was lower. And so it has gone, back and forth.

In the legislative arena, the scenario has been similar. ACM supporters quickly found that it was easier to influence local than state, and state than federal, legislators. Also symbolic support was easier to obtain than substantive regulation. One early means of attacking "cults" they seized upon at the local level was ordinances to restrict public fundraising. At the state level, they initially sought legislation to outlaw "cults." When it became apparent that such legislation was patently unconstitutional, they sought bills that would force religious recruiters to identify themselves and their purpose, expand conservatorship powers, and preclude civil suits by individuals who were unsuccessfully deprogrammed. For their part, new religious groups discovered that they were more successful at the federal government level and in the appellate courts where constitutional and civil liberation concerns carried greater weight. They began assembling a network of academicians, clergy, political leaders, and attorneys who shared these concerns and would lobby against ACM-sponsored legislation and represent them in litigation. And they sought precedent-setting decisions, usually at the appellate level, that would close off the possibility of endless litigation in every state or community.

The overall result of a decade of skirmishing has been a standoff. Each side has had its share of victories and defeats, and neither has any immediate prospects of winning a decisive triumph. Both sides have moderated their stances to enhance their public respectability. New religious groups have accommodated to conventional society in a number of respects, and the ACM has begun backing away from its vigilante-style tactics. Still, the ACM has continued to hold the upper hand. There is widespread public perception that indeed a "cult problem" exists. The fear and mistrust of "cults" has led to a continuing barrage of negative media coverage, governmental investigation, litigation, and "educational" campaigns, all of which have kept these groups on the defensive. Although the conflict no longer occupies the center stage of public attention, new religious groups continue to operate under the onus of public stigma.

INSTITUTIONAL STAGE

Both new religious groups and the ACM are fast approaching a watershed, at least for the near term. For the new religious groups, there are a host of organizational problems, outlined in the preceding papers, that they must resolve if any of them are to rival contemporary major denominations. History suggests there will be few, if any, success stories. The problems confronting the ACM are at least as acute. While there have been numerous anticult-style movements throughout American history, none has become institutionalized as a major social force. It is intriguing to ponder whether the ACM has any chance at all of socially projecting itself beyond the confines of the current cult controversy. Attempting to forecast the course of a countermovement like the ACM is, of course, perilous given the spontaneous, serendipitous nature of all social movements' development. It was predictable that some type of countermovement would emerge in response to the challenges posed by "cults." It is even possible to anticipate certain features of countermovements, such as apostates, atrocity stories, and some type of countermovement operatives (like deprogrammers). Whether a countermovement will resolve key organizational problems at pivotal points in its development is much more difficult to foresee. The following discussion, therefore, is intended as illustrative of alternatives and possibilities rather than as predictive.

The most likely outcome is that the ACM will fail in the long run to become more than an inconspicuous protest group. There are a myriad of groups that opposed earlier waves of new religious movements (for example, Mormonism, Christian Science, Jehovah's Witnesses). Many of these continue their efforts, and, by and large, they resemble ACM groups in a number of important respects. These oppositional groups form a network of independent entities, each run largely on the entrepreneurial drive of one person or a small group of individuals. They cooperate to a limited extent, but each preserves its own organization and autonomy. The most successful oppositional groups are those targeting new religious groups with aggressive recruitment campaigns that also have (in part as a result) higher rates of defection. Appeals are directed to disgruntled members and former members, families of converts, members of competing religious groups, and the public at large in areas where the groups have heavy concentrations of members, economic enterprises, converts, or political influence. Charges of a heretical theology, official greed and corruption, deception and exploitation of members, and increasing group economic and political power are standard fare. Major distinguishing characteristics between these older oppositional groups and the ACM are that the former no longer have very much visibility or impact and the more coercive tactics of the ACM are avoided.

If the ACM indeed founders in the years ahead, it will be because it has not adequately addressed developmental problems on the horizon. Although organizational and resource-generation difficulties remain, these do not appear to be the central questions facing the ACM. Rather, the primary issues confronting the ACM relate to its ideology and to its mandate. From one perspective, organizations constitute the answers to problems; and from this perspective the problem to which the ACM addresses itself—as well as its analysis of and remedy for that problem—is limited and fraught with obstacles. First, the ACM has defined its target as ''cults,'' but the definition of ''cult'' is always vulnerable to challenge because the groups the ACM seeks to encompass under that rubric are in fact so diverse. Indeed, the credence presently granted the ACM is a product more of public fear and ignorance than commonly shared charateristics or any objective threat posed by ''cults.'' The fact is, what sustains a countermovement during a period of high public alarm will not provide an organizational mandate when the controversy has cooled.

Second, the ACM has sought to maintain a high profile by demonstrating that cultlike groups are far more widespread than is generally recognized. However, this natural proclivity of oppositional groups to expand the number of subversives holds little promise as a long-term tactic. The history of countermovements reveals that the more who are accused of being witches, communists, or cultists, the more tenuous linkages become and the more are moderates aroused in opposition. Third, cult groups' size and recruitment success, upon which the ACM claim is staked, are in decline. Claims of manipulative recruitment and socialization practices may be even more difficult to mount if new religious groups continue to seek accommodation with conventional society and radical theological themes become muted.

Fourth, the ACM's ideological underpinnings are vulnerable, as the ''brainwashing'' explanation for ''cult'' membership finds little confirmation in a mounting body of social science research findings. Finally, current ACM ideology and practice run afoul of recent judicial trends. Arguments that ''cults'' are pseudoreligions, for example, run counter to recent Supreme Court decisions that broaden the range of beliefs and practices accorded religious status, and the justices remain reluctant to construct a definition of religion. Up to the present, at least, all of the major "cults" whose status as religious groups has been challenged have passed court tests. Brainwashing and deprogramming cases also indicate that the ACM faces significant legal problems. Despite ACM claims that both brainwashing and deprogramming are neutral procedures and bear no relation to the substantive content of religious belief and practice, in fact both challenges to recruitment/socialization techniques and attempts to induce members of "cults" to renounce their affiliations inevitably involve inquiry about or challenge to religious beliefs and practices. Federal courts in particular have stood firm in not allowing erosion of rights in this area.

There is some evidence that the ACM is exploring alternative strategies that offer greater potential for broadening its influence while avoiding some of the pitfalls of its current strategies. Some ACM proponents have begun focusing attention on abuse of children, spouses, and elderly members in small religious groups, with child abuse the dominant issue (Rudin, 1982). Although this new focus is still very tentative, it offers the ACM a clearer field to exploit. There is widespread American mistrust of "radical" religion (as a result of the legacy of Jonestown, the excesses of the Islamic revolution, and the rhetorical hubris of the new Christian right) that is relatively independent of concerns about "cults." By emphasizing specific practices that might be regulated rather than attempting to define certain groups as pseudoreligions or "cults," the ACM could harness and channel these concerns. Child abuse has become a high-visibility issue in the United States, and recently there has been considerable media coverage of child "abuse" based on religious tenets ("Matters of Faith and Death," *Time,* 16 April 1984, 42; "Seven Million Dollar Lawsuit," *The Utah Evangel,* May, 1984; "The Rod of Correction," *Time,* 11 June 1984, 33). In addition, this new strategy offers the prospect for regulating behaviors irrespective of their avowedly religious context. There is already precedent, for example, to limit parental control over medical care given to children even when religious precepts govern parental decision making. So, for example, members of Jehovah's Witnesses and Christian Science may refuse medical treatment for themselves, consistent with their religious beliefs, even in life-threatening situations; but they may not refuse treatment for their children in similar situations. Finally, regulating specific practices of this genre offers the possibility for confronting a large number of groups not now designated as "cults." In fact, since practices and not groups are the ostensible target, mainline churches could be involved as well.

This single issue, of course, would not be sufficient to sustain the ACM; however, there is reason to believe that such a new agenda could be broadened once it is established. If, for example, present trends in social welfare thinking continue, abuse will involve psychological as well as physical components; such an expansion would offer virtually limitless opportunities to regulate family practices based on religious tenets. Further, because there has been so little governmental scrutiny of religion in America, there are myriad practices that might cause great controversy were they to be exposed to public debate. The recent outpouring of support for Reverend Moon (following his conviction on tax evasion charges) by mainline denominations reveals how vulnerable they perceive themselves to be with respect to tax and financial matters.

If the ACM were able to parlay some such set of issues into an organizational mandate, it could assume the form of a regulatory organization not too different from that which presently monitors the activities of charitable groups. Limited governmental regulation is supplemented by such private organizations, which draw up codes of proper conduct, establish public reporting practices, collect and publish fundraising and expenditure data, and sanction groups found not to be in compliance with accepted practices. Since suspicions are raised by refusal to release data for public scrutiny, charitable organizations may comply simply to avoid stigma. It is easy to imagine religious organizations making a similar accommodation in order to avoid controversy, particularly if the monitoring organization initially established itself to deal with emotionally volatile issues such as child abuse.

SUMMARY AND CONCLUSIONS

The ACM began as an effort by the families of converts to new religious groups to deal with the challenge that these groups posed to the family unit. During the formative stage, individual families located one another and slowly developed a common interpretation of the problem with which they were confronted. The development of the brainwashing/mind-control explanation for "cult" membership was the seminal accomplishment of this stage since it was this ideology that fostered the alliance of families of converts and that legitimated a means of resolving the families' problem (that is, deprogramming). During the expansionist stage, the ACM sought to find some means of controlling "cults" that would allow it to draw upon legitimate, institutionalized mechanisms of social control. There was a refinement of the brainwashing ideology, which facilitated an alliance with sympathetic behavioral scientists and clinicians, as well as the recruitment of apostates, whose convincing testimony about the manipulative, coercive mind-contol practices of cults provided the major impetus for governmental investigations of "cults." Although the ACM gained a decided advantage in the conflict during this period, the tactical sparring between the protagonists did not produce a clear-cut victory for either side. The ACM clearly has begun to face a long-term crisis since the public alarm on which its current successes are based ultimately will subside. It remains unclear how the ACM will resolve the challenges now confronting it. The most likely outcome is decline into relative obscurity and impotence, for the kinds of changes needed to insure future success involve disavowal of practices upon which past successes have been built. There is, however, a possibility that the ACM could develop into a regulatory organization with a public mandate to monitor deviant practices by a wide range of religious groups. Clearly, this would represent a major organizational innovation in America with potentially significant implications for religious practice. Although the probability of this outcome remains slight, it should not be discounted. As Coser (1956) has observed, one of the major consequences of social conflict is a realignment of institutional relationships.

REFERENCES

Boettcher, Robert, and Gordon L. Freedman
  1980   *Gifts of Deceit: Sun Myung Moon, Tongsun Park, and the Korean Scandal.* New York: Holt, Rinehart & Winston.

Bromley, David G., and Anson D. Shupe, Jr.
  1981   *Strange Gods: The Great American Cult Scare.* Boston: Beacon Press.
  1979   *"Moonies" in America: Cult, Church, and Crusade.* Beverly Hills CA: Sage.

Coser, Lewis
  1956   *The Functions of Social Conflict.* New York: Free Press.

Flowers, Ronald B.
  1984   "The Nature and Current Status of the Mail-Order Ministry Controversy." *Proceedings of the Association for the Scientific Study of Religion: Southwest.* Dallas, Texas.

Kelley, Dean, ed.
  1982   *Government Intervention in Religious Affairs.* New York: Pilgrim Press.

Pilarzyk, Thomas
  1978   "The Origin, Development, and Decline of a Youth Culture Religion: An Application of Sectarianization Theory." *Review of Religious Research* 20 (Fall): 23-43.

Rudin, Marcia
  1982   "Women, Elderly, and Children in Religious Cults." Paper presented at the Citizen's Freedom Conference, Arlington, Virginia, October 1982.

Shupe, Anson D., Jr. and David G. Bromley
  1981   "Apostates and Atrocity Stories: Some Parameters in the Dynamics of Deprogramming." In *The Social Impact of New Religious Movements,* edited by Bryan Wilson, 179-215. New York: The Rose of Sharon Press.
  1980   *The New Vigilantes: Deprogrammers, Anti-Cultists, and the New Religions.* Beverly Hills CA: Sage.
  1979   "The Moonies and the Anti-Cultists: Movement and Countermovement in Conflict," *Sociological Analysis* 40 (Winter):325-34.

Shupe, Anson D., Jr., David G. Bromley, and Donna L. Oliver
    1984   *The Anti-Cult Movement in America: A Bibliography and Historical Survey*. New York: Garland Publishing.

Time
    1984   "Matters of Faith and Death." 16 April.

    1984   "The Rod of Correction." 11 June.

Utah Evangel
    1984   "Seven Million Dollar Lawsuit." May.

CHAPTER SIXTEEN

A Historian of Religion Looks at the Future of New Religious Movements

Robert Ellwood

UNDERSTANDING THE ISSUE

Any debate on the future of New Religious Movements (NRMs) is bound to be deeply connected with the larger ongoing debate over secularization. Secularization has been defined by Peter Berger as "the process by which sectors of society and culture are removed from the domination of religious institutions and symbols," together with its subjective corollary, the "secularization of consciousness"—the notion that after such a removal, people also *think* less about religion and inwardly use religious concepts less as a real basis for making decisions or establishing values.[1]

Whether, or in what way, secularization is actually happening is an issue that has deeply divided commentators on the modern spiritual scene. For believers in secularization, the decline of religion in recent times is an obvious fact, the sort of thing that "everyone knows," and indeed they often respond to their critics with a hint of irritation that supposedly intelligent people should refuse to accept such a patent reality, as though talking to a flat-earther. On the other side, critics point to their own obstinate facts about the persistence and even prosperity of religion in the modern world, its amoeba-like ability to reshape and multiply itself to fill countless new niches in social ecology, and query whether a theory that requires so many qualifications and superimposed epicycles to make it fit the facts may not be a sociological equivalent of Ptolemaic astronomy.

---

[1]Peter L. Berger, *The Sacred Canopy* (Garden City NY: Doubleday, 1969) 107.

Nonetheless, secularization as an idea persists and in fact is accepted in some form by the majority of important sociologists and historians of religion. Such is the case no doubt first of all because, as Durkheim implied at the very end of *The Elementary Forms of the Religious Life*,[2] and as Bryan Wilson has more recently observed,[3] secularization is indicated by the very nature of the sociological enterprise. For if, as the latter must assume, religion can be interpreted—in part or in whole—by sociological analysis, then religion is dethroned as absolute monarch and subjected to a higher law. In Durkheimian language, if the real though unacknowledged object of religion is society itself, then religious knowledge can be replaced by sociological knowledge and must be when the latter arrives on the scene. The sociologist by the very act of sociologizing also secularizes, and insofar as his work has any impact on the attitudes of society as a whole, secularization is furthered.

To such sweeping pronouncements, the antisecularization theorist is likely to respond, "So what else is new?" He would point out that, for those who have cared to listen, the gods have been subject to the "higher laws" of critical analysis almost as long as there have been gods, in the West exercised by philosophers from Euhemerus and Lucretius on down. Even more to the point, he would argue that the ages of faith against which the secularizationist wishes to showcase the modern decline of religion are almost as much a "myth" as the recent "loss of faith." In a world packed with born-again Christians, Muslim fundamentalists, and stubborn churchgoers in lands that have been under Communist rule for more than a generation, it is hard to deny that secularization is, at the least, running well behind schedule.

Conversely, we may note with Mary Douglas that "there is no good evidence that a high level of spirituality has generally been reached by the mass of mankind in past times, and none at all that their emotional and intellectual lives were necessarily well integrated by religion . . . evidence for old-time sanctity comes from suspect sources such as hagiography, panegyrics, and sermons. If we were to read even that biased evidence more critically, we would notice the professionals upbraiding the mass of ordinary people for lack of faith, as if the gift of which, we are told, modernity has deprived us was always rather the exception."[4] The careful social history of recent decades,

---

[2] Emile Durkheim, *The Elementary Forms of the Religious Life,* trans. Joseph Ward Swain (New York: Collier Books, 1961). Original French ed., 1912.

[3] Bryan Wilson, "The Return of the Sacred," *Journal for the Scientific Study of Religion* 18:3 (September 1979): 268-80.

[4] Mary Douglas, "The Effects of Modernization on Religious Change," in Mary Douglas and Steven M. Tipton, eds., *Religion and America* (Boston: Beacon Press, 1983) 29.

such as that of the French *Annales* school, has tended to confirm a suspicion that, say, the unalloyed piety of the European Middle Ages is more an ideological fabrication of—for very different reasons—Whig and Catholic romantic historians than the way it was for "the mass of ordinary people."

For instance, Emmanuel Le Roy Ladurie's remarkable book *Montaillou,* describing the village of that name in southern France in the early 1300s, indicates that no more than half the population bothered to attend mass on an ordinary Sunday, and for some populations, such as shepherds in the hills, churchgoing was very uncommon.[5] Attitudes that would later be called anticlerical were far from unknown, priests being derided for sexual misconduct and otherwise leading an unworthy life. So was all-out disbelief possible, such as that of a peasant who said the soul consisted merely of blood and so simply disappeared after death. "Heaven was when you were happy in this world, Hell was when you were miserable, and that was all."[6]

To be sure, Montaillou had been swept by the Cathar or Albigensian movement, and our remarkably detailed information on the religious stance of its ordinary medieval people is derived from court testimony taken by Jacques Fournier, Bishop of Parmiers, in the course of that zealous churchman's harrying of heretics. Many had consider the Goodmen who had come to teach the Cathar gnosticism better exemplars of spirituality than their Catholic counterparts, and not a few had joined them. By the time of the testimony, the religious views of the folk in Montaillou doubtless labored under a double disillusionment: first, their disenchantment with the established church led to the appeal of the apparently holier Cathar evangelists, and then the persecution and near-extermination of those same evangelists left people cynical about religion in general. Nonetheless, the testimony makes clear two important facts: that far-reaching religious skepticism and nonparticipation were possible in the Middle Ages; and that new religious movements—as one may surely call Albigensianism so far as its social role in France at the time is concerned—were part of a fluid and ambiguous spiritual situation, both attracting faith and sowing seeds of later disillusion.

In sum, the antisecularization camp appears finally to be saying not so much that religion is powerful today—an excessive generalization if there ever was one—as that it really wasn't all that powerful in the past either. It does not deny that institutional religion played a different, and seemingly more puissant, role in outward society in some past eras. Bishops (like Fournier) were often political figures with real power, and religious elites often had a

---

[5]Emmanuel Le Roy Ladurie, *Montaillou,* trans. Barbara Bray (New York: Vintage Books, 1979) 305.

[6]Ladurie, *Montaillou,* 320.

near-monopoly on education and the publication of books, thus controlling at least the terms of reference for worldviews. Nevertheless, the hold of established religion on the "ordinary masses" was far from uncontestable. Not only were there rival religions such as Albigensianism and significant remnants of pre-Christian faith, usually in the form of folk magic; it is clear also that many people were simply more interested in other things than religion. Work, family, lust, food and drink, and fatigue took precedence. The church's real rivals were not alternative worldviews or rival religions but its ancient foes, the world and the flesh, though with the right goading rivals could take the paradoxical form of an ascetic faith like that of the Cathars.

Again, one wonders if the situation with religion is really so different today. Although we have more entries, perhaps, in the spiritual and worldview marketplace than medieval France (though, if Fournier's testimony is any guide, the number then is not to be underestimated), it is not at all clear that religious competition works to the detriment of religion as such. Peter Berger feels that pluralism works to the eventual discrediting of religious worldviews,[7] but Andrew Greeley[8] and David Martin[9] have argued the opposite: that it creates a situation of ferment from which many competitors will profit. The most important worldview clash, and one that has been held to challenge the earlier worldview hegemony allegedly exercised by the church, is the celebrated "science and religion" conflict. Yet one suspects that this is not an agonizing issue for more than a few people today and that most resolve it about like medieval people resolved the also real conflicts between pre-Christian and Christian values, between religious and feudal values, and (for the educated) between classical and Catholic learning. That is to say, they took what they needed from both, giving one or the other practical or theoretical primacy, and let it go at that. Thus, a medieval man could employ magical folk remedies while also affirming the healing power of Christ, and it no longer amazes that an American fundamentalist can drive a car running on petroleum whose discovery employed the same geology on which evolutionary theory rests.

The real crunch is not between religions and worldviews, then, but between religion and individual priorities, individual budgets of commitment to various areas of life—between the spirit and the world and flesh. Here our indications are that human nature is not so different; and whether or not a

---

[7]Berger, *Sacred Canopy*, 145.

[8]Andrew Greeley, *Religion in the Year 2000* (New York: Sheed and Ward, 1969) 97ff.

[9]David Martin, *A General Theory of Secularization* (New York: Harper and Row, 1978).

bishop or a Communist sits in a national cabinet, or universities are taught by monks or agnostic professors does not make much difference. State policies are about equally likely to be calculating, and students divide their attention roughly the same between drink, sex, philosophizing, and prayer.

As the foregoing discussion has perhaps made evident, my position is that there is truth to both the secularization and antisecularization sides, but that the "continuationists"—as those may be called who hold that the position of religion has not changed as much as secularizationists would say and that it is going to be with us in approximately its present strength for as long as one can now foresee—bespeak a more fundamental reality. Religion is infinitely adaptable and will continue to change—sometimes radically, sometimes in the direction of trenchant conservatism—to meet those new realities of which secularizationists talk. But there is little to suggest that it is going to disappear or diminish greatly; something identifiable as religion, and continuous with what is ordinarily known as religion in the past, will persist. (Although this discussion may call for a definition of religion, to undertake an elaborate argument on that notoriously tricky topic would be too much of a digression here. Briefly, I am assuming religion refers to social and subjective structures that take simultaneously Joachim Wach's three forms of religious expression—theory, practice, and sociology—and point to transcendent or nonordinary realities that can bestow power and enhance the meaning of human life.)

In a word, religion will bend but not break under the pressure of change in the "outside" world it inhabits: the world of changing technology, medicine, political realities, economics, and the rest. As indicated, its changes may be either (or both) radical adjustment and conservative reaction; it answers to deep-seated needs to which both respond. It will not change at the same rate in all areas of its life either. Thinking of Wach's three forms of religious expression, the sociology (though not necessarily the institutional and leadership structures) of a religion may change most rapidly, the practical forms of expression next, and the theoretical (that is, myths and doctrines) most slowly. To take but one example: in the twentieth century the Roman Catholic Church has changed dramatically sociologically, from a largely peasant and immigrant church to one basically middle-class in Europe and America, and "third world" (with all that implies) elsewhere. Its practical forms of expression—worship—have changed significantly but somewhat more cautiously. Its theoretical expression is in principle unchanged, although important shifts of emphasis obtain. In the case of new religious movements, of course, the opposite prioritization may show itself. They may pride themselves on a fresh doctrinal outlook, yet their worship and sociology may reveal continuities as well as breaks with their spiritual milieu. We must now return to the position of new religious movements in a world of secularization/continuation.

THREE POSSIBILITIES

Let us begin by granting for the sake of argument the truth of each side and see what it would mean for NRMs. If secularization is in any sense a significant reality of our times, NRMs could have, it seems to me, three sorts of interaction with it.

First, they could articulate reaction against secularization. When society and subjectivity are "removed from the domination of religious institutions and symbols," some people are bound to feel loss. It will appear to them that the bestower of meaning and giver of power that was the transcendent has been expunged from human life, leaving them with no meaning and no power. For the brave claim of secularists that, with God pensioned off, humanity can now "come of age" and take charge of its own destiny is, for all but an elite, at best a mockery; even if the average person in a modern democratic society can to some extent manage such personal areas as family and career, he still experiences such larger matters as war and peace, economic tides, and the self-perpetuating onrush of technological "progress" as things that happen *to* him, for good or bad as the case may be. He knows he has no real control over them, no more than paleolithic man over the fortunes of the hunt, save through magic by whatever name it goes; and no modern cant is likely to convince him otherwise.

In the modern world, the ideas of secularization and progress are inseparably intertwined. While it is possible to find spokesmen for one who disdain the other, in both the popular and academic mind the two have generally been viewed, whether with enthusiasm or alarm, as implying each other. As Robert Nisbet has pointed out, triumphalist progress has generally been seen as bearing freedom and power[10]—two gifts that traditional religion offers subjectively by supernatural means—through science and social engineering. They are this-worldly rather than inward or other-worldly benefits, brought about through means that work from different, if not necessarily incompatible, sorts of information and techniques than those of traditional religion. Thus, progress so understood inevitably removes sectors of society and culture from religious domination. Insofar as they experience change in the name of progress, then, people tend to assume it is change in the direction of secularization: religion, ostensibly based on a different sort of information and usually experienced as something coming to us out of the past, would be thought unlikely to produce *directly* the scientific and social changes regarded as progress. (This is despite the efforts of many to *reconcile* the two: to give progress religious impetus, as in the "social gospel" movement; or to argue the indirect influence of religion

---

[10]Robert Nisbet, *History of the Idea of Progress* (New York: Basic Books, 1980).

on progress, as in the oft-debated connection of biblical religion with the rise of science and historicism in the West.)

But as we have noted, progress as change in the direction of power and freedom—and secularization—is experienced ambivalently by many people. Few would deny that science and social engineering have indeed produced important novel forms of the two, but rapid change itself engenders its own forms of powerlessness and with it inner loss of freedom. Further, insofar as it is associated with secularization, progress appears to destroy the possibility of another kind of power and freedom—a kind that might counter the destructive side of progress, namely, religion's subjective supernatural power and freedom. Whether modern progress has really brought secularization or whether that notion is only a form of the ancient myth—as old as Confucius and the Hebrew prophets—that people were more pious in the past than today is beside the point for the moment; the fact is that many people experience the destructive side of change as negative secularization.

In this situation, NRMs will have an opportunity. When a society is widely believed to be secularizing, inevitably the mainstream religious bodies will be thought tainted by the process too. In their very Troeltschian function as "church," custodians of a culture's values and spiritual home of most of its people, they will seem ineffective opponents if not covert allies of secularization, bound overall to sail with the prevailing winds.

What the truly afflicted modern wants is not accommodation but the stock-in-trade of "strong" religion in all times and places—subjective supernatural power and freedom, or to put it another way, magic and soul: power to overcome or abide that which is uncontrollable in one's fortune and inner reality having free access to ultimate reality.

In a secularizing situation, NRMs can offer these bounties with particular effectiveness because they present marked discontinuity with the environment and thus are clearly uncontaminated. Further, their charateristics of intensity and charisma make it seem that they are centrally concerned with the business of magic and soul, and are good at it. For the person upon whom the paradoxes of progress weigh heavily, who wants the goods of modernity without loss of magic and soul, NRMs can make a strong appeal.

A movement like Nichiren Shoshu, for example, offers a near-magical key to health and success in the world of the vibrant, aggressive, up-to-date young people who figure so prominently in its literature. Hardly less attuned to generating prosperity supernaturally amid the skyscrapers of modern corporations are several movements of the positive thinking type, practical meditation methods like TM, and the "human potentials" groups. Others, such as western Zen, Vedanta, and the Neo-Pagans, are more concerned with the "soul" side of the problematic, tapping supernatural resources not so much to solve problems and generate success as to enhance one's inner reality in a "one-dimensional" world.

This brings us to a second sort of interaction between secularization and NRMs. Not only do they offer ways to react against it; they also provide spiritualizing interpretations of secular values, frequently claiming to do so in a more up-to-date way than conventional faiths. Thus, for example, the frequent use of "science" in their titles: Christian Science, Divine Science, Scientology, and so forth. Some make much today of convergences between their worldviews and that of the "new physics," those of Eastern background understandably appreciating popular books like Fritjof Capra's *The Tao of Physics*.[11] Nonetheless, it is doubtful if the appeal of the interpretative role runs as deep as the reactive impulse. Acquaintance with the "science" NRMs assures us that their heart remains magic and soul, not the compatibility of quantum theory with Buddhism, though of course the validity and importance of such dialogue are real.

Third, if we take secularization as a real and ever-growing phenomenon, it will catch up with NRMs as with everything else. Despite their call to those distressed by the loss of magic and soul, and their efforts to interpret the world of secularism religiously, they will be undercut by an irresistible devaluing of religious and transcendent language and concepts. In a truly secular society, religion would have no accessible vocabulary. Words like God might remain in the dictionary, but, emptied of strong meaning by a universal budgeting of attention elsewhere, they would mean no more than the names of Egyptian gods to most of us.

If such a secular black hole is the ultimate fate of religion's star, NRMs could contribute to the burning-out of religious language that made it possible. The decay of gods is essentially a linguistic rot. Even the relative success of NRMs at one point in the process—the present—could contribute to religion's final illness if the proliferation of religious vocabularies and agendas they interject should result in such confusion as to devalue all religious language. If the emperor says he has not one but a thousand new suits, he may keep people wondering a little longer; but when he's finally called on it, none of them is likely to look like more than thin air.

ANOTHER INTERPRETATION

But what if our other contention is true, and secularization is a learned myth? What if the current religious situation is really not much different from its customary wont, and, while things may change, the overall relation of religion to human life is going to stay about what it is? What about NRMs then?

---

[11]Fritjof Capra, *The Tao of Physics* (Boulder CO: Shambhala, 1975).

Secularization theory really depends on a crisis-response model of religion in society. So does a good deal of anthropological interpretation of religious movements, such as cargo cults and nativist revivals. Something has happened in outer history, they say, that has provoked this religious response: the crisis of European contact, the crisis of faith engendered by science.

Some commentators, however, have pointed to limitations in this model. The extrinsic-cause model does not explain why some crisis-situations give rise to much NRM activity, while others do not. W. E. H. Stanner some years ago pointed out that cargo cults (like millennial movements in general) really create their own crisis, as much as they respond to imposed crises, by provoking civil disobedience and economic disruption, and above all by raising eschatological expectation to a high pitch.[12] While we cannot here discuss the matter in detail, it is clear that a full interpretation of any NRM must concern itself not only with immediate synchronic stimuli, but also with the general dynamics of its religious milieu: the character of existing religious institutions, the traditional role of charismatic leadership, the attitude toward sectarianism. Above all, we must look at the internal dynamics of religion, both those of the NRM as it creates and resolves its own crises and those tensions in need of resolution within the major religious tradition. For important religious movements, such as the Protestant Reformation in Europe and Kamakura Buddhism in Japan, are manifestly not only responses to changed external conditions but also attempts to deal with unresolved problems latent in those movements from their beginnings.

It is evidently with such considerations in mind that Rodney Stark speaks in this volume of secularization producing its own countervailing trends in the religious economy, most commonly through sect formation. As we have seen, those who most deeply feel the ambiguities of secularization are likely to find established religion too compromised, so this outcome is understandable. In time, those sects may join the establishment, leaving space—sure to be filled, for religion like nature abhors a vacuum—for new entries to arise. This may be called a "steady-state" theory of religious change.

As I have indicated, I perceive both secularization and continuation or steady-state themes in religion today, with the latter the more underlying reality, but the former are affecting in significant ways the style of religion.

It is undeniably true that religious influence, in the form of religious persons, institutions, and worldview models, has receded markedly in some sectors of society. The road to modernity has been marked by mighty and often traumatic struggles to remove such influence from government, education, and the eco-

---

[12]W. E. H. Stanner, "On the Interpretation of Cargo Cults," *Oceania* 29 (1958): 1-25.

nomic sphere. While issues remain, it can hardly be denied that in those areas it's a different world from the Middle Ages. Even religion itself, paradoxically perhaps, had felt this "secularizing" withdrawal. In our own day, it could be contended that the great denominational institutional expressions of religion that paralleled the great institutions of government, education, or economic life have declined in apparent power, the real center of spiritual life moving more to local and private spheres. By the same token, mature dialogue between religion and those institutions, or between religion and the cultural and intellectual mainstream they presumably represent, is in decline. What theologians today have the popular cachet or academic prestige of Barth, Tillich, or the Niebuhrs a generation ago? Yet clearly religion persists—if anything, more flourishing than ever on the popular level—even as its moorings to the rest of the "establishment" seem to be cut. What can we make of this situation?

GREAT TRADITIONS AND LITTLE TRADITIONS

To my mind, a highly appropriate model could begin with Robert Redfield's concept of Great and Little Tradition.[13] What we have, I think, is a religious Little Tradition continuing unabated while its corresponding Great Tradition is atrophying under the acids of secularization.

First, let us review some essential features of a Great Tradition. In religion, it means the dominant faith as it is borne by its highly educated elites, usually professionals. In traditional societies, these elites can wield appeciable political and economic power and may well be closely associated with the kings and aristocrats who patronize them and make the Great Tradition's learning and culture ornaments of their courts. The Great Tradition elites' version of the religion is highly literate, historically aware, engaged in scriptural and philosophical study, and transmitted through education.

In premodern societies, the Little Tradition includes the same religion as it is understood and experienced by peasants who, being illiterate, know things only as they are in the present or transmitted in myth and folklore. It has little concern with formal philosophy or history; it is oriented to cosmic rather than historical time, concentrates on worship and experience more than theory, and is communicated through family, community, charismatic figures such as shamans, and local priestly representatives of the Great Tradition.

Thus, Little Tradition religion will center around seasonal festivals like Christmas, around family and village folkways, around things *done* like pil-

---

[13]Robert Redfield, *Peasant Society and Culture* (Chicago: University of Chicago Press, 1956, 1973) 41ff. The distinction, of course, is not new; see Max Weber, "Castes, Estates, Classes, and Religion," ch. 7 in *The Sociology of Religion*, trans. Ephraim Fishoff (Boston: Beacon Press, 1963).

grimage and rite, and nonrational experience like miracles and mystical states. Little Tradition people are likely to feel, fundamentally, that they cannot really affect the course of society as a whole or the policies of the highly placed except by provoking a miracle—say a peasants' revolt or a crusade—rather than rational means.

The feelings of Great and Little Traditions for each other are likely to be ambivalent. Great Tradition elites are likely to waver between concept for the naivete and "superstition" of the latter and bouts of imagining such "simple faith" to be really deeper than their own. Peasants, on the other hand, may well cheer or venerate their alleged betters one day and inwardly hate them the next. Nonetheless, the two levels continually interact, as concepts, practices, and even persons go up and down.

But, as Redfield also points out, a Little Tradition can continue with a vigorous life of its own long after the Great Tradition that nurtured it has vanished and perhaps been superseded by another. The villages of Mayan Indians in Yucatan that he studied, though superfically touched by the Catholic Great Tradition, still preserve Little Tradition usages grounded in the long-vanished Great Tradition of the Mayan Empire. "The shaman-priests of the villages," he reported, "carried on rituals and recited prayers that would have their full explanation only if we knew what were the ritual and the related body of thought at Chichen Itza or Coba."[14]

Something like a lingering Little Tradition—a technological society's version of peasant religion, perpetuating itself in a steady-state—may be what we have in a society like America as the intellectual and other Great Tradition ramifications of the dominant religion seem to be running out of steam. It is precisely in those places where the Little Tradition is always strongest that religion today has its strength: family and local community, inward experience (meditation or being "born again"), seasonal festivals (such as Christmas), charismatic transmission (including TV shamans), emphasis on miracle and nonrational authority, the crusade approach to social change, a deepseated suspicion of elites combined with a sense of aura about the great and the learned with whom one has rapport. This Little Tradition version of religion, of course, has always been there; now it comes into prominence because the usually more visible Great Tradition is fading and leaving the scene to it by default, or historical necessity.

What does this split-level religious scene, secularized above and steady-state below, mean for NRMs? Fundamentally, it means good prospects. As in Montaillou, folk or popular religion has always been more receptive to new forces than elite religion has been. They can offer vehicles for the popularist's covert dislike of elites, and his regard for charismatic leadership and em-

---

[14]Redfield, *Peasant Society and Culture*, 46.

phasis on experience rather than history also coverge with the NRM's modes of operating. Most of Stark's eight points for success in NRMs refect conditions common to popular religion or easily generated within it: cultural continuity; a medium level of tension with the surrounding environment ("deviant but not too deviant" is tacitly understood in popular religion—it sets itself apart from elitism and values charisma or "calls," but it also values relative homogeneity within its own communities); effective mobilization (this requires charismatic leadership as well as structure and so is a variable); normal age and sex range (goes without saying); a favorable ecology (in popular religion today the religious ecology is indeed unregulated, and conventional faith, that is, The Great Tradition, is weakened); maintenance of dense internal networks (common in popular religion); resistance to secularization; and adequate socialization of the young (another variable).

Thus the tinder in popular religion is ready for the spark in the form of a charismatic leader who can mobilize a following around an NRM, produce at least local success, and socialize the young into it. The basic ways of understanding religion in the Little Tradition are highly congenial to the worldviews and rhetorical styles of NRMs.

Some limitations to this success do obtain, though, and they focus around Stark's important point that successful NRMs must have some cultural continuity with their environment and maintain only a medium level of tension with it. This is more important, I would say, in popular than elite religion. While a well-educated elite may allow their spiritual interests to range through time and space, as free to settle in ancient India or Egypt as in their own tradition, the popular religionist is more apt to feel a new movement ought at least to come from the same place he does. To speak more concretely, the secularization of the Great Tradition will probably mean that future NRMs are less likely to be Oriental or otherwise exotic than in the Great Tradition past and more likely to be new versions of the popular believer's Christianity. This is heralded by the fact that since the sixties Eastern NRMs have yielded center stage to Christian-based Pentecostal, biblicist, and "success" movements. At the same time, these are likely to be much more diverse and nonnormative than when a Christian Great Tradition, with an educated mainstream theological elite, was more of a felt presence in national life.

Some NRMs may attempt to fill niches abandoned by the Great Tradition, relating religion to science, philosophy, education, or economics—as religious schools and communes are already doing on a small scale. Some, like the Unification Church, may come in from missionized areas overseas. And before long we may see in America some of the rich indigenous versions of Christianity founded in Africa and the West Indies. Some, like the Native American Church, may build on what have become Little Traditions in America other than Christian: native, Asian, popular Jewish. But they are likely to be inescapably American in style and content, "deviant but not too deviant." They may not all be sects or cults in any formal sense. They will nonetheless show that nothing is more American than the continual formation of NRMs.

WHAT, THEN, THE FUTURE?

Now let us reflect briefly on the possible future of some specific New Religious Movements. In the case of Krishna Consciousness, Larry Shinn has pointed out that its assets for long-term survival lie in the depth of individual commitment, a strong yet reasonably flexible institutional structure, and increasing support from the ethnic Hindu community in America. To this Steven Gelberg adds the appeal of an inherently "interesting" doctrine, surely an important value insofar as an NRM's office is to offer deeply subjective bulwarks against secularization. On the other side, it is recognized that the high degree of alienness of the "Hare Krishnas" within the American scene will provide difficulties in terms of Stark's first requirement, retaining cultural continuity, even though the same cultural features augur well for some success in India, affording them there a continuing reservoir of strength for their world mission.

Nonetheless, in light of the present discussion, the prospects for conspicuous success by Krishna Consciousness in America are not bright. Because of its already cited strengths and its international base, it will survive, but I would not expect it to gain much more numerical or institutional strength than it presently enjoys. While the religion certainly counters secularization as vehemently as any, it is particularly vulnerable to the decay of religious language that ultimately contributes to that which it opposes. The name Krishna and its Sanskrit terminology are foreign at best and contribute to religious linguistic confusion.

Krishna Consciousness is also vulnerable as American religion becomes more and more a Little Tradition severed from a Great Tradition. As we have noted, the appeal of what is perceived as "exotic" or "Eastern" is diminished among people of Little Tradition religious orientation compared to Great. It is hard to imagine Little Tradition religionists in America ever sensing much cultural continuity with Krishna Consciousness or sensing an identity of its devotionalism with their own Christian variety, at least so long as it retains so much of the externals of Indian culture.

Here, however, Krishna Consciousness is faced with a difficult conundrum. One can freely agree with John Lofland that survival means change, yet also agree with the opposite truth—that for religion, resistance to change also has survival value. People often look to religion to image that Eternity which changes not, preserve ethnic and cultural roots, and show that some things don't change in a world of baffling future shock. This will be particularly true of a religion like ISKCON, which professes to teach some quite specific eternal truths, and is both highly liturgical and committed to highly distinctive dress, food, and life-style. The whole point of liturgy and separatist life-styles is that they are supposed to change only very slowly if at all; as Roman Catholics have discovered, even fairly moderate change in these areas can be quite upsetting for many believers and potentially discrediting in an institution that had claimed absolute truth. As E. Burke Rochford notes, ISKCON now faces the delicate task of maintaining sufficient tension with environing society to maintain its uniqueness while not inviting excessive opposition. With the support of the ethnic Indian community, it may succeed to about the extent of American Buddhism and Sikhism, which also have both Asian-American and occidental communalist components.

Theoretically, the Unification Church ought to have brighter prospects. Being Christian (if non-normatively) and in some ways Protestant-evangelical in style and capable of flexibility, it should have less cultural continuity problems with Krishna Consciousness. Indeed, the three authors in this volume treating of it envision the Unification Church surviving, though changing to do so. But there are also difficulties, and much depends on how the church confronts them.

Michael L. Mickler has interestingly presented four options for the Unification Church at what he perceives to be its present "crucial point" of transition to a more formalized stage of church life. We can only point out here that this decision also implies a decision whether to opt for a Great Tradition or Little Tradition sort of image and style. Again suggesting a church very much in transition, present indications go both ways. If the church moves toward the sort of concern with world issues in the reformist sense suggested by the first two of Mickler's categories and toward the emphasis on "mainstream" theological education and intellectual symposia of recent trends, that would imply a Great Tradition move. If our position is correct, such a move would be against the stream of what American religion is doing, but that might not be to the church's disadvantage if it means there is a vacuum to be filled. What other church today is trying with the assiduousness of the Unification church to engage in dialogue with the intellectual main currents? Nonetheless, the church is not likely as a result to grow tumultuously but could eventually end up a small, somewhat "different," but not disrespectable denomination like the Swedenborgians. Such a move would, as Eileen Barker points out, require loosening of both cultural and doctrinal rigidity, as it did for many other groups making the same transition in the past. There is a danger here of the classic split between liberals and "holdfasts," which the Swedenborgian "New Church" also experienced. Like them, the Unificationists are too small and too committed to the "family" idea to suffer such a schism without much trauma and loss, yet it would not be unlikely.

If, on the other hand, the church goes the Little Tradition route, which is strongly implicit in Mickler's last category, "cultic," it would remain theologically uncritical, and evangelistic in style. It would then, ideally, slowly win acceptance as a popular religious form as have once controversial groups ranging from the Salvation Army to the Mormons. Oddly enough, the incarceration of Sun Myung Moon for tax evasion could actually help in this process. The support of him by evangelicals on religious freedom grounds has been impressive and, to me at least, surprising, and in the Little Tradition milieu there is always a latent opposition to "the government" that can be sparked by the right symbols (including persons as symbols) to advantage.

Like the other writers on the subject in this book, I do not wish to go farther in predicting the future of the Unification Church. It is in flux and is presently being wrought by conscious and unconscious decisions. Probably it will survive, but not grow dramatically; I do not see conditions being right for *any* dramatic shifts in religious allegiance in America in the foreseeable future.

Less need be said about two other movements discussed in this volume, Nichiren Shoshu and Scientology. All in all, the prospects of Nichiren Shoshu are perhaps comparable to those of Krishna Consciousness. Like the latter, it has commitment, good institutional organization, and both ethnic and occidental-convert support. It has the additional advantage, as David Snow points out, of a dense but open social network. Because of the simplicity and alleged immediate benefit of its practice, it has had an appeal in the Little Tradition milieu probably unmatched by ISKCON. Yet it also suffers from lack of cultural continuity despite strenuous efforts to Americanize, has had much in-and-out membership, and probably will not again flourish as it did in the yeasty late sixties and early seventies.

The same is probably true of Scientology. Quite apart from all its adverse publicity and the easily dated and ambiguous quality of the "science" imagery to which Roy Wallis and William Bainbridge allude, it suffers from lack of identity in Great Tradition/Little Tradition terms. Little Tradition people, in the modern American context, expect technological products from science but not cosmic or personal meaning answers; those they want from religion. (It would not be entirely incorrect to say the reverse is true of some Great Tradition elites.) Scientology endeavored to give scientized religious-type meaning and power to a Little Tradition clientele, in a culturally discontinuous manner; unlike Christian Science with which Roy Wallis has compared it, it has not established reassuring churchlike edifices with Protestant-style services, nor made itself a reading-room presence in conservative middle-class neighborhoods, nor drawn much adherence from such neighborhoods unless in the form of transitional young people. Because of its inconsistencies and the exceptionally high tension around and within it, despite some parallels I would expect Scientology to decline even faster than Christian Science.

Most of the movements discussed in this book were conspicuous successes among NRMs in the late 1960s and the 1970s, when they received much publicity. That publicity was certainly not unrelated to the fact that, like most of what was then called the "counterculture," they had appeal for young people of the middle and upper classes, that is, religiously of Great Tradition orientation. Not surprisingly, given that clientele and the temper of the times, most of these groups have in common importation from Asia; even Scientology is said to have been influenced by Buddhism.

But if our hypothesis is correct, the NRM future does not lie with imports of this type. I would like to conclude by suggesting that future research look increasingly at NRMs of deep Little Tradition background. Some that are not conventionally Christian or Jewish (broad categories these days) with potential for growth in coming decades include Neo-Paganism; "No church" Christianity; explicitly or implicitly Gnostic groups; quasi-Christian movements of Native American, West Indian, or African background; and Satanism. Research should be particularly organized to test hypotheses concerning Little Tradition values and modes of transmission, and the importance of cultural continuity and relative tension for success.

CHAPTER SEVENTEEN

A Sociologist of Religion
Looks at the Future
of New Religious Movements

Benton Johnson

My task in this chapter is to examine the future possibilities of new religious movements by drawing on the material presented by the other contributors to this volume and on my own judgment as a sociologist of religion. I will begin by taking a critical look at Rodney Stark's theoretical model of how new religions succeed. After that I will discuss the prospects for the three new religious movements most extensively treated in this volume, namely Scientology, the International Society for Krishna Consciousness (ISKCON), and the Unification Church, taking into account Bryan Wilson's general warnings and the specific analyses of part two.

In my opinion Stark's model of religious success is a tightly assembled inventory of factors that can help systematize existing knowledge in this area and provide a focus for future research. One of its principal merits is that it integrates conceptual elements familiar to sociologists of religion with elements drawn from sectors of social science they have tended to avoid or ignore. For example, Stark's inclusion of material from the recent social movement organization literature should help end the long-standing insulation between that field and the sociology of religion. And his inclusion of material from economics, with its emphasis on markets, firms, and the degree of their regulation, puts sociologists of religion in touch with variables that they have treated pejoratively when they have treated them at all. The result of these infusions is a rich mix that will be a source of fresh perspectives on the study of religious development. Another merit of Stark's model is that it is grounded in a more general set of theoretical assumptions from which he and his collaborators have already derived a number of hypotheses that have led to intriguing empirical discoveries.

Stark does not claim that his model incorporates all the major factors involved in religious success. He claims only that it is an inventory of necessary, not sufficient, conditions. Moreover, the model is undergoing refinement and elaboration, for Stark has recently added to it the factor of the socialization of offspring; and he seems ready, albeit reluctantly, to add yet another, namely the character of religious ideology. Several of the contributors to this volume have made suggestions for the model's further improvement, and I have a few suggestions to make myself. My first suggestion concerns the matter of religious success; my second concerns religious ideology.

ON RELIGIOUS SUCCESS

Success, in Stark's model, is defined as a continuous variable representing ''the degree to which a religious movement is able to dominate one or more societies.'' Both Bryan R. Wilson and Steven J. Gelberg, however, object to such a definition. They argue that religious movements differ in their objectives and hence in their conceptions of success and that some of these conceptions are not amenable to empirical investigation. For example, Prabhupada, founder of ISKCON, ''often affirmed that he was more interested in having a few sincere disciples than in achieving mass popularity.'' In other words, in defining success one must take seriously a movement's own perspective. It seems to me that Stark is justified in constructing a model to explain differences in the ability of religious movements to dominate one or more societies but that Wilson and Gelberg are also correct in asserting that religious movements have differing conceptions of success. The root of the issue between them is Stark's choice of the terms success and failure for his dependent variable. They are not good choices. For one thing, they have no clear meaning except in reference to some standard of performance, and clarity requires that the standard be specified. For another, the two words have strong evaluative connotations that make them poor candidates for technical terms in a scientific model. Controversy, including the hairsplitting that Stark dislikes, can be avoided by renaming the dependent variable *domination,* or perhaps *impact.* Then the goals of each religious movement can be factored into the model as independent variables. It makes sense to assume, for example, that a movement will not achieve a high degree of impact on a society if its goal is merely to prepare twenty pure souls for existence on a UFO scheduled to make a single visit to earth in 1990.

THE POWER OF RELIGIOUS IDEOLOGY

The most frequently voiced complaint about Stark's model is that it contains no systematic treatment of the role of theological or ideological variables in developing religious commitment. Perhaps his neglect of these variables reflects his reliance on the popular resource mobilization perspective. As David A. Snow points out, this perspective, which was originally developed in the study of secular social movements, emphasizes organizational and macrosociological variables and treats belief systems as "relatively unimportant determinants of movement emergence, mobilization, and success." Snow makes a convincing case that the study of religious mobilization cannot afford to overlook ideological variables. He is correct to observe that even the best designed organizational structure can fail to utilize support if its leaders are unable "to develop and maintain a sense of enthusiasm and anticipation" among those it wishes to enlist. The current decline of liberal Protestant denominations, for example, is not the result of faulty organizational structure or a lack of material resources. The decline reflects the inability of these bodies to devise messages and programs that are compelling to young middle-class adults. Religions vary in the *power* their beliefs and values have to generate human energy and direct it toward certain objectives.

What are some of the ingredients that make a religious belief system powerful? One of them may be its ability to interpret all aspects of life in terms of a single cosmic scheme that is portrayed vividly and dramatically. The ideology of Nichiren Shoshu of America (NSA), graphically described by Snow, is an excellent example of such a scheme. NSA teaches that its founder, Nichiren Daishonin, was the "new Buddha" prophesied by the original Buddha some 2,000 years earlier as the sole agent of true Buddhism in the age of Mappo, the age in which humanity now lives. In this age, the essence of Buddhism—including all its teachings, its commentaries, and its spiritual exercises—is contained in a simple chant: *Nam-Myoho-Renge-Kyo.* Those who repeat this chant are the Bodhissatvas of earth in the present age. Other religions have equally colorful ideologies. Followers of the Rev. Moon regard themselves as the vanguard of a new world order that will restore Edenic paradise spoiled by Satan's seduction of Eve. Gelberg reports that ISKCON's "cosmology is teeming with demigods, demons, incarnations, heroes, heroines, and saints." Snow has identified another ingredient of the power of religious ideology, namely, its ability to provide personal incentives for collective action. The members of NSA receive many benefits by chanting to the *GOHONZON,* but their benefits will multiply greatly if they also act on behalf of the movement as a whole. For example, if NSA succeeds in its project of reinvigorating America by restoring its lost pioneer spirit, many of its members expect to gain positions of great power and influence. Surely one source of the current decline of Protestantism is the collapse of its cosmology and its inability to offer personal rewards to its members.

John Lofland, has, in my opinion, put his finger on yet another ingredient in the power of religious ideologies, namely, the extent to which the culture of a movement is *elaborated.* Elaboration refers to "the sheer quantitative dimension of culture . . . how much of it there is and to what range of matters it is applied.'' Most human action takes place under conditions that do not guarantee its expected outcome. Disappointment, challenge, and surprise are inevitable by-products of action. Success is rarely a simple matter of following a recipe in a mechanical fashion. Interpretation, innovation, and reflection are also required. New movements, whether religious or not, face this basic condition of life in exaggerated form. Whatever their goals, their success depends to some extent on the availability of a wide range of recources to deal with it. This is another reason why Stark is correct to suggest that cultural continuity facilitates the success of new religious movements, for the larger the inventory of resources for action, the easier the task of problem solving becomes. Moreover, as time goes on, those movements that manage to remain vigorous become increasingly elaborated, either by further cultural borrowing or by internal development. If they are to survive, new religious movements cannot remain ''pure,'' that is, unelaborated beyond the time of their founding. Needless to say, the more numerous and difficult their goals, the more they must elaborate and hence the more they must change.

Lofland is also right to emphasize that elaboration entails the risk of secularization. For new religious movements, however, it seems to me that elaboration entails more serious risks of a different sort. First, it entails the risk of innovations that may jeopardize its effectiveness and even its very survival. This risk is greatest in movements that emphasize loyalty to a single leader who is responsible for all major policy decisions. As Eileen Barker makes clear, the fortunes of authoritarian movements led by charismatic figures depend a great deal on the personal qualities of the leader. The fatal ending of Jim Jones's People's Temple movement is a tragic case in point. On the other hand, more decentralized or consultative decision-making procedures entail the risk that the process of elaboration will move along divergent paths, and this may lead to conflicts that absorb the energies of the movement and eventually cause it to splinter. In fact, most new religious movements that attain size and influence have splintered at one time or another. This is true of Buddhism, Christianity, and Islam; and it is even true of Mormonism, Stark's modern exemplar of a vigorous and expansive movement. Although schism destroys a movement's unity, it need not destroy the movement itself, for it can give the leaders of a promising tendency free rein to build an organization even stronger and more aggressive than the original one.

Finally, a particularly important empowering ingredient in the ideology of any religious movement that hopes to conquer the world is the ability to include as equals within the religious community anyone who meets uniform requirements without regard to the communal barriers that divide the human race. Religious movements that have swept over large areas of the world have all been universalistic in this sense. As Stark notes, it was the achievement of Christianity to provide cultural unity within the bounds of the Roman Empire, a feat that would have been impossible had the Pauline church not broken with the particularistic tendencies of Palestinian Judaism. In this connection it is significant that Mormonism has recently dropped its ban on blacks in the priesthood.

THE FUTURE OF SCIENTOLOGY

Roy Wallis's illuminating discussion of the prospects of Scientology, together with a number of points Wilson makes, furnishes a good basis for predicting that this movement will experience rough sledding in the future. Despite remarkable growth in adherents and income over the first quarter century of its existence, despite the ingenious inventions of its founder and leader, L. Ron Hubbard, and despite an effective organizational structure, Scientology faces the threat of stagnation and decline unless it can overcome some formidable obstacles.

When Hubbard can safely be presumed dead, Scientology will face the crisis of authority undergone by all religious movements founded by charismatic leaders with autocratic tendencies. This crisis will be aggravated by two other problems peculiar to those contemporary movements that Wilson refers to as therapeutic. The first stems from the fact that such organizations have difficulty building a stable pool of devoted members because the bulk of them are essentially fee-paying clients who are attracted by the promise of personal growth to empower them in their careers and intimate relations. Except for staff and those who aspire to staff positions, their mobilizing potential is low. Scientology, Transcendental Meditation, and other spiritually tinged therapeutic movements do not have the mobilizing power of Mormonism or even of Nichiren Shoshu. In Durkheim's terms, Scientology is a "church" only in an equivocal sense—in fact much less a church even than Christian Science, which in historical perspective may be regarded as a living relic of the earliest stage of an evolutionary process from religious denomination to therapeutic business firm.

The second problem stems from the intensely competitive character of organizations that offer therapeutic services. Even if Scientology manages to avoid costly litigation and to continue the elaboration process at which Hubbard excelled, it will face a wide range of new challenges from entrepreneurs who have learned from him and from others and who have done some innovating themselves. There is a wide-open market in the area of commercialized therapeutic services, and brand loyalty is weak. But perhaps this very condition, which was not readily apparent sixty years ago, may spur Hubbard's successors to remain more competitive than Mrs. Eddy's were.

The low mobilizing potential of the competing firms in the therapy market is a sufficient reason for asserting that it is exceedingly unlikely any movement like Scientology or Transcendental Meditation will achieve a high impact on American society. To be sure, competition sometimes results in the domination of a market by a handful of firms, but the low start-up costs and the difficulty of keeping trade secrets will probably prevent this from happening in the therapy industry. Firms with new ideas and new techniques will have the competitive edge. At present *est* is declining, and Neuro-Linguistic Programming is on the rise. Firewalking seminars are the coming thing. It may be true, as Wallis remarks, that there is nothing so outmoded as yesterday's science, but in the meantime a firm may well gain market share by exploiting the latest scientific cosmologies. In my opinion the possibilities described by William Sims Bainbridge are both intriguing and real.

Even though no one firm may achieve market dominance, the emergence and growth of a market for therapeutic services is a cultural development of the first importance. Wallis considers it a response to the process of rationalization, a position reminiscent of Talcott Parsons's astute analysis of the strains accompanying modern and scientific development—an analysis as plausible today as it was forty years ago. To date, in American society, the dominant response to rationalization has not been a turn toward fascism or socialism or the strengthening of traditional solidary ties (for example, to family, church, and nation), though there were some tendencies in the latter direction during the early cold war period, and there was the brief but dramatic upsurge of radicalism in the late 1960s. The dominant response has been for people to accept the process of rationalization and to equip themselves as individuals to meet its opportunities and disappointments as resourcefully as they can. This has entailed the cultivation of personal power and the expansion of individual options, including those of changing careers, partners, and life-styles. This response has been centered in the middle class and reflects the remarkable vitality of the two cultural motifs that Reinhold Niebuhr long ago identified as the real faith of the modern bourgeoisie, namely, a belief in progress and human perfectability. It is, in Wallis's phrase, a world-affirming faith. Niebuhr did his best to drive it from the liberal churches and replace it with a sterner creed. It lives on, however, outside these now stagnating institutions in a myriad of "New Age" tendencies dedicated to the proposition that the world will be better and that humanity is divine.

THE FUTURE OF ISKCON

The great youth rebellion of the late 1960s known as the counterculture had both a negative and a positive side. Its negative side was a protest against virtually every major social institution and every dominant motif of American culture, particularly middle-class culture. Its positive side was a search for radical alternatives—a search that generated a bewildering array of tendencies, many of them incompatible. The new religious movements on which sociologists of religion have focused so much attention represent only one direction the search took. Another direction, much less studied, was toward radical politics. Now, nearly twenty years later, most members of the counterculture generation have, in varying ways and degrees, made their peace with American society and culture.

The International Society for Krishna Consciousness was one of a number of religious groups able to grow and attain public notoriety because they attracted counterculture youth who were looking for a truly radical alternative to conventional middle-class life. No doubt, as Gordon Melton points out, two other factors also contributed to whatever growth such groups achieved, namely, the fact that many middle-class Americans were already aware of and receptive to certain Oriental religious themes and the fact that the supply of teachers from the East had recently increased. Even so, neither ISKCON nor any other radical religious movement that recruited in the 1970s ever attracted more than a large handful of followers, and many they did attract appear to have dropped out. For one thing, their demanding and radically distinctive regimen appears far too costly to most people, at least as a full-time life-style. For another, as Bromley and Shupe point out, they have been the target of a great deal of abuse. For these and a variety of other reasons related to Stark's model, it can be said with certainty that unless ISKCON transforms itself in unlikely ways, its impact on American society will continue to be exceedingly low.

On the other hand—as the richly informative papers by Steven Gelberg, Larry D. Shinn, and E. Burke Rochford, Jr., show—ISKCON is in no imminent danger of collapse and may well be on the road to creating a secure little niche for itself in American society. Thanks to the foresight of its founder, Prabhupada, it seems to have weathered the crisis of his death. As Shinn documents in detail, the Governing Body Commission has emerged as an effective centralizing force that has set limits on but not destroyed the traditional authority of the gurus. Provided this force remains effective, ISKCON's decentralized decision-making system may actually prove beneficial, for it will allow local leaders to try out a variety of new ideas for strengthening the movement without committing the entire organization to any one of them. ISKCON's apparent success in coping with the transfer and routinization of authority stands in the sharpest contrast to the experience of The Children of God, another world-rejecting religious movement that also recruited counterculture youth seeking radical alternaives. As Wallis shows, its founder, Moses David, seems incapable of relaxing his iron grip on the organization, of grooming a leadership cadre to succeed him, or of modifying his prediction of Christ's return in 1993—a prediction that is bound to have a demoralizing effect in the not-so-distant future.

ISKCON could clearly benefit from a more secure financial undergirding, from an expanded membership base, and from better public relations. Its increasingly close ties with the Indian immigrant community, many of whose members are affluent professionals, have already yielded a flow of needed contributions. Since a substantial influx of new devotees seems out of the question for the foreseeable future, the further development of lay support groups, including groups of part-time devotees, would seem advisable as a source of revenue, public support, and an occasional recruit. The surprising popularity of Prabhupada's palace in the West Virginia hills as a tourist attraction and the recent opening of the Bhaktivedanta Cultural Center in Detroit hold out the prospect of an early improvement of ISKCON's public image. Offering seminars and celebrations for outsiders in a pleasant resort setting could produce both income and good will. Before his forced departure from the United States, Bhagwan Sri Rajneesh was able to attract thousands of paying guests for trainings and festivals at his commune in Oregon. As Gelberg notes, however, innovations such as these smack of accommodationism and will provoke further resistance from those who believe that accommodations have already undermined the prestige and purity of communal life. Yet more innovations along these lines have to be encouraged to secure the survival of the communal life itself, though they will make for internal tensions that could lead to schism.

THE FUTURE OF THE UNIFICATION CHURCH

Like ISKCON, the Unification Church offered a radical alternative to existing society that appealed to the contingent of counterculture youth who were really serious about finding a totally new way of life. It, too, has a fairly meager membership base in North America, a poor public image, and has recently suffered losses. Moreover, both movements have important sources of support overseas. But here the resemblances end. Unlike ISKCON, the Unification Church has not established a workable and broadly acceptable governance structure to replace its founder's authority after his death. The most important difference between the two movements, however, concerns their basic teachings and objectives. ISKCON draws on those aspects of Hinduism that consider a cloistered existence to be essential for true spirituality. It is relatively uninterested in political action. The Unification Church, on the other hand, is inspired by Korean cultural motifs and by the militant millennialism of pre-twentieth-century Anglo-American Protestantism. It wants to dominate the world by direct action. As long as it persists in this ambition, it will face a barrage of challenges from which ISKCON will be spared.

One truly formidable challenge that the Moonies have hardly begun to face is how to defeat communism and create a workable plan for a new political and economic order. A more immediate set of challenges is to avoid costly mistakes in deciding where to concentrate their energies. For example, should they disperse their limited human resources all over the country in such projects as CAUSA, a Church-supported front organization designed to combat communist ideology? If they do, they risk spreading their resources too thin to accomplish much. But if they do not, large sections of the country will be left with no Unification presence at all. One major objective has been to settle intact families in neighborhoods all over the country. If this goal continues to be deferred, many Unification women will be past their prime childbearing years. But if it is not deferred, the church will face a host of new problems, for example, how to maintain dense ties among the members, how to educate the children in an alien environment, and how to devise a credible explanation for the fact that many of these children will seem sinful in the eyes of the world. There is much room for error in facing up to any of these problems.

In meeting these challenges, the Unification Church will be able to draw on an already well elaborated culture that continues to be enriched by new inputs not only from Rev. Moon and his closest associates but from the cadre of young intellectuals the church has deliberately developed and from the advice of the many outside intellectuals whose opinions it has often solicited. Indeed, the apparent openness of church influentials to the views of outsiders is one of the most remarkable features of the Unification Church. Michael Mickler's informative paper, written from the privileged perspective of an insider, reveals that the process of elaboration has already generated four basic tendencies, which he calls ''ideological subgroupings,'' concerning the issue of which direction the church should take in the future. The leadership therefore has a wide range of options to choose from in charting its course.

Mickler is fully aware, of course, that divergent tendencies can also be a source of disruptive conflict. Although he does not emphasize the point, it seems clear both from his paper and Barker's that for the foreseeable future the most serious factional disputes will be between the church's Korean leadership and its cadre of American intellectuals. It also seems clear that in case of a showdown the Koreans will have the upper hand. For one thing, their membership base in Korea and Japan is larger and better established than the American one. Even more important is the fact that they command the bulk of the church's financial resources. It is no longer a secret that the movement's American operations, including its much publicized acquisitions of property, have been heavily subsidized from abroad. A schism would therefore deal a staggering blow to the American branch of the church. Moreover, neither of the two ideological subgroupings preferred by the American cadre would provide a solid basis for the substantial growth of a schismatic American-based church because both of them are accommodationist and hence carry the seeds of secularization. One tendency accommodates to the culture of ''yuppie'' careerism and demythologized religion, and the other accommodates to the culture of leftist political activism. Neither tendency offers exciting alternatives therefore. The two Korean tendencies, by contrast, retain much more distinctively Unification themes. In my opinion, they point the way toward whatever impact the church can achieve.

CONCLUSION

Sociological prediction is an inexact science, as inexact as long-range weather forecasting. All one can say for sure is that there is a high probability that certain patterns will prevail under specified conditions that cannot be taken for granted. If current social conditions persist, it is reasonable to predict a growing market for the services of therapeutic business firms. Whether Scientology will remain a leading firm will depend on its ability to keep on the right side of the law and to create new products that give it an edge over its competitors. The prospects of ISKCON and other commune-based Hindu imports appear modest but promising, provided they improve their public image, an achievement that need not be difficult. The future of the Unification Church and other world-transforming movements is far bleaker because of the sheer complexity of their task, the resistance they will provoke, and the large risk they run of committing disastrous errors. But current social conditions may not persist, for the world is moving along a dangerous and uncharted course that can provide opportunities for ambitious movements like the Unification Church that are clever and forceful enough to seize them. No one predicted the change of climate that led to the current spate of new religions; no one can predict with certainty what their fortunes will be at the turn of the century and beyond.

CHAPTER EIGHTEEN

Cultural Consequences of Cults

Phillip E. Hammond

INTRODUCTION

The prospectus sent to participants in the conference on the future of new religious movements included the statement that we were "to anticipate what the future holds for these groups and, by extension, *for American society as a whole.*" Those underlined words are the subject of this essay, the only essay in the volume that blithely ignores the new religious movements themselves, so to speak, and instead speculates generally about America in the twenty-first century in light of the fact that NRMs came on the scene during the final third of the twentieth. How might the culture and institutions of this country—and not just *this* country, but, by extrapolation, any country that has experienced the influx of NRMs during the 1960s and 1970s—be influenced? One consequence, of course, has already been discussed: the emergence of an anticult movement, which may leave residues of its own. What might be other consequences?

My concern here will be focused on socio-cultural reverberations somewhat removed from the NRMs themselves. Because of the distance between cause and effects, therefore, the links may be less observable—requiring an analysis such as this even to make visible their potential—but, at the same time, those links may be decidedly more vulnerable to manifold other influences. What appears in the mid-1980s to be a plausible and likely fallout of NRMs into the broader culture may, because of the multitude of these intervening factors, develop along paths quite at odds with the projections here.

Nonetheless, if for no other reason than the "spirit of the game" invites it, some speculation into the direct influences of NRMs on the broader society seems appropriate in a book such as this. It should be clear that I am estimating neither what the future holds for today's NRMs—the proper task of virtually all the rest of this volume's essays—nor the likelihood of the

NRM's own goal achievement, a somewhat different issue. Rather, I am trying to assess what, if any, unintended cultural consequences will follow from the fact that during the 1960s, 1970s, and into the 1980s, the industrial nations of the world experienced a range of new religious movements in their midst. As J. Milton Yinger tells us regarding "deviant religious groups" generally, their importance rests "on the nature of their cultural challenges, not their memberships." (Yinger, 1982:233) We might expect, therefore, that it is precisely in the arena of unintended outcomes where impact will, in the long run, be more lastingly felt. Such, in any event, is what this essay is about.

THE AMERICAN PAST AND ITS TRAJECTORY

Benton Johnson, writing in 1981 about the NRMs, notes that, generally speaking, they have no "adequate theory of society," and thus—even though they may have revised some people's religious consciousness—they are unlikely to produce the social changes they themselves seek (Johnson, 1981:62). As he recognizes, however, to assert that NRMs will fall short of *their* societal aims is not at all to say that they will have no societal *impact*. Assessment of impact is, to be sure, the privilege of the historian looking backward. But, if American history is any guide, one can venture some guesses in our day, informed by the unintended consequences of prior periods when new religious impulses were felt and expressed.

Thus, during the First Great Awakening (c. 1730-60), the ostensible theological thrust was evangelical, but the unintended consequence was the further (and irrevocable) disestablishment of Puritan Protestantism. During the Second Great Awakening (c. 1800-1830), the theological impulse was again evangelical, but the broader outcome was a pattern of religious voluntarism that has persisted to this day. Similarly, in the decades following the Civil War, the theology took a radical turn in the direction of liberalism, but the more lasting impact could be said to be the institutionalization of religious pluralism. If one were to summarize two centuries of religious change, then, one might say that whatever their theological intentions, the periods of religious ferment led to ever greater levels of individual choice.

And what of the present period? Accepting McLoughlin's analysis (1978) that the current scene is, indeed, a period of religious ferment—a period in which the ostensible thrust is toward "eastern," "mystical," or at least unconventional theologies—we might note that the long-range consequences of this thrust may well be quite otherwise. Just as the previous awakenings have capitalized on an ever-increasing individualism—whatever their doctrinal definition of the situation—so, too, do the NRMs of the current day not only flow from this individualism but also help institutionalize it at yet another notch higher. Their impact on the culture at large, then, may lie not so much with the substance of their novel theologies as with the increased demands they make on the ethic of individualism.

A GENERAL CULTURAL OUTCOME

A first observation to be made, therefore, stems from Rodney Stark's point in the first chapter of this book regarding the regulation of the "religious economy": just as new religious movements have greater chance of emerging and thriving in a relatively unregulated religious economy, so does the appearance of NRMs serve to further deregulate that economy. At the individual level, this increase in individual religious choice means simply that even greater choice—in whether and how to be religious—is likely to ensue. At the *cultural* level, however, it may mean more. It may, by offering novel religious choices, be offering broader value choices as well. Thus Glock and Wuthnow, after comparing the "conventionally" religious and the "nonreligious" with the "alternatively" religious in their Bay Area survey, note:

> By and large, to be alternatively religious represents a sharper and more pervasive break with the conventional than does being nonreligious. The differences between the conventionally and alternatively religious on canons of personal morality are in every instance greater than between the conventionally religious and the nonreligious. The same applies to political outlook and political attitudes. . . . Unlike the nonreligious, the alternatively religious break with the conventionally religious in other realms of life. Thus, the alternatively religious in all comparisons are the least likely of the three orientations to attach great importance to the "creature comfort" items. . . . Openness to alternative life-styles is also more characteristic. . . . These results . . . are not an artifact of group age. . . . Among both youth and matures, the alternatively religious are more sharply and pervasively in conflict with the conventionally religious on all of the issues examined. . . . (1979:62-63)

One might say, using the parlance coming out of the 1960s, that NRMs have provided an avenue for a counterculture to take root and be expressed. The consequence in the next century will be a yet more variegated culture.

More precision than this is desirable, however, because, over and beyond the sheer addition of religious options, might there be a multiplier effect with reverberations felt elsewhere in society as well? I think at least two such reverberations can be identified and predicted with fair accuracy. They are; (1) the further weakening of the link between religion and family, and (2) the further erosion of "established" religion. In neither instance can these outcomes be said to be intended by any NRM, yet both will be more characteristic of our society in the next century, in part because of the NRMs in this one. No doubt there will be many other cultural consequences as well, but these two seem almost certain.

THE LINK BETWEEN RELIGION AND FAMILY

In one of the most seminal essays in all of sociology of religion, Talcott Parsons wrote that

> it is to be taken for granted that the overwhelming majority will accept the religious affiliations of their parents—of course with varying degrees of commitment. Unless the whole society is drastically disorganized there will not be notable instability in its religious organization. But there will be an important element of flexibility and opportunity for new adjustments within an orderly system which the older church organizations . . . did not allow for (1963:65)

The "element of flexibility" Parsons had in mind is the ease with which persons can switch denominations without family heresy. For the Lutheran-raised son or daughter, a change to the Methodists is not a rejection of parental religion, for example, but merely an exercise in culturally circumscribed choice. Similarly, Catholics raised in an ethnic parish can remain Catholic even while leaving their ethnic parochial background, and Jews have at least Orthodox, Conservative, and Reform options without dropping out of their familial faith. However wrenching individual cases may be, the religious culture of America, Parsons asserted, made room for adjustments in the religion-family link; one did not have to reject the latter in order to make a change in the former.

All of this flexiblity rested on a fairly low rate of defection from all religion, however. That is to say, the assumption that one denomination is about the equivalent of any other presumes only a few in each generation will exercise the option of rejecting religion altogether. Otherwise, an important cultural feature of Americans—visible at least since de Tocqueville's visit in 1831—would be seriously challenged. "Each sect worships God in its own fashion," de Tocqueville observed, "but all preach the same morality." (1969:290) President Eisenhower was merely echoing the same sentiment in 1952 when he declared our government to be "founded in a deeply felt religious faith—and I don't care what it is." (Quoted in Herberg, 1960:84)

New religious movements in the sixties, seventies, and eighties *have* challenged this cultural assumption, however. Surely it is no coincidence that the strongest expressions of anticult feeling come not from established churches but from families who, in seeing their children join a religious group outside of the mainstream, regard those children as somehow "lost." Cults, in other words, call into question the link between religion and family.

And well they might. While the number of cult members is still so small as not to show up in samples of the national population, we can nonetheless see that the cultural assumption of only negligible defection from all religion is seriously in doubt. The next two tables provide the evidence.

Table 1 makes clear that defection among Catholics and Jews has risen from the generations born before 1931 to the generations born since. Approximately one in ten in the older group departed their religious legacy whereas nearly two in ten, and then one in four, in subsequent groups have done so. Protestants, however, show no such trend. Is this because they are religiously more loyal? Probably not, inasmuch as their "defection" rate, while not increasing through time as do those of Catholics and Jews, is consistently much higher. The explanation would seem to be in the far greater options available to Protestants to change from parental denomination while still remaining Protestant. If, therefore, we look not at all kinds of defection from parental religion but just at the proportion of such defections that constitute departure from all religions, we find that Protestants are not that different from Catholics and Jews.

Catholics and Jews lead the way, of course; their choices remain restricted once departure from parental religion occurs. Nonetheless, the figures of Table 2 are remarkable across the board because *in every denomination defection into no religion is on the increase among those departing from parental religion.* Moreover, these defections double and then triple across the three age cohorts. The strong if flexible link Parsons could assume in 1963 is now obviously weakened to a great degree.

Where do new religious movements fit in? They would appear to be both product and producer of this weakened link. First of all, only with the link weakened were NRMs able to recruit members and become a visible force.

TABLE 1

THE PROPORTION, BY YEAR OF BIRTH, OF CATHOLICS AND JEWS AND PROTESTANTS (AGE 18 +) WHO DO NOT SHARE THE RELIGIOUS AFFILIATIONS OF THEIR PARENTS*		
	YEAR OF BIRTH	
PARENTAL RELIGION	1931 OR EARLIER	1932-1946	1947 AND SINCE
Catholic	13 (1122)	17 (764)	22 (827)
Jewish	10 (135)	16 (56)	25 (57)
Protestant	35 (2361)	37 (1239)	33 (1090)

* These data (and those of table 2) are derived from the combined 1973-1980 General Social Surveys of the National Opinion Research Center of the University of Chicago. They were made available through the Inter-University Consortium on Political and Social Research of the University of Michigan, and their analysis is the work of Samuel Mueller of the Department of Sociology, University of Akron. Professor Mueller's aid is gratefully acknowledged. It must be noted that the right-hand-most column contains those who, by their youth, have not yet lived through their "high-risk" defecting period (and thus deflate the true percentage) plus those who, because of their young adulthood, have not yet returned to the fold (and thus inflate the true percentage). The trend is nonetheless clear for Catholics and Jews in table 1 and for all in table 2.

Second, their very success no doubt contributes to the further weakening of the family-religion link. It is important to recognize that this last assertion is cultural, not individual, however. No doubt the enthusiastic early generations of NRM members will take great care to raise *their* children in the parental religion. The proximate consequence for members of NRMs may therefore be fewer defections from parental religion. But the wider consequence—of demonstrating that, indeed, children can depart markedly from parents' affiliations—is surely to weaken even further the tie between family and religion.

One might raise the question, therefore, following Parsons's trenchant analysis early in the 1960s, whether or not we have experienced a "notable instability in . . . religious organization." In other words, have new religious movements contributed to the disruption of a long-standing cultural pattern in the United States linking the family with religion? Robbins and Anthony, who have followed closely this particular aspect of NRMs, would suggest the answer is yes.

> Cults operate as surrogate extended families and, moreover, provide novel therapeutic and spiritual mystiques which confer meaning on social processes . . . no longer . . . easily legitimated by . . . traditional ideologies. In so doing, however, they exploit the weaknesses of existing institutions (churches, nuclear families, psychiatry) and perhaps pose a threat to these institutions. (1979:88-89)

One cultural consequence of the emergence of new religious movements in the 1960s, 1970s, and 1980s, therefore, will probably be a dramatic further loosening of the link between religion and family.

TABLE 2

THE PROPORTION, BY YEAR OF BIRTH, OF THOSE WHO, HAVING DEFECTED FROM PARENTAL RELIGION, HAVE DEPARTED RELIGIOUS AFFILIATION ALTOGETHER		
	YEAR OF BIRTH	
PARENTAL DENOMINATION / 1931 OR EARLIER	1932-1946	1947 AND SINCE
Catholic — 23 (13)	47 (17)	55 (22)
Jewish — 33 (15)	69 (16)	64 (25)
Methodist — 8 (39)	13 (31)	29 (24)
Lutheran — 9 (22)	21 (28)	40 (30)
Presbyterian — 7 (41)	15 (54)	28 (46)
Episcopal — 21 (34)	38 (42)	48 (40)
White Baptist — 9 (33)	13 (31)	29 (24)
Black Baptist — 18 (18)	29 (21)	39 (18)

EROSION OF ESTABLISHED RELIGION

A second cultural consequence of current new religious movements will likely be the erosion, through legal decision making, of the power of those religions with long-standing roots in the American culture—the so-called mainline denominations, including Catholicism and Judaism. More accurately, perhaps, what will happen is the *further* erosion of such religion, because what is occurring is, in reality, but another step in the same direction established religion has already been forced to go on previous occasions. Thus, in a quite literal sense, when the framers and ratifiers agreed on the No Establishment Clause of the First Amendment, they assured a decline in the power and prestige of whichever denomination *would* have been chosen had establishment been allowed. Similarly, the passing of all vestiges of state establishment—completed finally in Massachusetts in 1833—left all denominations on a voluntary footing, a decline in power if not in prestige.

The kind of legal erosion being brought on by contemporary NRMs is more subtle than in these earlier instances, however. A closer parallel with the present is the case of Mormon polygamy, wherein the court, confronted by the unprecedented claim to plural marriage (Reynolds v. United States, 98 US 145 [1879]), responded not only by declaring the practice unconstitutional but also by making explicit the fact that governments, not churches, determine which behaviors are acceptable. Churches retained their power to *preach* doctrines of choice, then, but it was now clear they had lost the power necessarily to *act* on them. In a similar fashion, I would argue, the great number of legal challenges brought by new religious movements in our own day—even though, by and large, the courts have upheld the right of NRMs to be different—will have the consequence of further eroding religious power.

The context for this argument is the well-known tension between the Free Exercise Clause and the No Establishment Clause of the First Amendment. Put baldly, the argument is that every extension of what is permitted as free exercise of religion by *individuals* leads to a diminution in the rights of religious collectivities because it calls into question their prior privileged position. The more widespread a benefit becomes, in other words, the less value that benefit will have to those who were earlier its sole beneficiaries. This argument is complicated, however, and no doubt controversial as well, so we must proceed slowly.

The idea is hardly new that legal decisions may lead unintentionally to consequences quite at odds with those decisions' stated purposes. Thus, for example, court cases enabling Native Americans to extend their tribal sovereignty give rise to that sovereignty's possible arbitrary use, which gives rise to the need to protect individual rights, which then undermines tribal sovereignty (Medcalf, 1978). The decision is made that children attending schools in poor districts are entitled to the same enriched education received by students in wealthy districts, but local communities therefore no longer control admissions, curriculums, or standards of excellence. This notion—that individual rights are won at the expense of those collectivities intermediary between persons and central governments—is well known.

In the church-state scene, however, there is an additional element inasmuch as the individuals whose rights get recognized in ground-breaking cases are oftentimes representatives of the religious collectivities whose power *as collectivities* is being compromised. As James A. Beckford says, "Religious groups . . . voluntarily take their testimony into courtrooms and are thereby seduced into rationalizing their deepest convictions in return for legal credibility." (1983: 10 MS.)

This phenomenon is easier to see *ex post facto,* of course. Thus, in upholding the right to proselytize in hostile neighborhoods, the court made explicit the right of government to control proselytizing. (Cantwell v. Connecticut, 310 U.S. 296 [1940]) Or in granting conscientious objector status to persons not "religiously" motivated, the court took on the *de facto* task of defining religion (United States v. Seeger, 380 U.S. 163 [1965]); Welsh v. United States, 398 U.S. 333 [1970]), a task it had hitherto assiduously claimed to avoid (United States v. Ballard, 322 U.S. 78 [1944]). Viewing with alarm these threats to "established" religious communities that often result unintentionally from the further broadening of individual rights, some "conservationists" have called for a purposive strengthening through legal recognition of so-called "mediating structures." Inevitably, however, such an argument runs into the problem I have identified here.

> In general, we are more relaxed about "no establishment" than is the present approach of the courts, and more adamant about "free exercise." We would wish the courts to take more seriously the institutional integrity of religion, rather than its current tendency of privatizing religion by focusing on individual beliefs and motivations. (Kerrine and Neuhaus, 1979:14)

Such is the wish, perhaps, but it is not at all clear how one can be "more adamant" about individual free exercise and at the same time insist on continued (or renewed) recognition of religion's "institutional integrity"—not, at least, if religion retains a single meaning. If the courts will grant the right of conscientious objection to someone who does not believe in God, what special right can be claimed by someone who does? Or by one belonging to a group based on such a belief?

New religious movements, I am asserting, have intensified this process by requesting—and, for the most part, being granted—extensions of religious rights. Thus, on issues not only of evangelizing but also of soliciting funds, tax exemption, and political involvement by religious groups, NRMs have stretched existing boundaries, with the consequence that government feels the need (or is asked) to intervene in matters that once were entirely internal to churches. (See Kelley, ed., *Government Intervention in Religious Affairs,* 1982, for discussions of these matters.) Ironically, it is a No Establishment case involving Transcendental Meditation that allows us to see how this erosion process works.

The circumstances of this case were peculiar, to say the least. Followers of Maharishi Mahesh Yogi were teaching meditation techniques in five public schools in New Jersey. Upon examination by the Federal courts, this practice was declared "religious" and thus in violation of the No Establishment Clause. All three judges agreed that TM is religious because its "substantive characteristics" resemble those of other systems found to constitute religion in prior cases. For one of these concurring judges, however, this "look-alike" test was not enough.

> I am convinced that this appeal presents a novel and important question that may not be disposed of simply on the basis of past precedent. Rather . . . the result reached today is largely based upon a newer, more expansive reading of "religion" that has been developed in the last two decades in the context of free exercise . . . cases but not, until today, applied by an appellate court to invalidate a government program under the establishment clause. (Malnak v. Yogi, 592 F.2d 197 [1979])

Judge Adams then proceeded to write a fairly lengthy opinion that at the end, offers a legal definition of religion, precisely an outcome established religious traditions would avoid and will no doubt resist. Along the way, however, the judge considers the "mediating structures" position of two understandings of religion—a "broad" one with respect to Free Exercise issues so that individual conscience is given greatest rein and a "narrow" one with respect to No Establishment issues, thus protecting the favored status of religious collectivities clearly recognized as such. The result, he says, would be a "three-tiered system of ideas": (1) those that are unquestionably religious and thus free from government interference but also barred from government support, (2) those that are unquestionably nonreligious and thus subject to government regulation and eligible for support, and (3) those that are religious only under the dual definition, thus free from government regulation but eligible for government support. The hypothetical outcome is that the third category would get favorable treatment, which leads to clearly unconstitutional preferences.

The point is, something like this situation already occurs, leading the government to outlaw more and more of what is religious on No Establishment grounds *because* it has been recognized as religious on Free Exercise grounds. Thus, says Beckford, many govenments used to justify a variety of arrangements for giving *bona fide* (i.e., generally recognized) religious groups a number of official privileges. Indeed, the privileges used to make very good sense from the States' point of view at a time when religious groups served as the foremost defenders of general culture and as agents of socialization (1983:7MS)

Insofar as the substance of "general culture" is *challenged,* however, then the "official privileges" are also challenged.

In the realm of education alone, first publicly funded but church-operated schools, then clerical teachers, then a religious curriculum, then sponsored devotionals, have been outlawed from public schools because the *de facto* Protestant nature of such things was challenged by Catholics, Jews, and non-believers whose Free Exercise rights had permeated the culture. (See my discussion [1984] of a 1920s Georgia Supreme Court "Bible-reading" issue for a clear illustration of how a case decided on Establishment grounds arose from such Free Exercise considerations.)

After the fact, the process is not mysterious; the particularism assumed to be universal is shown to be a particularism by the act of recognizing yet other particularisms. New religious movements since the 1960s, I am suggesting, are hastening this process by revealing in yet new ways how "Judeo-Christian" has been our conception of religion. As non-Judeo-Christian variations gain legal status, therefore, the effect will be further erosion of heretofore established religion.

There is an even larger irony on this point, exposed by those fundamentalists who would reimpose school prayer, declare this nation to be "Christian" or otherwise restore religious particularism—of just what stripe they, of course, dare not say. The irony comes from the failure of these people to recognize their lineage in the left-wing, arminian, egalitarian, nonconforming, and sectarian branch of Protestantism that was at least half of the impulse for the First Amendment in the first place. What Robert Bellah (1982) calls "romantic cultural particularism" joined forces with secular individualism two centuries ago to create the church-and-state situation we have today. Considering the path of development since 1789, NRMs are hardly unusual, then, but instead represent simply further occasions by which established religion is eroded.

CONCLUSION

If the above two predictions can be made with some confidence, one might generalize further. New religious movements in the last third of the twentieth century will lead to yet another increase in institutionalized individualism, just as previous episodes of religious ferment did. And if this is so, are we not led to conclude even more generally that, just as NRMs could take root and grow only in an already secularized soil, so does the success of those NRMs—however limited—indicate even further secularization? After all, we have just argued that individuals will experience even greater freedom from families, and churches will experience even greater loss of influence. Is it not reasonable to conclude, therefore, that religion will decline yet another step?

A coauthor here, Bryan Wilson, has been the most eloquent spokesman for this point of view (Wilson, 1975;1976;1979), and probably the majority of sociologists of religion agree. Yet the appearance of NRMs on the contemporary scene has led some observers to the opposite conclusion—that the "sacred" may be "returning" (for example, Bell, 1977. See also Anthony, Robbins, and Schwartz, 1983, for a summary of the debate.) Surely both sides cannot be correct.

Or can they? Perhaps the arguments advanced in the foregoing pages suggest a resolution of this apparent dilemma. Imagine that the "sacred" is always and everywhere being encountered. That is to say, with Durkheim, social life lived entirely on the profane level is impossible, which means that the "unquestioned" is forever intruding in human affairs. But whether this sacred is regarded as "religion" depends upon the accretion of a number of other characteristics, foremost among them being the degree to which the sacred impinges upon lives and the degree to which it is expressed in supernatural terms.

Looking backward, moreover, we can see yet other accretions: (1) the supernatural expression of the sacred has often been elaborated into systematic theology, (2) which, in the West, has been largely Christian, (3) embodied primarily in the church, (4) the "purest American" branch of which is Protestant evangelical. As long as religion, with these accretions, remained highly institutionalized—as long as Protestant evangelicalism retained a near-monopoly, to use Rodney Stark's formulation—then as new encounters with the sacred occurred, they were likely to be perceived in the culturally prescribed manner, and one person's God resembled the next person's God, one church acted much as all other churches, and so forth.

Given this view, secularization might thus be conceived as the systematic dismantling—or "unpeeling"—of these accretions. Thus in America, Protestant evangelicalism lost hegemony; the church had to compete with other Christian bodies; Christianity became but one religion in the marketplace; and informal expressions of the sacred came to exist alongside systematic theology, much of which could in fact be rendered in "natural" terms, which finally may have lost all relevance in some people's lives. This development did not mean the disappearance of the sacred but rather the loss of its accretions and thus its recognizability as religion.

In the resulting "secular" setting, new encounters with the sacred may take place, but—insofar as they draw upon cultural traditions some distance from Western Christian traditions—they appear to some as not religious at all and to others as a "return" of the sacred. The new religious movements of the 1960s and 1970s seem to have met with such mixed reactions, as indeed they would if they are simultaneously two things: (1) authentic efforts to express the sacred, and (2) believable *because* of the dismantling of previous accretions of the sacred.

The NRMs can never duplicate the course taken by, say, Christian sects in America, therefore. Even more doubtful is their likelihood of achieving cultural hegemony. But the new religious movements of the final third of the twentieth century must be seen nonetheless as intrusions of the sacred into cultural life, even if they are, at the same time, both products of the secularization preceding their appearance and facilitators of yet more to come. Even if the NRMs manage to hang on as religious alternatives, in other words, they carry the cultural implication not that sacralization is taking place but quite the opposite.

REFERENCES

Anthony, Dick T. Robbins, and P. Schwartz
    1983   "Contemporary Religious Movements and the Secularization Premise." *Concilium* vol. 161 (January): 1-8.

Beckford, James A.
    1983   "The State and Control of New Religious Movements." *Acts of the 17th International Congress for the Sociology of Religion.* Paris.

Bell, Daniel
    1977   "The Return of the Sacred?" *British Journal of Sociology* 28:4-14.

Bellah, Robert N.
    1982   "Cultural Pluralism and Religious Particularism." In *Freedom of Religion in America,* edited by Henry B. Clark, III, 33-52. Los Angeles: Center for Study of the American Experience, University of Southern California.

Glock, Charles Y., and Robert Wuthnow
    1979   "Departures from Conventional Religion." In *The Religious Dimension,* edited by Robert Wuthnow, 47-68. New York: Academic Press.

Hammond, Phillip E.
    1984   "The Courts and Secular Humanism: How to Misinterpret Church/State Issues." *Society* vol. 21, no. 4 (May-June): 11-16.

Herberg, Will
    1960   *Protestant, Catholic, Jew.* Garden City NY: Doubleday Anchor.

Johnson, Benton
    1981   "A Sociological Perspective on the New Religions." In *In Gods We Trust,* edited by Thomas Robbins and Dick Anthony, 51-66. New Brunswick NJ: Transaction Books.

Kelley, Dean M., ed.
1982   *Government Intervention in Religious Affairs.* New York: The Pilgrim Press. Is a good description of the range of issues wherein government is asked (or feels the need) to intervene in religious activity brought on by NRM's "free exercise": methods of solicitation, tax exemption, political involvements of religious bodies, evangelizing.

Kerrine, Theodore M., and Richard John Neuhaus
1979   "Mediating Structures: A Paradigm for Democratic Pluralism," In *The Annals of the American Academy of Political and Social Science* 446 (November): 10-18.

McLoughlin, William G.
1978   *Revivals, Awakenings, and Reform.* Chicago: University of Chicago Press.

Medcalf, Linda
1978   *Law and Identity: Lawyers, Native Americans, and Legal Practice.* Beverly Hills CA: Sage Publications.

Parsons, Talcott
1963   "Christianity and Modern Industrial Society." In *Sociology Theory, Values, and Sociological Change,* 33-70. edited by E. A. Tiryakian, New York: The Free Press.

Robbins, Thomas, and Dick Anthony
1979   "Cults, Brainwashing, and Counter-Subversion" in Dean M. Kelley, ed., *The Annals of the American Academy of Political and Social Science* 446 (November): 78-90.

de Tocqueville, Alexis
1969   *Democracy in America.* Edited by George Lawrence. Garden City NY: Doubleday Anchor.

Wilson, Bryan
1975   "The Secularization Debate," *Encounter* 45: 77-83.

1976   *Contemporary Transformations of Religion.* Oxford: Oxford University Press.

1979   "The Return of the Sacred," *Journal for the Scientific Study of Religion* 18: 268-80.

Yinger, Y.M.
1982   *Countercultures: The Promise and the Peril of a World Turned Upside Down.* New York: Free Press. Re "deviant religious groups": "Their importance rests on the nature of their cultural challenge, not their membership" (233).

• INDEX •